The Toyota Way of Dantotsu Radical Quality Improvement

Sadao Nomura

Introduction by John Shook and Toshiko Narusawa

Lean Global Network

Routledge
Taylor & Francis Group

A PRODUCTIVITY PRESS BOOK

First edition published 2021
by Routledge
52 Vanderbilt Avenue, New York, NY 10017

and by Routledge
2 Park Square, Milton Park, Abingdon, Oxon, OX14 4RN

Routledge is an imprint of the Taylor & Francis Group, an informa business
© 2021 by Taylor & Francis Group, LLC

ISBN: 978-0-367-67238-6 (hbk)
ISBN: 978-0-367-67236-2 (pbk)
ISBN: 978-1-003-13039-0 (ebk)

Foreword

As many have said, process improvement is a journey not a destination. Our journey with Mr. Nomura has been nothing but exceptional for the improvements we have seen. His most unique capability is to "Stand in the Circle" and observe every detail of what is happening in a process or area. For the uninitiated it can be quite disquieting, as it takes patience and is strictly pragmatic in identifying the opportunities for improvement. Mr. Nomura has developed a simple but powerful recipe for step by step implementing TPS, but most importantly training those willing to commit to the journey and the discipline to persevere. The compendium of the recipe contained herein, allows an organization to accomplish goals previously not thought possible: independent of global location, customs and norms. For us this was one of the most difficult challenges to rise to, in that the direct approaches used in Japan were not natural for a U.S. manufacturing organization. So we had to commit to understanding the goal of each step in the process and explaining to our teams not only how to do something, but why we're doing it. My belief is that translation and commitment must come from top level leadership in an organization—you must own it. Some actions that you will take to reduce waste and achieve the next level of performance, can look to be bad short term financial decisions. This is where he reminds you of the goal of "Zero Defects". The implicit assumption being that the customer wants a perfect product and if you are able to deliver it, many good things happen throughout the value chain. After practicing TPS for a long period, since 2006 for us, you realize that the vision of "Zero Defects" is what is important—not if and when you actually achieve it.

Some results we achieved in our journey (so far) are:
- The Raymond Team achieved a defect reduction from a baseline average in 2006 of 1.23 defects per unit down to 0.0036 defects per unit in November of 2019
- In one Raymond facility we increased production from 4,000 units shipped in 2008 to 22,000 units shipped in 2019 within the same MFG square footage (450% increase), optimizing before we automate

- Our Raymond associates have generated over 100,000 kaizen suggestions from the inception of the Kaizen program in 2007
- The Raymond Greene Plant received the 2015 Toyota Industries President's Award in recognition of our exceptional achievements and contribution toward the Global TOSO Paint Improvement Project activity

I strongly recommend you consider the "Nomura Method" to help you implement TPS. It has allowed our organization to rise to new levels of lean management expertise, from the plant floor to the back office, including optimizing our distribution companies and even helping our suppliers and customers to do the same. We are living proof that an organization can reinvent itself using this method, even as we approach our 100 year anniversary! Thank you Mr. Nomura.

Michael Field
President and CEO, The Raymond Corporation
- a Toyota Industries Company

Introduction

by John Shook and Toshiko Narusawa

Welcome to a story of remarkable quality improvement inside the world's best quality manufacturer. Even the best can get better. As you will learn in these pages, not only can they get better, the best can get extremely better.

Quality at Toyota Logistics & Forklift

You have surely heard of the Toyota Production System and its two pillars of JIT and Jidoka and of its foundation of stability from standardized work and continuous improvement & innovation. As Toyota explains TPS on its website:

> *The Toyota Production System (TPS) was established based on two concepts: "jidoka" (which can be loosely translated as "automation with a human touch"), as when a problem occurs, the equipment stops immediately, preventing defective products from being produced; and the "Just-in-Time" concept, in which each process produces only what is needed for the next process in a continuous flow.*

Just as TPS begins with Jidoka, any effective system of production begins with building in quality. The Toyota approach to quality has its origins in the founding of the Toyoda group of companies during its formative period in the late 19th and early 20th centuries. Sakichi Toyoda (1867-1930) is as known in Japan as perhaps Eli Whitney in the US or James Watt in the UK. Sakichi was struggling to follow in the footsteps of his father as a carpenter when he was bitten by the inventor's bug. Sparked by two inspirations, one personal and one of national ambition, Sakichi got a patent for his Jidoka invention in the first decade of the 1900s, an important milestone but just one step in over three decades of tireless effort to attain his goal of producing the world's best automatic loom, which he introduced to global acclaim in 1924.

His first inspiration was a very personal one, with images of his mother and other women weavers in his hometown in Japan's current Shizuoka Prefecture struggling at their hand-operated wooden looms. But, his more immediate inspiration was one of national ambition as Sakichi was emboldened by new Japanese government policies to encourage local invention in order to compete in a global economic and political environment in which Japan was seemingly hopelessly behind.

Along the way, Sakichi founded a few companies. One of them is Toyota Industries Corporation from which Toyota Motor Corporation was spun off in 1937 and today is the parent of the TOYOTA Material Handling Group, widely known as the Toyota Logistics & Forklift Company (TL&F). It is only fitting for TL&F to be ground zero for the most important advances in quality improvement since the Deming-inspired quality improvements of the post-WWII Japanese economic miracle. Those advances are the story of this book.

The author of the book, and progenitor of the story, could be recognized as a latter-day J. Edwards Deming. Over a period of almost ten years, Sadao Nomura led TL&F through a series of activities and discoveries that radically raised the quality level of their products and, more importantly for us, along the way instituted a replicable process—replicable by any manufacturer. The process is replicable only with diligence and persistence along a journey of extreme quality improvement that begins with cutting in-process defects (reduced at TL&F by 98%), putting the brakes on customer claims (reduced at TL&F by 93%), and instituting upstream design engineering processes to prevent defects from occurring in the first place.

To state it as succinctly as possible: follow the steps laid out in detail within these pages and you will enjoy the same radical improvements in quality as Toyota Logistics & Forklift and other companies.

Jidoka—A Concept for the 21st Century

The Toyota Production System and your production system should begin from the same starting point: building in quality. Achieving perfect quality that is built-in—not reworked upon later inspection—is one of the two basic purposes of Jidoka. The other purpose is a matter of respect for humanity. But, first, a word on this curious word "Jidoka".

Jidoka as a term can cause confusion even in Japan because it is a made-up Toyota term (a Japanese portmanteau) that is based on the Japanese word and kanji for automation.

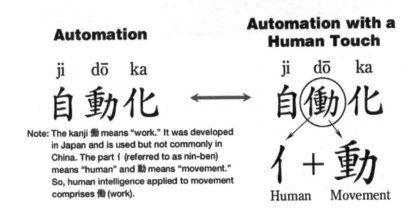

Automation

ji   dō   ka

自 動 化 ⟷

Note: The kanji 働 means "work." It was developed in Japan and is used but not commonly in China. The part 亻 (referred to as nin-ben) means "human" and 動 means "movement." So, human intelligence applied to movement comprises 働 (work).

Automation with a Human Touch

ji   dō   ka

自 働 化

亻 ＋ 動

Human   Movement

Reprinted with permission from *Kaizen Express*, Lean Enterprise Institute, 2009.

The work of a machine—or the function of any technology—should be separated from the work of humans, with assurance made that machines or any automation should work for humans—not the other way around! This respect for humanity, and this way of thinking about the design of work, is the foundation of all work at all Toyota companies.

The automatic shuttle-changing mechanism fitted to this loom enabled automatic shuttle replacement and supplying weft yarn without any loss of speed during high-speed operation. Other features included a shuttle-change guide, weft break auto-stop, warp break auto-stop and other devices to provide automation, protection, health and safety. This loom delivered the world's top performance in terms of productivity and textile quality. An engineer from Platt Brothers & Co., Ltd. of England, one of the world's leading manufacturers of textile machinery at the time, admiringly referred to this loom as "the magic loom." Following the successful development of the automatic loom, on November 17, 1926, the incorporation meeting of Toyoda Automatic Loom Works, Ltd. (now Toyota Industries Corporation) was held at the head office of Toyoda Boshoku in Nagoya City.
Source: https://www.toyota-industries.com/company/history/toyoda_sakichi/
Reproduced with permission of Toyota Industries Corporation

Dantotsu

Following Jidoka, a second Japanese concept has been appropriated that constitutes the core concept of this book and the 21st century production system of the Toyota Logistics & Forklift Company. Dantotsu is a colloquialism that means something like "extreme" (think "Extreme Programming") or "awesome" or "radical". So, Dantotsu quality is quality performance that is extremely better: Radical Quality Improvement.

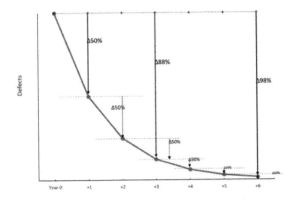

Radical Quality Improvement Curve

Sadao Nomura began his work with TL&F upon request in 2006 following a career with Toyota Motor Corporation that spanned more than four decades during which he experienced a wider-then-usual variety of responsibilities from manufacturing to quality assurance to support for suppliers and global operations. Notably at the Motomachi Plant, Nomura-sensei promoted development of key quality and productivity performance improvement processes that led to best-ever new vehicle launch performance with full-scale production volume stability attained in the first month of production for Toyota's best-selling 6th generation Mark II (known in some markets as the Cressida) mid-size passenger car.

The principles and methods introduced by Sadao Nomura led directly to remarkable quality improvement inside the world's best quality manufacturer. Nomura-sensei and TL&F proved that even the best can get better. As they did, you also can get *radically better*.

John Shook, Cambridge USA
Toshiko Narusawa, Kawasaki Japan

Introduction

Many companies seem to be in trouble because their product quality is not getting better despite company-wide quality improvement efforts under the "quality first" policy.

Even if it is known that the poor quality is due to something missing or wrong with the current quality improvement efforts, it is not easy to identify the real cause.

So, based on my hands-on experience and expertise gained at several domestic and overseas Toyota Motor plants, I would like to introduce some examples of activities that brought about significant effects on quality improvement at the Industrial Vehicle Division of Toyota Industries Corporation. I wrote this book hoping that you discover "what is really needed" by comparing my experience with your company's quality activities. I hope it will be helpful to you.

June 2016

Sadao Nomura

Toyota-Style "Dantotsu Quality Activities"

Contents

Part 1 Target Setting

Part 2 Standardization and Human Resource Development

Part 3 Weak-Point Management and Quality Creation

Chapter 9 Reduction of in-process defects (Type Ⓐ defect)

Chapter 10 Change-point control

Part 4 Always Respect the Basics

Chapter 11 2S (*Seiri* and *Seiton*)

Chapter 12 Stabilization of production line

Part 5 Systems for Continuation and Deepening

Motivation enhancement through global quality improvement competition

—Toyota Motor and Toyota Industries

In July 2006, upon request from Toyota Industries Corporation, I was inaugurated as a quality advisor for its Industrial Vehicle Division. The mission given to me was to provide guidance about quality improvement to three industrial vehicle manufacturers that the company acquired in 2000 in Sweden, Italy and the United States and their suppliers. In addition, I was also requested to give guidance to directly operated plants and their suppliers in Japan, France and the United States.

It seems to me that such an important mission came to me because of my experience with teaching quality improvement at Toyota Australia and Toyota South Africa, in addition to the on-site management experience based on the Toyota Production System at the Toyota Motomachi Plant. This book describes my experience.

Full view of the Takahama Plant of Toyota Industries Corporation

(1) Assigned to Toyota Australia (February 1989 - December 1991)

General Motors decided to close its Dandenong Plant (located in the suburbs of Melbourne city) due to aging; and therefore, by taking over the plant and its employees, Toyota launched a "New Corolla Production Increase Project," in which I participated as a manufacturing leader. Despite unfavorable conditions, such as old facilities and employees accustomed to the GM culture, we were able to reduce quality defects by 90% and achieve a market share expansion.

(2) Assigned to Toyota South Africa (April 1997 - August 2002)

At that time, nearly all of the cars produced by Toyota South Africa were sold to the local market, boasting an overwhelming market share. However, three German manufacturers, BMW, Mercedes-Benz and VW, which also had production bases in South Africa, rapidly expanded vehicle exports by taking advantage of export incentives promoted by the Mandela administration, launched after the abolition of Apartheid (a system of institutionalized racial segregation and discrimination). By using the incentives, they curtailed the local sales prices of their vehicles to expand their market shares. As a result, Toyota South Africa's market share declined and business conditions deteriorated gradually. To raise the performance of Toyota South Africa to compete with the three German manufacturers, exporting was indispensable, but the quality of the company's cars was the worst among Toyota's overseas plants, so the company was unable to obtain export permission from the Toyota head office.

In that situation I was appointed to work for Toyota South Africa with the mission of "improving its quality and achieving exports". Although it took five and a half years, I succeeded in achieving the goal and making Toyota South Africa a global export base. (For more details, see Chapter 15.)

In both of the above two cases, the goal was the improvement of each plant of each company. In order to achieve it, I worked inside as a member of the company for several years and built good relationships with the employees by living and sharing joy and sorrow with them. In cases where improvements did not proceed at all, it was possible to do it by myself as a last resort.

However, what Toyota Industries expected me to do at six companies (seven vehicle manufacturing plants) and numerous parts manufacturers located in five countries was to give them guidance at the same time as an "advisor" without having any particular authority and bring about good results. It seemed to be an almost impossible mission for me. Nevertheless, I thought that I was fortunate to have the opportunity to try such a big job at the end of a salaried employee's

Chart 1 Industrial vehicle plants of Toyota Industries

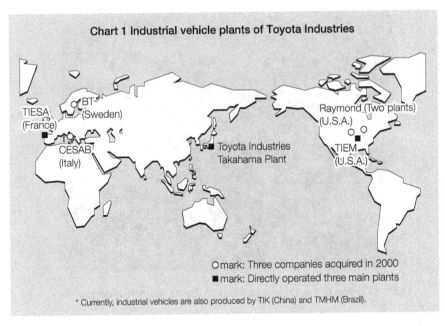

TIESA (France)

BT (Sweden)

CESAB (Italy)

Toyota Industries Takahama Plant

Raymond (Two plants) (U.S.A.)

TIEM (U.S.A.)

○ mark: Three companies acquired in 2000
■ mark: Directly operated three main plants

* Currently, industrial vehicles are also produced by TIK (China) and TMHM (Brazil).

Chart 2 World market shares of major forklift manufacturers (2014)

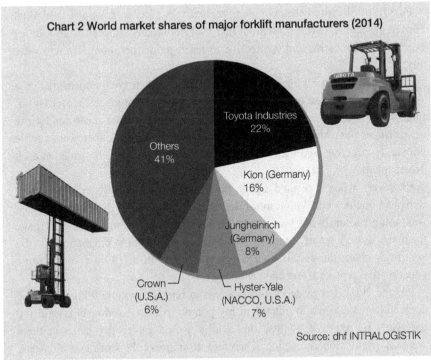

Toyota Industries
22%

Others
41%

Kion (Germany)
16%

Jungheinrich (Germany)
8%

Crown (U.S.A.)
6%

Hyster-Yale (NACCO, U.S.A.)
7%

Source: dhf INTRALOGISTIK

9

Assembly line at the Takahama Plant of Toyota Industries Corporation

life.

First of all, I visited each company regularly in order to grasp the individual current situations, and it turned out that every company suffered from a lot of poor quality problems and wanted me to teach proper solutions, if there were any.

Then, I wrote out all the problems I noticed and their countermeasures on a sheet of A3 size paper, explained them to the relevant employees in an easy-to-understand manner, and instructed them to implement those measures by my next visit as their homework. The measures I wrote on the paper were simple but surely effective, and their effectiveness had already been confirmed at each Toyota plant.

However, when I visited again three or four months later, everything remained unchanged. With a lot of defects still occurring, I did not know what was going on and what kind of countermeasures had been taken. So I gave them the same kind of English notes again and told them emphatically: "Be sure to do these things this time". However, even on my third visit the same situation was repeated, and one year passed.

In June 2007, I regarded it meaningless to repeat the same thing again and decided to make a major change in my policy. Even if I seriously considered the ways to improve quality, the quality would never get better without workers' motivation and action. Therefore, to improve the work consciousness and behavior of workers, I proposed the kick-off of *"Dantotsu* (unparalleled) Quality Activities" and received approval at Toyota Industries' global quality conference. The major points are described below.

Kick-off of Toyota Industries' "Dantotsu Quality Activities"

(1) Importance of quality
"Quality is the basic point for every manufacturer".
"The most important thing is to surpass rivals with quality".

(2) Recognition of the current state of quality
- Outflow of quality defects to the market did not stop, causing great inconvenience to customers.
- Quality defects did not decrease at vehicle manufacturing plants or suppliers, and continuously produced waste. Therefore, it was necessary to "go back to the basics of *monozukuri* (conscientious manufacturing)".

(3) Quality activity policy
- Since quality would not improve immediately, it was decided that the improvement activities would be continued for three years to get good results and maximize our superiority against competitors.
- We called the activities "Dantotsu (unparalleled) Quality Activities".

(4) Quality targets
Based on comparison with the results in 2006:
Quality defects at vehicle manufacturing plants and suppliers: To be halved each year × 3 years = -88%.
Market claims: To be halved within three years = -50%

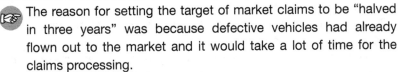 The reason for setting the target of market claims to be "halved in three years" was because defective vehicles had already flown out to the market and it would take a lot of time for the claims processing.

11

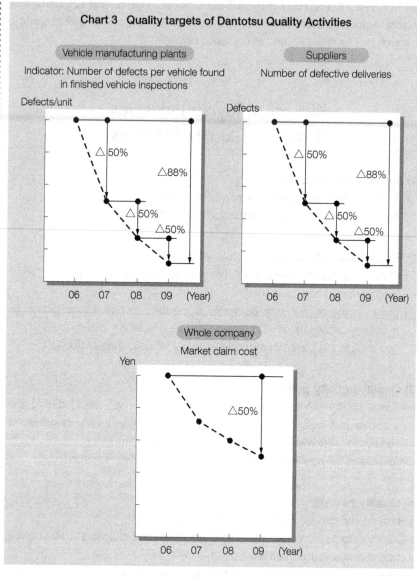

Chart 3 Quality targets of Dantotsu Quality Activities

Vehicle manufacturing plants

Indicator: Number of defects per vehicle found in finished vehicle inspections

Defects/unit

△50%

△88%

△50%

△50%

06 07 08 09 (Year)

Suppliers

Number of defective deliveries

Defects

△50%

△88%

△50%

△50%

06 07 08 09 (Year)

Whole company

Market claim cost

Yen

△50%

06 07 08 09 (Year)

(5) Progress follow-up

Progress of the entire group's quality activities was confirmed at the annual global quality conference.

(The conference was held at each company in rotation, and checking actual items at actual places, called *"GENCHI GENBUTSU"*, was also carried out.)

12

Through encouragement of the entire group to work toward the common target, as well as the announcement of good or bad results, each company started seriously preparing for quality improvement efforts. Thus, the foundation for group-wide quality improvement was established. The Dantotsu Quality Activities, which were initially planned for three years, proved to be steadily effective in reducing quality defects, although there were some ups and downs. Therefore, the activities were continued as Dantotsu-II from 2010 to 2012 and Dantotsu-III from 2013 to 2015, motivating the entire group to continue forward to achieve the ultimate goal "zero defects".

Quality defects occur unless all 4M elements (Man, Material, Machine and Method) are perfect. Therefore, it can be said that "quality is a barometer of a company's strength". The occurrence of quality defects indicates that a problem exists somewhere in the company. "Searching and identifying the problem and taking measures to prevent recurrence of it" is a true quality improvement activity. Working all together, honestly, steadily and thoroughly is the only way to improve the quality. There is no other way and there are no short cuts.

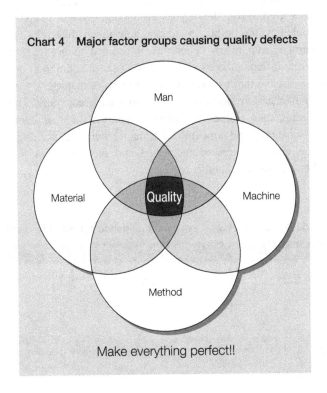

Chart 4   Major factor groups causing quality defects

Make everything perfect!!

However, there are countless routes for achievement, not only one. Nobody knows which route to approach the goal of "zero defects". Each of the companies had followed individual the routes they believed in; unfortunately however, good results did not come out. All of the employees had been making efforts for years, but had no favorable results. Therefore, they tended to think it meaningless to continue to do the same things, and they wanted to change something.

So, I explained what I had experienced at the Toyota Motomachi Plant, Toyota Australia, and Toyota South Africa; and asked them to practice straightforwardly in what I would teach them along with the "Dantotsu Quality Activities". Everyone seemed to only half-trust in it, but started the activity at last by saying "Let's do it anyway."

In order to deal with such a large number of students (companies), I prepared an A3-size text sheet, written in both Japanese and English about each step to teach, and traveled around domestically and abroad, giving *GENCHI GENBUTSU* lessons at each site eight hours a day using the text. The number of A3-size memos reached nearly 300 sheets, which have spread out all over the world known as the "Nomura Memo" or "Nomura Method".

For overseas employees, the Toyota Production System (TPS) seemed to have some unbelievable points, no matter how much they read the relevant books or learned from others. Therefore, I decided to hold a 2-week TPS training program in Japan three or four times a year in addition to the local on-site lessons, and gave that experience to 100 or more managers, team leaders, engineers, and other key persons coming from each company. Through this training program, they learned by actually seeing with their own eyes and experiencing what they had not believed through reading or listening. That kind of experience greatly increased the speed and motivation of their on-site activities after they returned home.

Chart 5 Annual quality improvement guidance schedule (example)

	Jan.	Feb.	Mar.	Apr.	May	Jun.	Jul.	Aug.	Sep.	Oct.	Nov.	Dec.
Business trip to EU	3W					3W		3W				
Business trip to U.S.A.			3W				3W				3W	
Giving lessons in Japan		2W			2W					2W		

*The time other than the above-indicated was mainly spent on providing guidance to domestic vehicle plants and suppliers, or creating texts.

The Dantotsu Quality Activities that had started in 2007 temporarily ended in March 2016. My long-term efforts for as many as nine years to strive to improve the quality honestly at seven forklift manufacturing plants and many suppliers scattered across Japan, the United States, Sweden, Italy and France finally bore splendid fruit that astonished everyone. And, since many people both at home and abroad who participated in the activities wanted me to summarize the quality improvement process into a book, I decided to create this book based on 300 sheets of A3-size memos I wrote in those days. The contents described here are all the things that proved to be effective in my experience, including ideas and knacks for quality improvement learned at each company. I have confirmed that the quality will surely improve if they are implemented, so please try them at your company. Now, I will explain the details of Dantotsu Quality Activities in line with the processes I actually implemented.

* The overseas base names have been changed since April 1, 2016 as follows, but in this book, the former names are used.

	Old names (used until March 31, 2016)		New names (used from April 1, 2016)	
	Abbreviations	Formal names	Abbreviations	Formal names
1	BT	BT Products AB	TMHMS	Toyota Material Handling Manufacturing Sweden AB
2	TIESA	Toyota Industrial Equipment S.A.	TMHMF	Toyota Material Handling Manufacturing France S.A.S.
3	CESAB	CESAB Carrelli Elevatori S.p.A.	TMHMI	Toyota Material Handling Manufacturing Italy S.p.A.

Part **1**

Target Setting

Chapter 1

Setting concrete targets to achieve zero defects

1. Flow of quality information and definition of defects

Depending on where a defect is found, the seriousness of the defect will change greatly. First of all, it is necessary to draw a diagram showing the material flow and quality information flow in the entire group, and to standardize a defect classification method indicating the seriousness depending on where each defect was found (Chart 1-1).

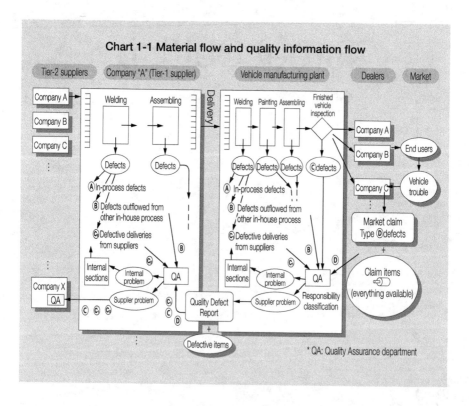

Chart 1-1 Material flow and quality information flow

It is very important to clarify the definitions of terms to be used in group-wide quality activities involving a large number of companies. At Toyota Industries, those terms are defined as follows (Chart 1-2).

Chart 1-2 Definitions of different types of "defects" classified in quality activities

Defect classification	Parts manufacturer	Vehicle manufacturing plants
	(Tier-1 supplier)	
	In-process defects	←
Ⓐdefects	In shop floor	Defects found by the worker who caused them or others on the same shop floor and not outflowing to the subsequent process.
Ⓑdefects	Internally found defects Defects not detected in the relevant shop but found in the internal subsequent process and not outflowing to the outside of the company.	← Defects not detected in the relevant shop but found in the internal subsequent process and not outflowing to the finished vehicle inspection process.
Ⓒdefects	Externally found defects Defects not detected in the company but found in the customer's manufacturing process Ⓒ or in the finished vehicle inspection Ⓒ (Defective deliveries from Tier-2 supplier shall be indicated by "Ⓒ".)	Defects found in finished vehicle inspection Defects not found in the manufacturing process but detected in the finished vehicle inspection line of the quality assurance department.
Ⓓdefects	Market defects Defects not detected in the company or by the customer and outflowing to the market, resulting in vehicle trouble during use by end users.	← Defects not detected in the manufacturing process or the finished vehicle inspection line and outflowing to the market, resulting in vehicle trouble during use by end users.

- Not only users in the marketplace, but also subsequent process workers should be regarded as "customers"!
  The outflow of quality defects to the subsequent process causes major inconveniences such as interruption of work and/or reworking of defects. Therefore, it is necessary to tackle zero outflow of any defects to anywhere including subsequent processes.
- Leadership in the quality assurance department is extremely important.
  In order to deliver products with zero quality defects to customers in the market, we need activities that can assure quality throughout all processes of the supply chain from material suppliers (first process) to dealers (final process). Therefore, the role of the quality assurance department, which is responsible for cross-sectional quality management, is very important.

2. Target Setting

(1) Target setting for vehicle manufacturing plants

The quality assurance department confirmed the annual quality performance data of the base (reference) year on each indicator mentioned in "Dantotsu Quality Activities" and set targets for the entire company and each department for the subsequent three years. It was determined as a rule not to change targets once they are set (even in the case of unfavorable results, one should never lower the target value in order to put up a front). The following are examples of target setting for our "Dantotsu Quality Activities".

1) Target: Reducing the market claim costs (example)

The target of reducing market claim costs was set up as follows (Chart 1-3).

Chart 1-3   Market claim cost reduction targets (example)

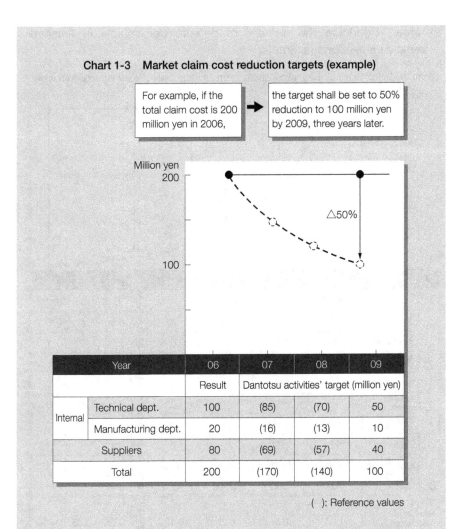

| For example, if the total claim cost is 200 million yen in 2006, | ➡ | the target shall be set to 50% reduction to 100 million yen by 2009, three years later. |

Year		06	07	08	09
		Result	Dantotsu activities' target (million yen)		
Internal	Technical dept.	100	(85)	(70)	50
	Manufacturing dept.	20	(16)	(13)	10
Suppliers		80	(69)	(57)	40
Total		200	(170)	(140)	100

(   ): Reference values

- The general managers of technical and manufacturing departments broke down their respective department targets, determined individual sections' targets within each department, and instructed each section manager to start the three-year Dantotsu Quality Activities.
- The quality assurance department prepared a market claim amount chart for 2006 by supplier. For the top-thirty suppliers that showed the worst results, the department presented a 50-percent reduction target to each company, and supported the claim reduction activities.

2) Target: Reducing the number of defects per vehicle in finished vehicle inspections (example)

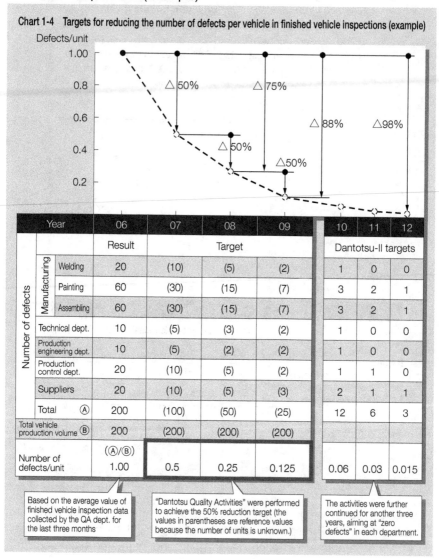

Chart 1-4   Targets for reducing the number of defects per vehicle in finished vehicle inspections (example)

Year		06	07	08	09	10	11	12
		Result	Target			Dantotsu-II targets		
Manufacturing	Welding	20	(10)	(5)	(2)	1	0	0
	Painting	60	(30)	(15)	(7)	3	2	1
	Assembling	60	(30)	(15)	(7)	3	2	1
Number of defects	Technical dept.	10	(5)	(3)	(2)	1	0	0
	Production engineering dept.	10	(5)	(2)	(2)	1	0	0
	Production control dept.	20	(10)	(5)	(2)	1	1	0
	Suppliers	20	(10)	(5)	(3)	2	1	1
	Total (A)	200	(100)	(50)	(25)	12	6	3
Total vehicle production volume (B)		200	(200)	(200)	(200)			
Number of defects/unit		((A)/(B)) 1.00	0.5	0.25	0.125	0.06	0.03	0.015

Based on the average value of finished vehicle inspection data collected by the QA dept. for the last three months

"Dantotsu Quality Activities" were performed to achieve the 50% reduction target (the values in parentheses are reference values because the number of units is unknown.)

The activities were further continued for another three years, aiming at "zero defects" in each department.

- The target for each section was based on the 2006 results for the number of defects per day because the value would become too small if it were based on the number of defects per vehicle. Setting the reference values in parentheses as targets makes it easier for on-site workers to understand the targets. Each section manager decided this and informed all members in the individual sections. (Chart 1-4)

3) Target: Reducing the number of supplier-related* defective deliveries

Chart 1-5 Worst supplier list

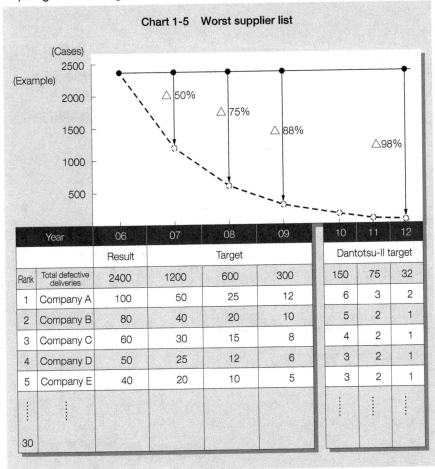

Year	06	07	08	09	10	11	12
	Result		Target		Dantotsu-II target		
Rank / Total defective deliveries	2400	1200	600	300	150	75	32
1 Company A	100	50	25	12	6	3	2
2 Company B	80	40	20	10	5	2	1
3 Company C	60	30	15	8	4	2	1
4 Company D	50	25	12	6	3	2	1
5 Company E	40	20	10	5	3	2	1
⋮	⋮				⋮	⋮	⋮
30							

- The quality assurance department checked the number of defective deliveries from suppliers in FY 2006 and prepared a worst suppliers list. For the top-thirty worst suppliers, the department set Dantotsu activity targets, presented respective targets to each company, and supported their reduction activities. (Charts 1-5 and 1-6)

* "Supplier-related" means "the suppliers were responsible for the defects".

Chart 1-6   Tips for successful quality improvement activities by suppliers

Get the commitment of the top management of each supplier!

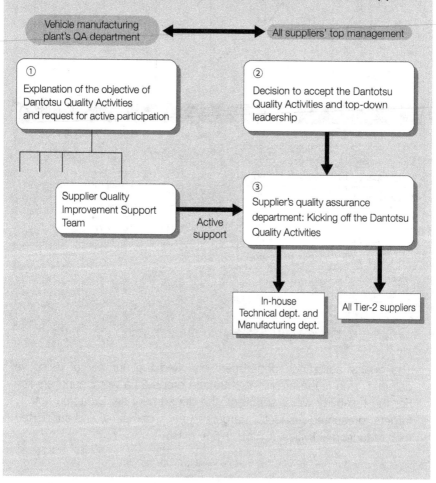

Vehicle manufacturing plant's QA department ⟷ All suppliers' top management

① Explanation of the objective of Dantotsu Quality Activities and request for active participation

② Decision to accept the Dantotsu Quality Activities and top-down leadership

Supplier Quality Improvement Support Team → Active support

③ Supplier's quality assurance department: Kicking off the Dantotsu Quality Activities

In-house Technical dept. and Manufacturing dept.

All Tier-2 suppliers

(2) Target setting for each parts manufacturer

We considered that the "Dantotsu Quality Activities" started by Toyota Industries Group was also a good opportunity for each supplier (parts manufacturer) to dramatically improve quality. Therefore, we decided to extend the activities to all suppliers (Chart 1-7).

Chart 1-7   Flow of quality defect information viewed from parts manufacturers

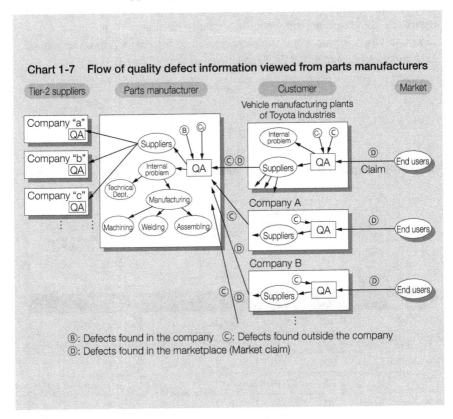

ⓑ: Defects found in the company   ⓒ: Defects found outside the company
ⓓ: Defects found in the marketplace (Market claim)

1) Target of reducing market claim costs by parts manufacturers

• The quality assurance department checked the total market claims cost informed by customers in 2006, and also checked individual amounts related to technical departments, manufacturing departments and suppliers, respectively. Based on those results, the quality assurance department set a 50-percent reduction goal for the subsequent three years and presented it to each department. The setting method is the same as in the case of the vehicle manufacturing plants. Please refer to "(1) Target setting for vehicle manufacturing plants" in this chapter "2. Target Setting".

2) Target of reducing defect outflow by parts manufacturers (example)

The quality assurance department checked the total number of Type C defects found externally (outside the company)" and informed by customers in 2006, as well as the results by responsible department. Based on the results, the quality assurance department set a 50-percent reduction target for each shop for the subsequent three years and presented it to each in-house department. With regard to the relevant suppliers, the quality assurance department set a reduction target for the worst suppliers, presented it to the top management of each supplier, and supported their reduction activities (Chart 1-8).

Chart 1-8   Target of reducing defect outflow by parts manufacturers (example)

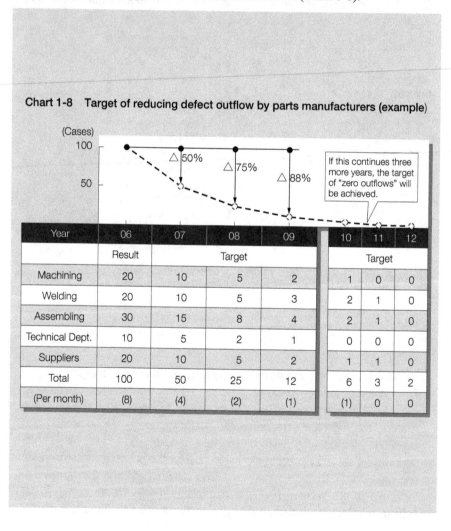

Year	06	07	08	09	10	11	12
	Result	Target			Target		
Machining	20	10	5	2	1	0	0
Welding	20	10	5	3	2	1	0
Assembling	30	15	8	4	2	1	0
Technical Dept.	10	5	2	1	0	0	0
Suppliers	20	10	5	2	1	1	0
Total	100	50	25	12	6	3	2
(Per month)	(8)	(4)	(2)	(1)	(1)	0	0

(Cases)
100
50

△50%   △75%   △88%

If this continues three more years, the target of "zero outflows" will be achieved.

Chapter 2

Visualization of defects

"Visualization" is a key factor that determines the success or failure of quality improvement activities. The quality assurance department set up a defect visualization system with the aim of efficiently and surely achieving milestone targets and the final goal of "zero defects".

1. Installation of Quality Management Board

A "quality indication stand" was set up in the central area of each plant so that anyone can see the quality status up to the previous. In this way, it became possible for everyone to see whether the product quality of the entire company was improving or not. One of important roles of this board was to make the departments that frequently caused defects feel a sense of crisis and feel, "This is bad. We must do something now!" (Chart 2-1).

(1) Quality Management Board for vehicle manufacturing plants

- Changes in quality status were visualized at three levels (Chart 2-2).
- A long-span transition of more than five years was visible, allowing for determination of appropriateness of the quality activities (Chart 2-3).
- It enabled workers to see details without using a computer.
  It's true that there is no tool as convenient as a computer from the viewpoint of data management. However, if it is only the supervisor who looks at it, and workers who actually make products and engineers who draw designs do not see it, the quality will definitely not get better.
- In principle, the current state of quality was written by hand.
  If a computer is used, a series of the procedures, "input → print → change of paper", will be required, which causes a waste of time and paper. In contrast, handwriting takes only three to five minutes.
- The Type ⓓ defects found in the marketplace were visualized on another board.

- Because the Type ⓓ defects were defects found in previously produced vehicles, it was easier to manage them on a different board from the one used for Types ⓑ and ⓒ defects that were found in currently produced vehicles.

Chart 2-1 Quality Management Board for the vehicle manufacturing plant

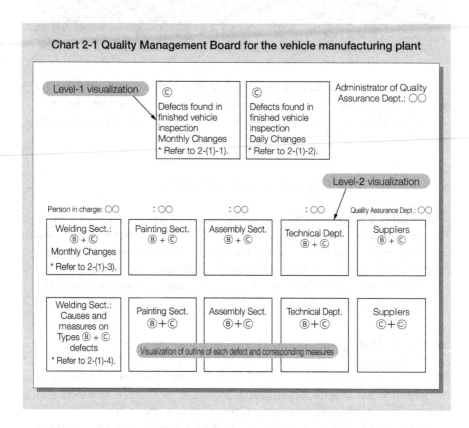

Chart 2-2   Changes in quality status visualized at three levels

Level	What to visualize
I	Trend in the whole plant
II	Trend in individual sections
III	Trend in individual sections' weak points

Chart 2-3   Visualization of quality activities

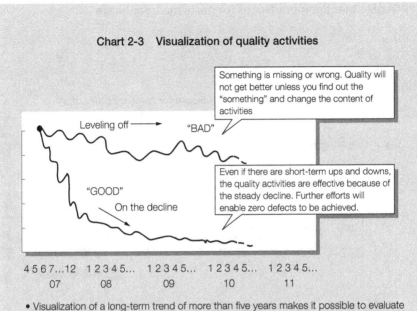

• Visualization of a long-term trend of more than five years makes it possible to evaluate the effects of the quality activities.

Quality Management Board at CESAB (Italy)

(2) Quality Management Board for parts manufacturers

Chart 2-4   Quality Management Board for parts manufacturers

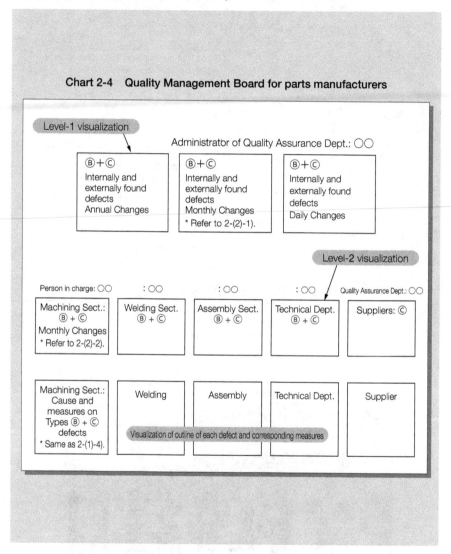

- For Types ⒷⒷ and ⒸⒸ defects related information that is provided by customers and internal departments, the quality assurance department's person in charge of the management board immediately filled it in the relevant sheets and contacted the responsible department (Chart 2-4).

2. Defect Outflow Visualization Sheet

The information that should be displayed first on the quality management board is defect outflow. The following are examples of defect outflow visualizations at a vehicle manufacturing plant and a parts manufacturer, respectively.

(1) "Defect Outflow Visualization Sheet" for a vehicle manufacturing plant
1) Monthly changes for Type © defects found in finished vehicle inspection ... Level-1 visualization (whole plant) (Chart 2-5)

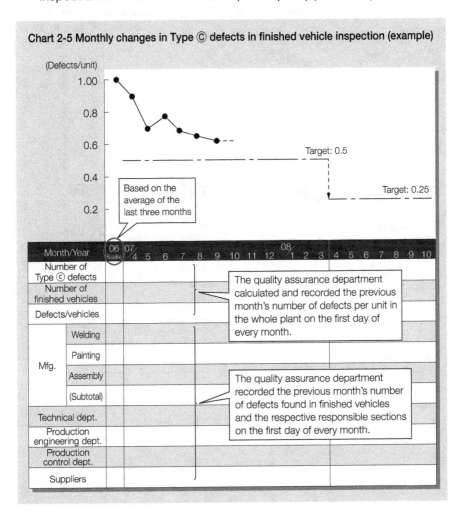

Chart 2-5 Monthly changes in Type © defects in finished vehicle inspection (example)

2) Daily changes for Type © defects found in finished vehicle inspection ... Level-1 visualization

The daily changes in occurrence of Type © defect were visualized in the same way as shown above (Chart 2-6). As it was easier to see the daily changes by the "number of defects", the left scale was set to "number of defects", while the right scale indicated "defects per vehicle".

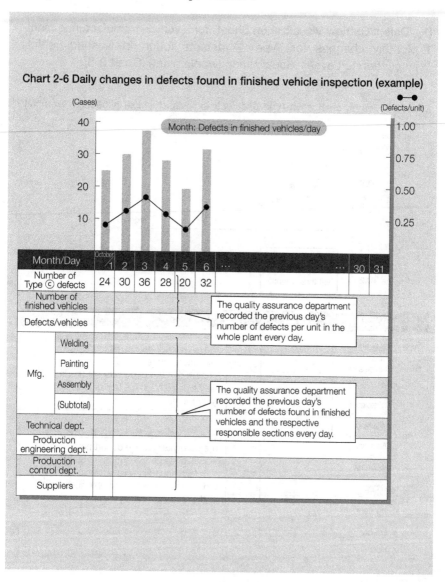

Chart 2-6 Daily changes in defects found in finished vehicle inspection (example)

Month/Day	October 1	2	3	4	5	6	...	...	30	31
Number of Type © defects	24	30	36	28	20	32				
Number of finished vehicles										
Defects/vehicles										
Mfg. Welding										
Mfg. Painting										
Mfg. Assembly										
Mfg. (Subtotal)										
Technical dept.										
Production engineering dept.										
Production control dept.										
Suppliers										

The quality assurance department recorded the previous day's number of defects per unit in the whole plant every day.

The quality assurance department recorded the previous day's number of defects found in finished vehicles and the respective responsible sections every day.

3) Monthly changes in Types Ⓑ and Ⓒ outflow defects from each department ... Level-2 visualization

The following were checked at each section:

• What kind of defect outflowed?

• From which team did it outflow?

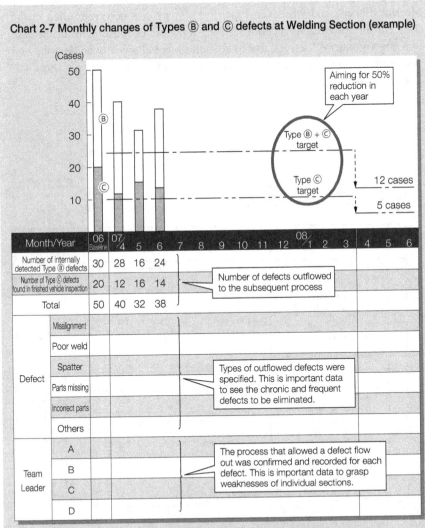

Chart 2-7 Monthly changes of Types Ⓑ and Ⓒ defects at Welding Section (example)

* A quality manager who would record and manage quality data was appointed at each section for accurate and timely visualization of the state of quality.

They were visualized in order to grasp the weak points of individual sections, and then necessary measures were taken intensively to reduce the number of defects (Chart 2-7).

4) Visualization of countermeasures against each outflow defect

The quality assurance department prepared a "Quality Defect Cause and Measure Sheet", and whenever Type Ⓑ or Ⓒ defects occurred, filled in the sheet for the responsible department using a picture or illustration. In the case of a large number of defects, five to six items were allowed to be described on one sheet as shown in Chart 2-8 (in case of few defects, one item per sheet was also acceptable).

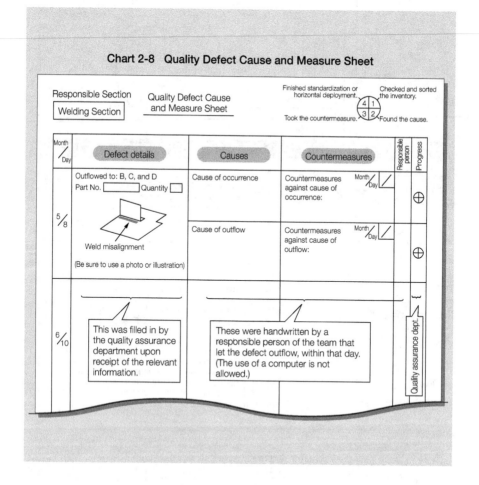

Chart 2-8   Quality Defect Cause and Measure Sheet

- When the same defect occurred repeatedly, the quality assurance department specified the number of occurrences in the defect description column.
- The responsible team leader reviewed the countermeasures that had been taken against the defect, discussed with workers why those measures failed to work, and implemented more effective measures that would surely prevent the recurrence of the same defect.
- The measures were taken to eliminate the causes of defect occurrence and defect outflow, respectively.
- If the problem was complicated, a "Weak-Point Management Sheet" (described later) was used to completely eliminate the causes of defects (see Chapter 8).

Visualization of countermeasures against each defect at CESAB (Italy)

(2) "Defects Visualization Sheet" for parts manufacturers
1) Monthly changes for defect outflow in the whole plant (Chart 2-9) ... Level-1 visualization

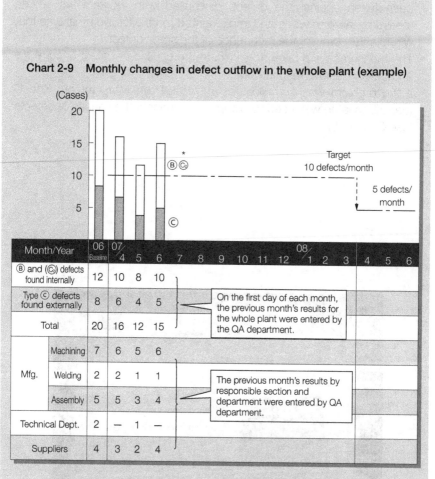

Chart 2-9   Monthly changes in defect outflow in the whole plant (example)

Month/Year	06 Baseline	07 4	5	6	7	8	9	10	11	12	08 1	2	3	4	5	6
Ⓑ and (Ⓒ₂) defects found internally	12	10	8	10												
Type Ⓒ defects found externally	8	6	4	5												
Total	20	16	12	15												
Mfg. Machining	7	6	5	6												
Mfg. Welding	2	2	1	1												
Mfg. Assembly	5	5	3	4												
Technical Dept.	2	—	1	—												
Suppliers	4	3	2	4												

On the first day of each month, the previous month's results for the whole plant were entered by the QA department.

The previous month's results by responsible section and department were entered by QA department.

* Type (Ⓒ₂) defects: They are defined as defective deliveries from Tier-2 suppliers. Improvement in the quality of outsourced parts is very important to ensure stable production, and it is necessary for the quality assurance department to have engineering staff for supplier quality improvement support and to provide suppliers with guidance.

2) Monthly changes for defect outflow from each department ... Level-2 visualization

A quality manager was appointed in each department to carry out quality improvement in cooperation with the quality assurance department. As parts manufacturers are generally small in organizational size, a team leader played this role in general.

For visualization, it is important not only to visualize the current state accurately and in a timely manner, but also to find weak points in each process

Chart 2-10   Types Ⓑ + Ⓒ defects found in machining process (example)

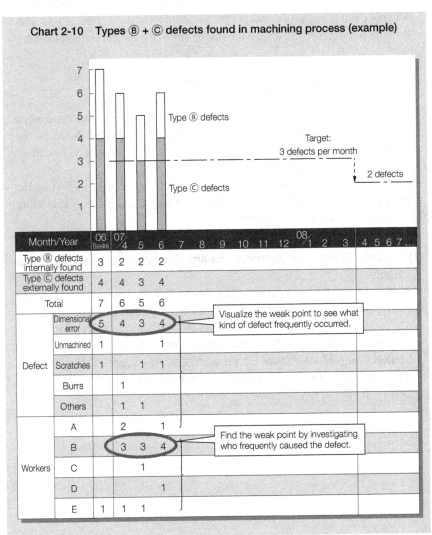

Month/Year	06 Baseline	07 4	5	6	7	8	9	10	11	12	08 1	2	3	4	5	6	7...
Type Ⓑ defects internally found	3	2	2	2													
Type Ⓒ defects externally found	4	4	3	4													
Total	7	6	5	6													
Defect — Dimensional error	5	4	3	4													
Defect — Unmachined	1			1													
Defect — Scratches	1		1	1													
Defect — Burrs		1															
Defect — Others		1	1														
Workers — A		2		1													
Workers — B		3	3	4													
Workers — C			1														
Workers — D				1													
Workers — E	1	1	1														

Visualize the weak point to see what kind of defect frequently occurred.

Find the weak point by investigating who frequently caused the defect.

from the sheet shown in the Chart 2-10 and to take proper preventive measures with workers against the recurrence of defects. For the sections that just filled in the sheet but did not utilize it, the quality assurance department staff went to the site to teach the team leader how to use it to prevent reoccurrence of defects, aiming to raise the overall awareness level of the worksite.

- Level-3 visualization was conducted after frequently occurring defects and the problematic processes were identified.
  For the defects found, the causes were written down on the Weak-Point Management Sheet (see Chapter 8) to eliminate them one by one. If you work hard for three years, you should be able to solve any complicated problems.

3. Market Claim Management Board

With respect to market claims that by their nature should not have occurred, a visualization on how much they were occurring was conducted based on the amount and the number of cases, and Dantotsu Quality Activities were carried out by all employees to reduce them.

It is important to consider the activities as "important activities affecting the company's fate" and conduct them to fulfill the target under strong leadership by the quality assurance department.

(1) Market Claim Management Board for vehicle manufacturing plants

- In the case of claims occurring due to outflow of quality defects to the marketplace, a large number of vehicles have already been shipped and so, even if countermeasures are taken promptly, it may take a long time to solve the trouble with all the target vehicles. For this reason, the Market Claim Management Board was used to visualize with a span of five years or more to take long-term measures aiming for "zero market claims" (Chart 2-11).

Chart 2-11 Market Claim Management Board for vehicle manufacturing plants (example)

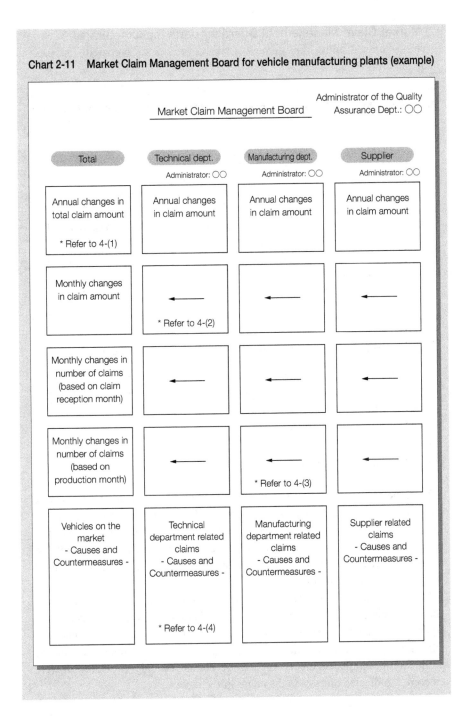

Market Claim Management Board

Administrator of the Quality Assurance Dept.: ○○

Total	Technical dept.	Manufacturing dept.	Supplier
	Administrator: ○○	Administrator: ○○	Administrator: ○○
Annual changes in total claim amount * Refer to 4-(1)	Annual changes in claim amount	Annual changes in claim amount	Annual changes in claim amount
Monthly changes in claim amount	← * Refer to 4-(2)	←	←
Monthly changes in number of claims (based on claim reception month)	←	←	←
Monthly changes in number of claims (based on production month)	←	← * Refer to 4-(3)	←
Vehicles on the market - Causes and Countermeasures -	Technical department related claims - Causes and Countermeasures - * Refer to 4-(4)	Manufacturing department related claims - Causes and Countermeasures -	Supplier related claims - Causes and Countermeasures -

(2) Market Claim Management Board for parts manufacturers

The Market Claim Management Boards were also prepared for parts manufacturers (Chart 2-12).

Chart 2-12   Market Claim Management Board for parts manufacturer (example)

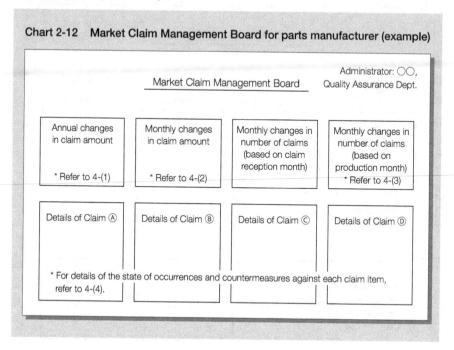

4. Market Claims Visualization Sheet

With the use of a "Market Claims Visualization Sheet", market claims were indicated on the Market Claim Management Board (Charts 2-13 and 2-14). This enabled us to see at a glance the trends in the amount and number of market claims, showing what kind of market claims occurred, when and how many they reached us, etc. It also visualized other information, such as "production month" and/or "relevant process".

In every plant, there are always some changes (model changes, minor changes, changes in tact time due to production increases or decreases, equipment changes or maintenance, work method changes, personnel allocation, etc.). We call them "change points" (see Chapter 10). In the production month-based chart, the "change points" (mainly big changes) were entered. It indicated hints as to the cause of the defect.

In addition to the change points, some market claims or complaints were attributable to "customer's usage time*"". By seeing the correlation between the customer's usage time and the production month on a scatter diagram for each "complaint item", it is possible to judge whether the countermeasure already taken has eliminated the root causes or not.

* Customer's usage time: Toyota Industries' products (forklifts) have a function to record how long the end user used them. With this record, higher levels of evaluation (more accurate analysis) is possible based on "how many hours" the product was used, instead of the "period" from the customer's start of use.

(1) Annual changes in market claim amount (Chart 2-13)

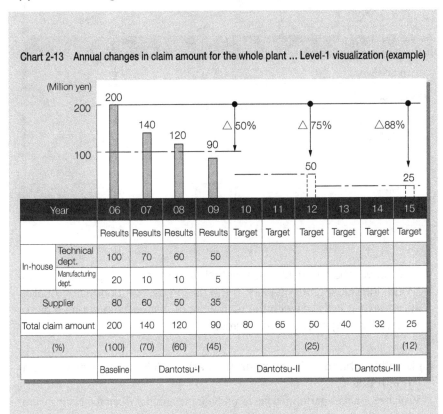

Chart 2-13   Annual changes in claim amount for the whole plant ... Level-1 visualization (example)

Year		06	07	08	09	10	11	12	13	14	15
		Results	Results	Results	Results	Target	Target	Target	Target	Target	Target
In-house	Technical dept.	100	70	60	50						
	Manufacturing dept.	20	10	10	5						
Supplier		80	60	50	35						
Total claim amount		200	140	120	90	80	65	50	40	32	25
(%)		(100)	(70)	(60)	(45)			(25)			(12)
		Baseline	Dantotsu-I			Dantotsu-II			Dantotsu-III		

(2) Monthly changes in market claim amount (Chart 2-14)

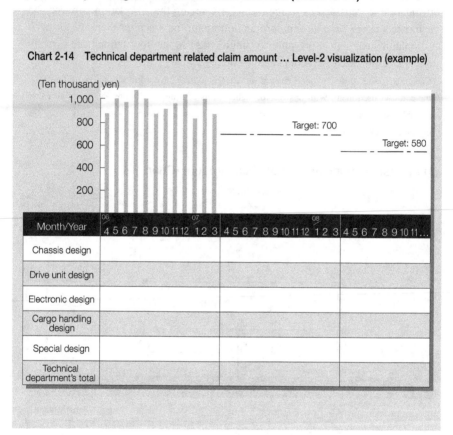

Chart 2-14   Technical department related claim amount ... Level-2 visualization (example)

- The above chart visualizes the actual values concerning each design group. Individual group leaders in the design section conducted quality improvement activities with the teamwork of respective groups so as to achieve the targets set for each group.

(3) Monthly changes in number of market claims on a production month basis

Visualization was performed based on both the months when the claims were received and when the relevant vehicles were produced. To determine the cause of the claim/complaint, it is effective to visualize what kind of change point(s) existed when the product or part was in production (Chart 2-15).

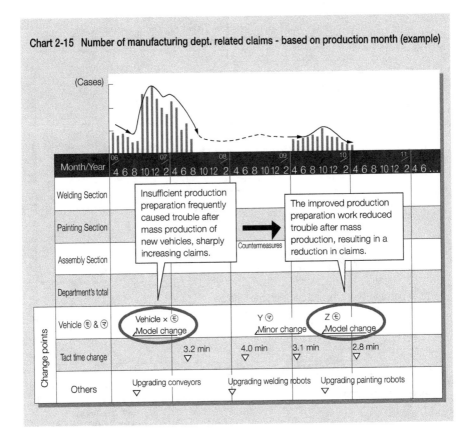

Chart 2-15 Number of manufacturing dept. related claims - based on production month (example)

- Visualization of big change points, such as a model change or tact time change due to a variation in production volume, makes it possible to facilitate identification of the causes especially when the number of complaints and claims is on the increase. If you can identify the cause and solve the problems one by one, the mountain of problems will surely get smaller.

(4) Details of each claim item ... Visualization on a sheet per claim

For each claim, the details of the defect and the number of claims based on claim reception month and production month were visualized, and changes in countermeasures were visualized on the usage time/production month scatter diagram (Chart 2-16). This sheet is very effective in identifying the cause of occurrence and judging the effectiveness of the countermeasure. This was prepared not only by the vehicle manufacturing plant, but also by parts manufacturers for all team members to consider countermeasures by looking at it.

Chart 2-16 Market Claim Visualization Sheet showing the state of occurrence and countermeasures against each claim item

Claim item [   ]   Person in charge: ○○

Part No.   Part name

1. Claimed defect

Illustrated	Details:

2. Number of claims based on claim reception month

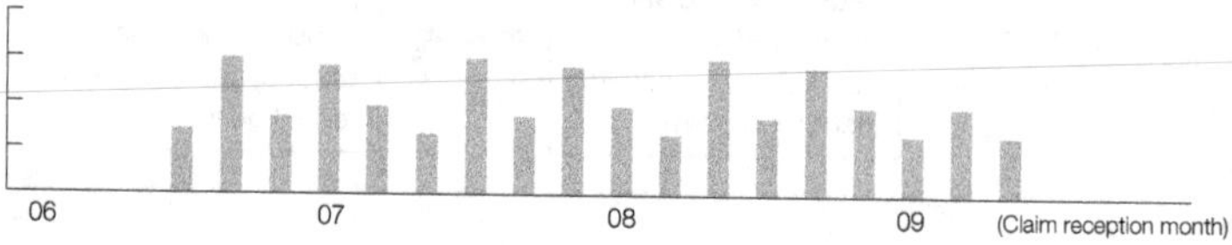

06   07   08   09   (Claim reception month)

3. Number of claims based on production month

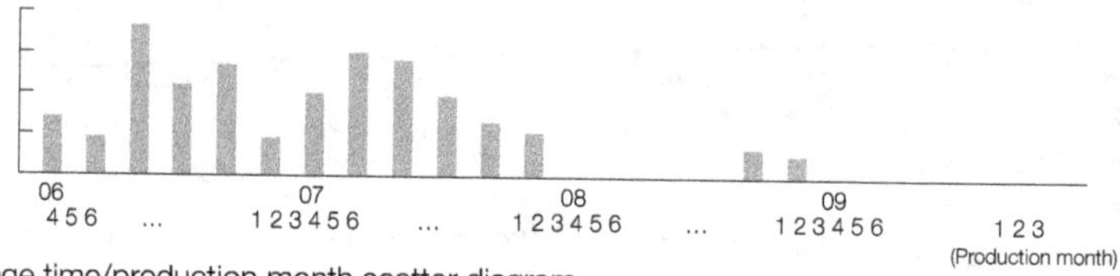

06   07   08   09
4 5 6   ...   1 2 3 4 5 6   ...   1 2 3 4 5 6   ...   1 2 3 4 5 6   1 2 3
                                                                (Production month)

4. Usage time/production month scatter diagram

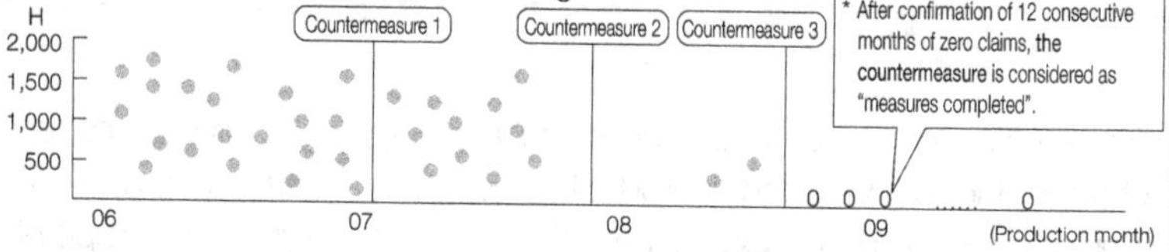

H
2,000
1,500
1,000
500

Countermeasure 1   Countermeasure 2   Countermeasure 3

* After confirmation of 12 consecutive months of zero claims, the countermeasure is considered as "measures completed".

06   07   08   09   (Production month)

* Each dot = Each claim

5. Cause and countermeasure

No.	Year/ Month/ Day	Problems	Causes	Countermeasures	Effects
I					
II					

44

Chart 2-17 How to view the scatter diagram (Based on production month)

① Constant occurrence

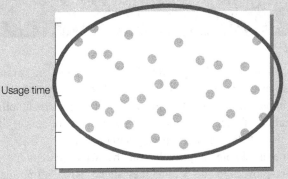

Usage time

Production month

If the claim occurrence indicates an evenly spread pattern
in a horizontal direction,
➡ the possibility of design problem is high.

② Intensive occurrence   * Each dot = Each claim

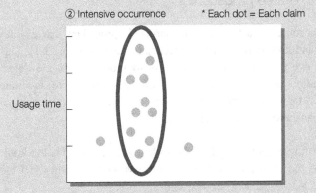

Usage time

Production month

If the claim occurrence indicates a vertical concentration,
➡ the possibility of manufacturing problems is high. It is necessary to
check if there were any change points or items at that time.

Chapter 3 "8-step procedure" for quality defect recurrence prevention
— For simplifying procedures

If you properly follow the "8-step procedure" for defect recurrence prevention, the number of defects will surely decrease. The "8-step procedure" is very effective and important not only to improve the company's profitability resulting from elimination of "defect creation" (the worst kind of waste), but also to increase customer satisfaction and expand your company.

Since this procedure is simple, big results can be achieved only if top management tells all employees to "do it", and they attend "*Asaichi* (morning) meeting" for 30 minutes. Therefore, I recommend this be implemented immediately.

1. What is the "8-step procedure"?

The "8-step procedure" is a type of "standardized" procedure that enables anyone to understand how to prevent a recurrence of defects (Chart 3-1). This procedure allows every section of the company to proceed with the defect recurrence prevention activity in the same way, as well as to facilitate evaluation of how far it is going or where the problem is, so that mutual learning in the organization becomes very easy.

- Troubleshoot today's defects by the end of the day ... Speed is the key! If you postpone the problem, another problem will arise tomorrow, so the work will pile up, leading to continuous waste.
  - → When. workers set their minds to finishing things by the end of the day, they were able to do it in Japan, the United States, and Europe as well. It was important to motivate them to try the "8-step procedure".
- Most companies seem to have already implemented the procedure from Steps ① to ⑤, but it is more important whether or not to implement sweeping measures including Steps ⑥, ⑦ and ⑧. Quality will surely improve by thoroughly addressing and solving the problems indicated

Chart 3-1　"8-step procedure" for defect recurrence prevention activity

① Actual defect check ➡ Immediately conducted by the team leader (TL)

Actual defective parts are checked to identify the process where the defect occurred.

② Stock check & sorting ➡ Conducted by TL immediately

Whether there are any other parts having the same defect in the stock shall be checked to make sure of the beginning and ending of the defect occurrence.

③ Cause investigation ➡ Implemented by TL within the day

The cause investigation is conducted through *GENCHI GENBUTSU* check. Also, the cause is investigated through interviews with the workers in the relevant process.

④ Countermeasure implementation ➡ Implemented by TL within the day

Against the causes of defect occurrence and outflow, respective countermeasures are implemented. Those actually implemented are written in the sheets on the *Asaichi* plastic board.

⑤ *Asaichi* report ➡ Reported by TL at the next *Asaichi* meeting

The relevant TL explains the cause and measures to all the members in an easy-to-understand manner, writes down any instruction or guidance on the sheet, and conducts follow-up activities.

⑥ Standardization and horizontal deployment ➡ Conducted by TL during the next day

Determination of work procedures and basic rules
　Is there any work standard? Do they understand it? Is just following it acceptable?
　→ If not, revise it immediately.
　　If not available, create it immediately.
　　Make it simple to enable them to understand it at a glance.
Listing of similar processes/items and implementation of horizontal deployment
　Zero defects cannot be achieved only by improving the process where the defect occurred.

⑦ Education and training ➡ Conducted by TL during the next day

Education is to teach people what is standardized.
Training is to enable workers to do what they were taught correctly in real work.
→ TL must make them promise to do what they were taught.

⑧ Daily management ➡ Checked by TL every day

TL checks whether members are actually doing as they were instructed
Check members' work through *GENCHI GENBUTSU* observation and make prompt corrections to defects if any.

by individual defects and implementing quality activities throughout the entire company, involving other processes, with strong determination to prevent the same defects from coming out again.

- The shortest way to reduce defects, if any, may be to implement the "8-step procedure" honestly, steadily and thoroughly. There are no shortcuts to quality assurance.

2. Details of the "8-step procedure"

Chart 3-2　Details of the 8-step procedure

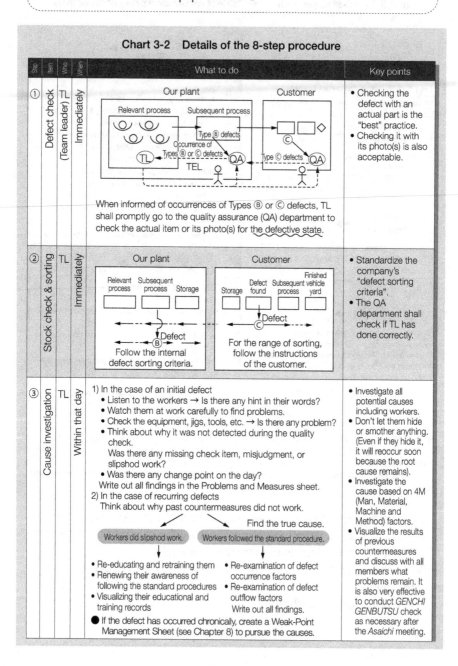

Step	Item	Who	When	What to do	Key points
①	Defect check	TL (Team leader)	Immediately	**Our plant** / **Customer** — Relevant process / Subsequent process; Type ⒷⓄ defects; Occurrence of Types Ⓑ or Ⓒ defects; QA; TEL; Type Ⓒ defects; QA. When informed of occurrences of Types Ⓑ or Ⓒ defects, TL shall promptly go to the quality assurance (QA) department to check the actual item or its photo(s) for the defective state.	• Checking the defect with an actual part is the "best" practice. • Checking it with its photo(s) is also acceptable.
②	Stock check & sorting	TL	Immediately	**Our plant** — Relevant process / Subsequent process / Storage; Defect Ⓑ; Follow the internal defect sorting criteria. **Customer** — Storage / Defect found / Subsequent process / Finished vehicle yard; Defect Ⓒ; For the range of sorting, follow the instructions of the customer.	• Standardize the company's "defect sorting criteria". • The QA department shall check if TL has done correctly.
③	Cause investigation	TL	Within that day	1) In the case of an initial defect 　• Listen to the workers → Is there any hint in their words? 　• Watch them at work carefully to find problems. 　• Check the equipment, jigs, tools, etc. → Is there any problem? 　• Think about why it was not detected during the quality check. 　　Was there any missing check item, misjudgment, or slipshod work? 　• Was there any change point on the day? 　Write out all findings in the Problems and Measures sheet. 2) In the case of recurring defects 　Think about why past countermeasures did not work. 　　　　　　　　　　　　Find the true cause. Workers did slipshod work.　Workers followed the standard procedure. • Re-educating and retraining them • Renewing their awareness of following the standard procedures • Visualizing their educational and training records • Re-examination of defect occurrence factors • Re-examination of defect outflow factors 　Write out all findings. ● If the defect has occurred chronically, create a Weak-Point Management Sheet (see Chapter 8) to pursue the causes.	• Investigate all potential causes including workers. • Don't let them hide or smother anything. (Even if they hide it, it will reoccur soon because the root cause remains). • Investigate the cause based on 4M (Man, Material, Machine and Method) factors. • Visualize the results of previous countermeasures and discuss with all members what problems remain. It is also very effective to conduct *GENCHI GENBUTSU* check as necessary after the *Asaichi* meeting.

Step	Item	Who	When	What to do	Key points
④	Countermeasure implementation	TL (Team leader)	Within that day	• For each problem for which a solution is found, necessary measures shall be taken within the day. If it takes time to implement the measures, provisional measures shall be taken to prevent recurrence. • The follow-up items shall be written in the Problems and Measures sheet, in detail with the responsible person and deadlines specified, and shall be followed up on until all items are completed. • Problems that cannot be solved by individual sections shall be discussed at the next morning *Asaichi* to be solved through teamwork. • The results shall be filled in "Quality Defect Cause and Measure Sheet". (Refer to 2-(1)-4) of Chapter 2)	• The measures shall be taken on the sources of not only occurrence but also outflow of defects. • As long as the root cause remains, the failure will reoccur. No one shall not cover up anything and shall disclose everything before implementation of countermeasures. • Necessary time for taking the countermeasure shall be provided to TL.
⑤	*Asaichi* report	TL	Next morning	• *Asaichi* meeting shall be held every morning at the predetermined time and shall be ended within 30 minutes. If there are many kinds of defects, discussion shall be started with the most serious one, with others to be followed up by the QA department. Place: in front of the Quality Management Board, Moderator: QA department member • The relevant TL shall explain the cause of and measures against the defect that occurred on the previous day, in front of the meeting members.	• Top management's participation boosts the morale of workers. Quick decision-making is possible. The levels of countermeasures can be upgraded.

• For any defect that occurred three or more times, the transition and countermeasures shall be explained with the use of the WPM Sheet (Weak-Point Management Sheet). (See Chapter 8)
• If necessary, *GENCHI GENBUTSU* check shall be conducted (to check the actual parts on site).
• The results of the follow-up items shall be confirmed at the time of the deadline. The moderator should contact the responsible person on the previous day to allow him/her to prepare to explain at the next *Asaichi* meeting.

Very Important

• Strictly prohibit "hiding". Even if they can escape from the spot, it will recur as long as the root cause remains. It is important for everyone to reveal everything before considering countermeasures.

Step	Item	Who	When	What to do	Key points
⑥	Standardization & horizontal deployment	TL	Within the next day	The solutions to "existing problems" indicated by defects shall be horizontally deployed to all similar processes and items to prevent similar problems from occurring. • Standard work procedure manual The key points shall be described in the procedure manual. In the case of manufacturing by looking at drawings, the drawings shall be completed in advance and used as work instructions. • Basic rules "What must be done" and "what must not be done" shall be standardized on each item. Example: Work interruption rule, etc. • Jigs, dies, tools, etc. Everything effective in preventing recurrence shall be horizontally deployed. A schedule shall be made and followed until everything is completed.	• Under the slogan "No improvements without standards", all work procedures shall be thoroughly standardized. • Standardization of work procedures is an important task of TL. • The basic rules shall be standardized as company rules to be followed by all employees.
⑦	Education & Training	TL	Within the next day	Education: Teach workers the standardized work. Properly teach each person why following the rules and work procedures is important and what will happen if they are not followed. Training: Train workers until they become able to do what they were taught correctly within the tact time in real work. Re-education and retraining For the workers who repeat negligence in their duty or violation of rules, while saying "I will follow the procedures and rules", a separate record of Individual education and training shall be prepared, and their words of promise shall be recorded each time re-education and/or retraining is conducted. It shall continue until those workers mend their ways. (See Chapter 7 for details.)	• Standardization of education and training systems. "Who, when and how to educate or train" shall be standardized. • Development of instructors and trainers. Good trainers and teachers shall be developed in the company. • Creation of a skill map. "Who can do what process" shall be visualized.
⑧	Daily management	TL	Every day	• TL shall check whether members are actually doing as they were instructed, correct mistakes, if any, immediately, and praise workers if they are doing good jobs. • TL shall make the "Problems and Measures" sheet available on work sites to enable any worker who noticed a problem to fill it in the sheet. At Yuichi (evening) meeting, TL shall decide the person who will take measures against the problem, as well as the deadline, and confirm implementation to prevent the occurrence of defects beforehand.	• "Praising" is very important! It can motivate workers most effectively. → Conduct proper education and training in which you can praise the trainees. • Do not leave the problem unsolved. If workers find that problems will be solved quickly, they will write more in the sheet.

50

3. Benefits of the "8-step procedure"

In every manufacturing company, various kinds of problems arise every day. In particular, quality defects are a kind of serious problem affecting the company's fate, so every company has been working on problem solving using its best method.

The Industrial Vehicle Division of Toyota Industries Corporation was also doing so, but unfortunately there had been no results for their efforts before I served as a quality advisor there. Therefore, I standardized the procedure for countermeasures against defects as the "8-step procedure", which I have taught to many companies including suppliers.

The following is an example of the result of defects found in finished vehicle inspections at Raymond Corporation (U.S.A.), which Toyota Industries Corporation acquired in 2000. Raymond, a prestigious forklift maker, was founded in 1922 and is older than Toyota Industries (1926).

It was in July 2006 that I visited the company for the first time. The plant overflowed with so many things that I could not quite see what was happening and where. Forklifts waiting for reworking were left abandoned, and the workers were running about in confusion to build vehicles.

So, the first thing I did was to set up the Quality Management Board mentioned in Chapter 2 to visualize defects found in the finished vehicle inspection. Then, I taught the 8-step procedure and started "*Asaichi* (morning meeting)". An assistant manager of the company's quality assurance department took great interest in this system and carried out what I taught promptly and correctly. I visited once every four months. And I wrote out the improvement points and how to improve them in English on a sheet of A3 size paper and handed the paper to the workers as homework. At the next visit I checked the results, and if there was a problem, I re-instructed them and gave them their next assignment. I taught the workers the points one by one tenaciously until they were able to do them properly. By following the "8-step procedure" throughout the plant, every worker began to share the awareness of improving quality and, in just two years from the start, the number of defects found in the finished vehicle inspection decreased by as much as 90%, which was also a surprising achievement for me. As a result of its long-standing efforts, Raymond won "Best Plant Award" from the American magazine INDUSTRY WEEK in 2014.

Similar results have been achieved not only in European and Japanese forklift vehicle manufacturing plants, but also at their suppliers, so it can be said that the "8-step procedure" is a very effective system to dramatically improve manufacturing quality.

The major benefits achieved by companies that introduced the "8-step procedure" are as follows.

Major benefits achieved by companies that introduced the "8-step procedure"

① **Simple and easy to understand**

It is a system that anyone can easily understand.

② **Enables quick countermeasures**

The pace of problem solving increased by making it a habit for "the team which caused a defect to take measures within the day".

③ **Improves the quality of countermeasures**

At the meeting, attendants including top management advised on important matters missing from the team leader's actions, and the effectiveness of countermeasures was improved through implementation of the advised matters.

④ **Motivates individuals to tackle quality improvement "more seriously"**

Any member who caused a defect had to explain it in front of other members at the next *Asaichi* (morning meeting), so everyone worked more seriously to avoid that. As a result, the number of defects sharply decreased.

⑤ **Improves cooperation among departments!**

Representatives of individual departments discussed the cross-organizational problem at the *Asaichi* meeting and decided what each department should do, so that the relationship among departments became closer and more cooperative throughout the entire plant to solve the problem.

⑥ **Enables prompt conveyance of top management's ideas to the bottom**

By attending the *Asaichi* meeting and interacting with each other, everyone could understand more accurately and agree with each other more quickly. The *Asaichi* is very effective as a place for communication improvement.

⑦ **Effective method for finding excellent human resources**

Through the 8-step procedure, it is possible to find good workers who are making honest and steady efforts.

Part **2**

Standardization and Human Resource Development

Chapter 4

Standardization of work

Standardization is an important task for managers and supervisors. For manufacturing, various kinds of operations are required as shown below.

For each operation, the following must be determined as a rule.

- What must be done
- What must not be done

By setting these as standards, and educating and training workers, it is possible to minimize the occurrence of quality defects.

This chapter describes how to standardize the work and operations according to the classifications shown in Chart 4-1 by defining those indicated by ① to ④ as "main work" and those indicated by "a" to "h" as "ancillary work".

Chart 4-1   Production flow and work classification - Main work and Ancillary work

Work \ Production sequence		Part A		Part B
Main work	Setup operations ——————→		Manufacturing operations	Setup operations ...
	① Equipment setup → ② Work setup →		First-part production --→ Final-part production ③ Standard work procedure manual ④ First & final part check	① Equipment setup ...
Ancillary work	A) Troubleshooting task		a) Equipment troubleshooting task b) Quality troubleshooting task c) Material flow troubleshooting task	
	B) Less-frequent work		d) Consumables replacement procedure e) Work delay recovery procedure f) Work interruption and resumption ... lunch time, short break, etc. g) Preventive maintenance for equipment h) Inspection of dies, jigs, tools, etc.	

1. Work manual for main work

(1) How to prepare the work manual for the main work (Chart 4-2)

Chart 4-2　How to create work manuals for the main work

No.	Work manuals	Key points of standardization	Problems without standardization
①-1	Equipment setup condition table	All information necessary for setup of part Ⓐ shall be visualized in the setup condition table. **Part Ⓐ Setup Condition Table** | No.	Part name	Location
1	Cutting tool holder	32
2	Cutting tool No.	○○
3	Jig No.	T-2
4	Program No.	No.10 | Holder storage: 31 | 32 | 33 | … Jig storage: T-1 | T-2 | T-3 | … Individual workplaces and processes shall be neatly arranged to allow workers to quickly find what they need by checking the location number and going to the specific storage areas.	• If workers work with only fragments of memory: ↓ Mistakes and misunderstanding ↓ A large number of defects • If the storage areas are messy: ↓ It is difficult to find the right item and the wrong one can be used. ↓ Waste of time searching for them and a lot of defects occur. Very frequently occurring cases
①-2	Equipment setup procedure manual	A setup procedure manual to minimize setup time and mistakes shall be created. • It shall be an easy-to-understand manual with many photos and illustrations inserted. • The previous setup errors shall be highlighted with a red pen in the procedure manual for visualization to call workers' attention to them during training in order to prevent recurrence.	• If there is no work procedure manual: ↓ Differences in performance among workers cause mistakes. ↓ Noticing mistakes only after occurrence of defects … Bigger waste
②	Work setup procedure manual	Preparatory procedures for what is necessary for mass production shall be standardized. 1) Taking out a necessary standard work procedure manual and attaching it on a board and checking the procedure. 2) Checking the location of necessary jigs, tools etc. shown in the standard work procedure manual and going for them. 3) Putting a quality check and record sheet on a table. 4) Collecting the parts. 　Checking the location in a parts collection list and collecting the right parts. Necessary parts / Standard work procedure manual or drawing / First & final parts quality check sheet / First & final parts master samples / Quality check table / Quality check tool area / Workbench or machine * After preparation of all necessary items for mass production, manufacturing shall be started.	• Availability of jigs • Availability of special tools } If there is no instruction: ↓ Non-use of them causes defects. • If there is no parts collection list: ↓ Rejection of an entire lot due to wrong parts inclusion • If a procedure manual and quality sheet are not accessible: ↓ Working with only fragments of memory, making defective products, and then noticing the mistake.

No.	Work manuals	Key points of standardization	Problems without standardization

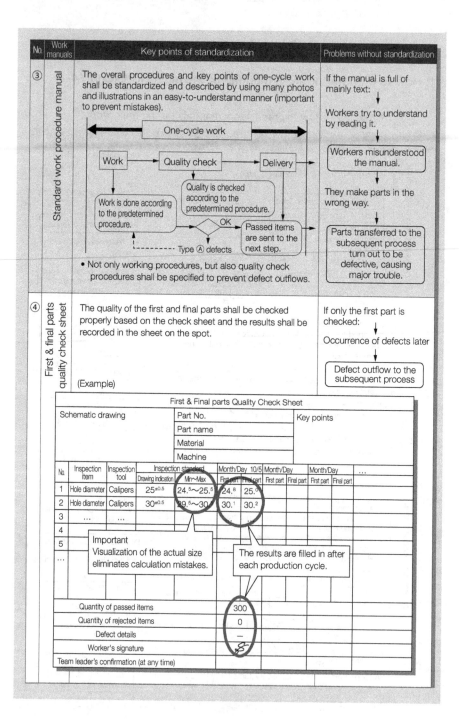

③ Standard work procedure manual

The overall procedures and key points of one-cycle work shall be standardized and described by using many photos and illustrations in an easy-to-understand manner (important to prevent mistakes).

One-cycle work

Work — Quality check — Delivery

Work is done according to the predetermined procedure.

Quality is checked according to the predetermined procedure.

OK → Passed items are sent to the next step.

----- Type Ⓐ defects

• Not only working procedures, but also quality check procedures shall be specified to prevent defect outflows.

If the manual is full of mainly text:

↓

Workers try to understand by reading it.

↓

Workers misunderstood the manual.

↓

They make parts in the wrong way.

↓

Parts transferred to the subsequent process turn out to be defective, causing major trouble.

④ First & final parts quality check sheet

The quality of the first and final parts shall be checked properly based on the check sheet and the results shall be recorded in the sheet on the spot.

If only the first part is checked:

↓

Occurrence of defects later

↓

Defect outflow to the subsequent process

(Example)

First & Final parts Quality Check Sheet

Schematic drawing			Part No.		Key points	
			Part name			
			Material			
			Machine			

No.	Inspection item	Inspection tool	Inspection standard		Month/Day 10/5		Month/Day		Month/Day		...
			Drawing indication	Min~Max	First part	Final part	First part	Final part	First part	Final part	
1	Hole diameter	Calipers	25±0.5	24.⁵~25.⁵	24.⁸	25.⁰					
2	Hole diameter	Calipers	30±0.5	29.⁵~30.⁵	30.¹	30.²					
3	...	...									
4											
5											
...											

Important
Visualization of the actual size eliminates calculation mistakes.

The results are filled in after each production cycle.

Quantity of passed items		300	
Quantity of rejected items		0	
Defect details		—	
Worker's signature			
Team leader's confirmation (at any time)			

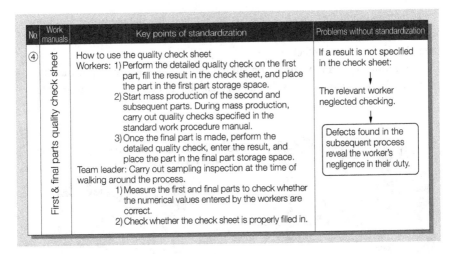

No.	Work manuals	Key points of standardization	Problems without standardization
④	First & final parts quality check sheet	How to use the quality check sheet Workers: 1) Perform the detailed quality check on the first part, fill the result in the check sheet, and place the part in the first part storage space. 2) Start mass production of the second and subsequent parts. During mass production, carry out quality checks specified in the standard work procedure manual. 3) Once the final part is made, perform the detailed quality check, enter the result, and place the part in the final part storage space. Team leader: Carry out sampling inspection at the time of walking around the process. 1) Measure the first and final parts to check whether the numerical values entered by the workers are correct. 2) Check whether the check sheet is properly filled in.	If a result is not specified in the check sheet: ↓ The relevant worker neglected checking. ↓ Defects found in the subsequent process reveal the worker's negligence in their duty.

(2) Quick access to the work manual

The work manual must be made available immediately when necessary. Then, does "immediately" in seconds? By defining it and other various kinds of criteria, we considered and determined a system that enables "quick access" (Chart 4-3).

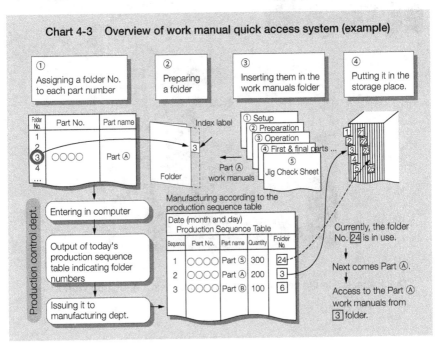

Chart 4-3　Overview of work manual quick access system (example)

If such a system for "quick access" is not defined, it will take time to look for necessary things to know, making workers tend to disregard the manual, which may lead to a serious defect.

The following is an example of a simple and highly effective "quick access" system. Such a system is considered indispensable to every manufacturing site.

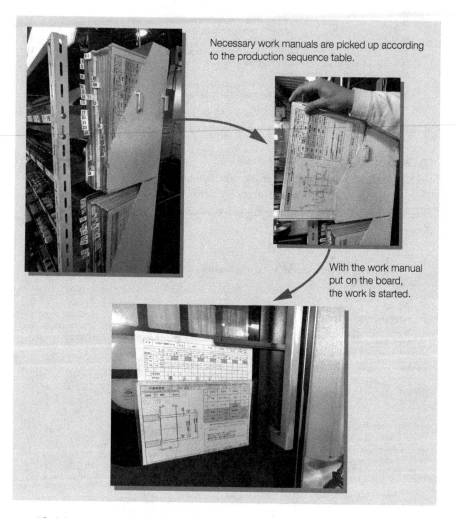

Necessary work manuals are picked up according to the production sequence table.

With the work manual put on the board, the work is started.

"Quick access" to the necessary work manual sheet—Ando Iron Works Co.

(3) Special models*: Important points for drawing-based production of small-volume large-variety products

Components of special model vehicles to be made through special orders from customers are generally produced only once and in small volumes. Therefore, it is difficult to prepare the related work manual in advance. The following describes how to cope with such a case.

* Special model (vehicles): Forklifts manufactured by Toyota Industries are classified into "Standard", "Option", and "Special" models.

1) Unfavorable case: If a worker makes the product by only using a customer's drawing (Chart 4-4), the following will happen.

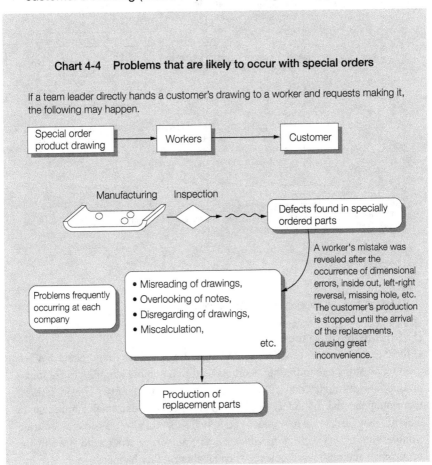

Chart 4-4   Problems that are likely to occur with special orders

If a team leader directly hands a customer's drawing to a worker and requests making it, the following may happen.

```
┌──────────────────┐      ┌──────────┐      ┌──────────┐
│ Special order    │  →   │ Workers  │  →   │ Customer │
│ product drawing  │      └──────────┘      └──────────┘
└──────────────────┘
```

Manufacturing   Inspection

Defects found in specially ordered parts

A worker's mistake was revealed after the occurrence of dimensional errors, inside out, left-right reversal, missing hole, etc. The customer's production is stopped until the arrival of the replacements, causing great inconvenience.

Problems frequently occurring at each company

• Misreading of drawings,
• Overlooking of notes,
• Disregarding of drawings,
• Miscalculation,
                                etc.

Production of replacement parts

2) Favorable case: The team leader adds necessary information to the customer's drawing so that it can be used as a work manual and quality check sheet, before handing it to the worker (Chart 4-5).

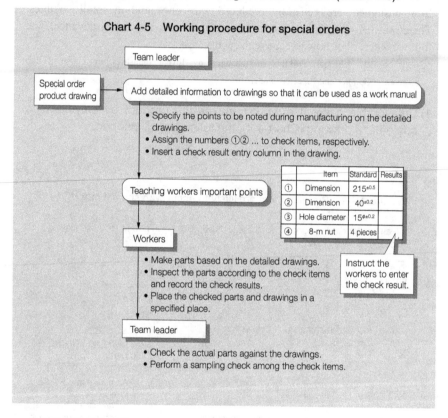

Chart 4-5   Working procedure for special orders

Team leader

Special order product drawing → Add detailed information to drawings so that it can be used as a work manual

- Specify the points to be noted during manufacturing on the detailed drawings.
- Assign the numbers ①② ... to check items, respectively.
- Insert a check result entry column in the drawing.

Teaching workers important points

	Item	Standard	Results
①	Dimension	$215^{\pm0.5}$	
②	Dimension	$40^{\pm0.2}$	
③	Hole diameter	$15^{\phi\pm0.2}$	
④	8-m nut	4 pieces	

Workers

- Make parts based on the detailed drawings.
- Inspect the parts according to the check items and record the check results.
- Place the checked parts and drawings in a specified place.

Instruct the workers to enter the check result.

Team leader

- Check the actual parts against the drawings.
- Perform a sampling check among the check items.

2. Standardization of ancillary work

(1) Troubleshooting tasks

In the process of production, various abnormalities may occur. When production stops due to trouble, workers tend to pay more attention to resuming production through quick troubleshooting than quality considerations, increasing the risk of defect outflow. Therefore, it is extremely important to clearly standardize what must be done for quality assurance during troubleshooting, as well as to educate and train every worker, to prevent the occurrence and outflow of defects when an abnormality happens.

Chart 4-6 Standardization of ancillary work

Item		Key points of standardization	Frequently occurring problems
a	Equipment troubleshooting task	Sometimes a machine suddenly stops abnormally during continuous production. In order to prepare for such a case, it is important to clearly state the material handling method (how to handle the workpiece or in-process parts in use) as the Step 1 in the "Troubleshooting procedure manual".	If a worker temporarily puts a workpiece (in his hand) or in-process part (in the machine) in the finished parts box for the purpose of troubleshooting:

Machinery — ② In-process parts inside the machine

A machine stops abnormally.

Put it in a defective parts storage place.

Workpieces box

Finished parts box

③ Parts in the finished parts box

Workers

① Workpiece held in worker's hand

Return it to the workpieces box.

Put a tag Sorting Required and sort the parts later.

Troubleshooting step 1 — Place all of ①, ② and ③ in the predetermined positions.

Troubleshooting step 2 — Perform troubleshooting within the permitted range.

Troubleshooting step 3 — If the machine is not reset, stop the operation, call the supervisor, and wait.

Implementation of troubleshooting

Reset of machine

Restart of production

Forgetting the temporary placement leads to defect outflows to the customer.

(Very frequently occurring mistake)

| b | Quality troubleshooting task | | If a worker finds defective parts and temporarily puts them on a workbench or the floor: |

Ⓐ Defect   Ⓑ Defect   ©Defect

A defective part was made.

A defect was found in the parts received from a preceding process or supplier.

Step 1 — The worker immediately attaches a defect tag to the part and puts it in a red box [See 2-(2)-© of Chapter 5].
(* Temporary leaving it on a workbench or the floor is strictly prohibited.)

Step 2 — The worker reports to the team leader (TL).

Step 3 — After confirming the Types Ⓑ or (©) defects, the TL contacts the QA dept.

Continuance of production

Forgetting the temporary leaving somewhere of defective parts, the worker mixed them with other parts in the finished parts box, resulting in the defect outflow.

(This is also a very frequently occurring mistake.)

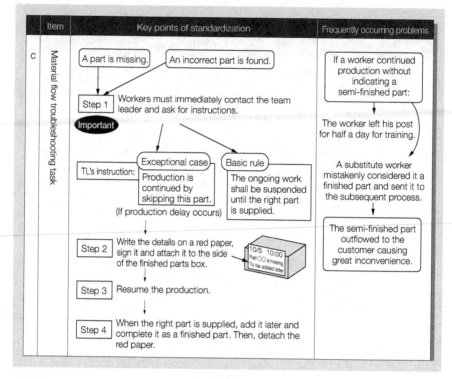

Item	Key points of standardization	Frequently occurring problems

c — Material flow troubleshooting task

A part is missing. / An incorrect part is found.

Step 1 (Important) Workers must immediately contact the team leader and ask for instructions.

TL's instruction:

Exceptional case — Production is continued by skipping this part. (If production delay occurs)

Basic rule — The ongoing work shall be suspended until the right part is supplied.

Step 2 Write the details on a red paper, sign it and attach it to the side of the finished parts box.

10/5 10:00 Part ○○ is missing To be added later

Step 3 Resume the production.

Step 4 When the right part is supplied, add it later and complete it as a finished part. Then, detach the red paper.

Frequently occurring problems:

If a worker continued production without indicating a semi-finished part:

The worker left his post for half a day for training.

A substitute worker mistakenly considered it a finished part and sent it to the subsequent process.

The semi-finished part outflowed to the customer causing great inconvenience.

(2) Less-frequent work

When consumables such as cutting blades, grinding wheels and welding tips are used beyond their limits, defects are more likely to occur. In addition, molds, jigs, tools, as well as various machinery and equipment, are subject to wear of the reference surface, loosening of the clamped portion, or air/oil leak as time passes, and when the individual limit is exceeded, a large number of defects will occur. In order to completely prevent the occurrence of such quality defects, the following must be carried out.

- Consumables: Standardization and implementation of a periodic or quantitative replacement system
- Work: Standardization of rules to prevent mistakes at the time of recovery from work delay or work interruption
- Molds, jigs, tools, and equipment: Standardization of the system for periodic or quantitative inspection and repair before exceeding limits for the elimination of defects

The following shows examples of standardization of some less-frequent work in which quality defects are likely to occur.

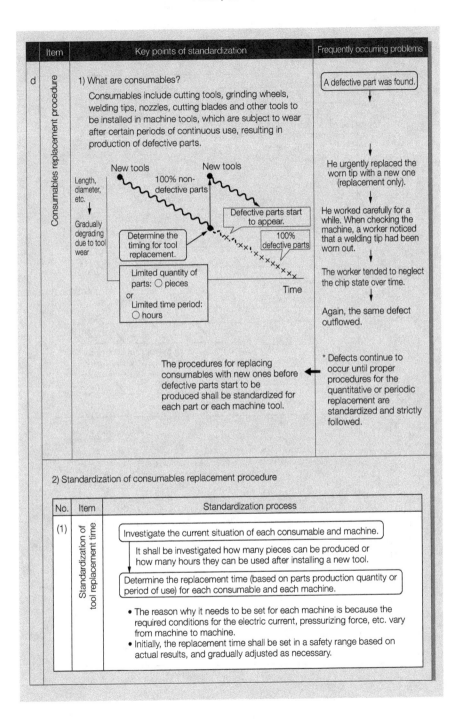

Item	Key points of standardization	Frequently occurring problems
d Consumables replacement procedure	1) What are consumables? Consumables include cutting tools, grinding wheels, welding tips, nozzles, cutting blades and other tools to be installed in machine tools, which are subject to wear after certain periods of continuous use, resulting in production of defective parts.	A defective part was found. ↓ He urgently replaced the worn tip with a new one (replacement only). ↓ He worked carefully for a while. When checking the machine, a worker noticed that a welding tip had been worn out. ↓ The worker tended to neglect the chip state over time. ↓ Again, the same defect outflowed. * Defects continue to occur until proper procedures for the quantitative or periodic replacement are standardized and strictly followed.

New tools — New tools

Length, diameter, etc.
↓
Gradually degrading due to tool wear

100% non-defective parts

Defective parts start to appear.

Determine the timing for tool replacement.

100% defective parts

Limited quantity of parts: ○ pieces
or
Limited time period: ○ hours

Time

The procedures for replacing consumables with new ones before defective parts start to be produced shall be standardized for each part or each machine tool.

2) Standardization of consumables replacement procedure

No.	Item	Standardization process
(1)	Standardization of tool replacement time	Investigate the current situation of each consumable and machine. It shall be investigated how many pieces can be produced or how many hours they can be used after installing a new tool. Determine the replacement time (based on parts production quantity or period of use) for each consumable and each machine. • The reason why it needs to be set for each machine is because the required conditions for the electric current, pressurizing force, etc. vary from machine to machine. • Initially, the replacement time shall be set in a safety range based on actual results, and gradually adjusted as necessary.

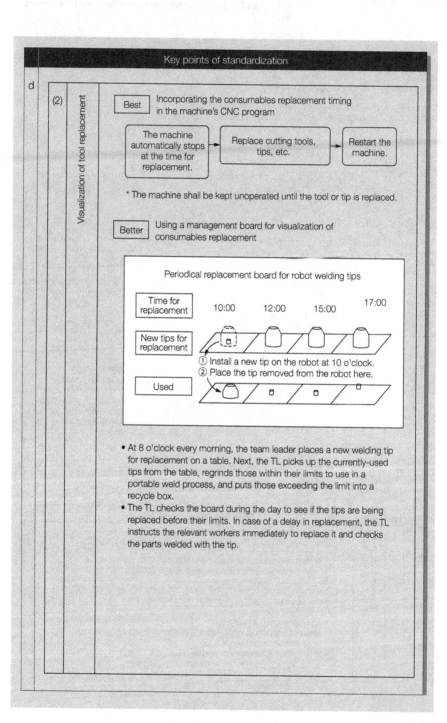

d

(2)

Visualization of tool replacement

| Best | Incorporating the consumables replacement timing in the machine's CNC program |

| The machine automatically stops at the time for replacement. | → | Replace cutting tools, tips, etc. | → | Restart the machine. |

* The machine shall be kept unoperated until the tool or tip is replaced.

| Better | Using a management board for visualization of consumables replacement |

Periodical replacement board for robot welding tips

| Time for replacement | 10:00 | 12:00 | 15:00 | 17:00 |

| New tips for replacement |

① Install a new tip on the robot at 10 o'clock.
② Place the tip removed from the robot here.

| Used |

- At 8 o'clock every morning, the team leader places a new welding tip for replacement on a table. Next, the TL picks up the currently-used tips from the table, regrinds those within their limits to use in a portable weld process, and puts those exceeding the limit into a recycle box.
- The TL checks the board during the day to see if the tips are being replaced before their limits. In case of a delay in replacement, the TL instructs the relevant workers immediately to replace it and checks the parts welded with the tip.

Key points of standardization

d   3) Centralized consumables management system

In general, the same types of welding tips, cutting tools, etc. are used in two or more processes, so it is necessary to establish a centralized consumables inventory management system.
- The consumables inventory volume shall be minimized.
- Production stoppages due to lack of consumables shall be eliminated.

Material flow chart for consumables

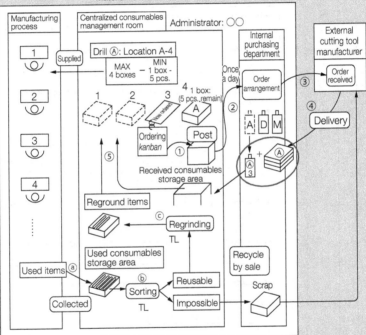

* There are many companies that do not have a centralized consumables management system.
   - In such companies, the same types of consumables are stored in multiple processes. Because the workers are afraid of a lack of consumables, they tend to have a lot, resulting in a large volume of consumables in the whole company (a bigger waste).
   - In addition, if storage conditions are bad, they are likely to use outdated consumables or similar ones, increasing the risk of producing defective products.

→ In order to eliminate such waste, a centralized management system needs to be established through top-down decision-making.

No.	Item	Implementation or standardization process
(1)	Centralized management room storage area arrangement	**Knowing the current state of consumables in use** • What consumables are used in which processes shall be checked, and how many per day? (They include what is necessary for manufacturing service parts.) **Creating a list of consumables basic units** ... This is used as a basis. • For each item of consumables, a list shall be created to indicate relevant processes, required quantity per day, purchasing method, etc. **Streamlining the storage areas for individual consumables** • Individual storage areas shall be determined with the respective location numbers assigned and displayed. • How to store items shall be determined by First-in First-out and easy access. • The maximum and minimum quantities to be placed shall be determined and displayed. **Collecting and sorting all consumables stocked in various places in the plant** • A certain quantity of what is really needed shall be stored in specific places. Surplus items shall be kept in a temporary storage place. • Unnecessary items shall be discarded. (They include those previously used, but now are unused.) • Unknown items shall be kept in the unknown item storage area for one year * Since the above cannot be done in a workers' spare time, full-time members shall be appointed to arrange the storage area in the shortest possible period of time.
(2)	Supplying & receiving control	Standardization of consumables supplying and receiving system (Example) MAX – MIN 4 boxes 1 box / 5 pcs. 1 2 3 4 Stock Order post Already supplied Already supplied Supplied Ordering Kanban **Step 1** When three boxes are supplied (timing for ordering), the ordering *kanban* shall be put at the post. A "Now ordered" *kanban* shall be left at the place.

No.	Item	Implementation or standardization process

Key points of standardization

d

(2) Supplying & receiving control

Step 2 The ordering *kanbans* at the post are collected by the purchasing department once a day at the predetermined time.

Step 3 The purchasing department places an order for them within the day. The ordering *kanbans* are stored on a specific board.

Step 4 When new consumables are delivered, move them to the received consumables storage area together with the ordering *kanban*.

Step 5 Replenish newly received consumables to specific places.

(3) Used consumables management

Some consumables collected from the manufacturing process are still usable, so it is necessary to establish a system to allow them to be used up to the limit through the sorting and re-grinding processes.

Used consumables collection → TL → Sorting → Reuse impossible → Recycle material disposal by sale
Sorting → Usable → TL → Regrinding → Reground items storage area

* The sorting criteria shall be standardized.

* The reground items are used only in specific processes. Since they are close to the usage limit, they shall be used in processes which do not require strict usage conditions.
(Example) The reground consumables are often used in manual work processes where the workers carefully check the wear condition and use them up to their limits.

Item	Key points of standardization	Frequently occurring problems

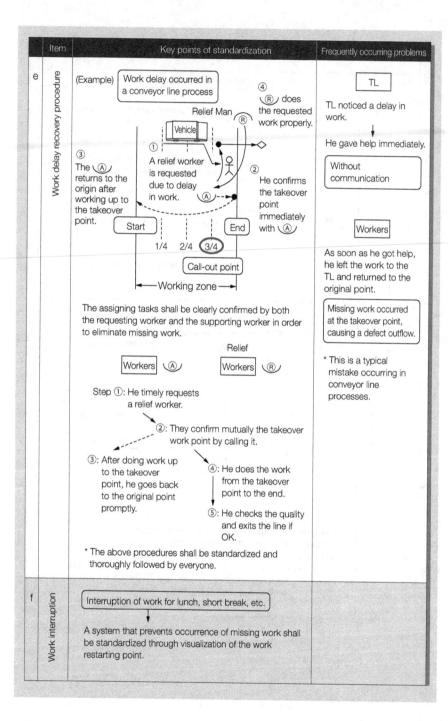

e — Work delay recovery procedure

(Example) Work delay occurred in a conveyor line process

Relief Man

④ ⓡ does the requested work properly.

① A relief worker is requested due to delay in work. ⓐ

③ The ⓐ returns to the origin after working up to the takeover point.

② He confirms the takeover point immediately with ⓐ

Start — End

1/4 2/4 3/4

Call-out point

←— Working zone —→

The assigning tasks shall be clearly confirmed by both the requesting worker and the supporting worker in order to eliminate missing work.

Workers ⓐ   Relief Workers ⓡ

Step ①: He timely requests a relief worker.

②: They confirm mutually the takeover work point by calling it.

③: After doing work up to the takeover point, he goes back to the original point promptly.

④: He does the work from the takeover point to the end.

⑤: He checks the quality and exits the line if OK.

* The above procedures shall be standardized and thoroughly followed by everyone.

Frequently occurring problems:

TL

TL noticed a delay in work.

↓

He gave help immediately.

Without communication

Workers

As soon as he got help, he left the work to the TL and returned to the original point.

Missing work occurred at the takeover point, causing a defect outflow.

* This is a typical mistake occurring in conveyor line processes.

f — Work interruption

Interruption of work for lunch, short break, etc.

↓

A system that prevents occurrence of missing work shall be standardized through visualization of the work restarting point.

68

Item	Key points of standardization	Frequently occurring problems
f	**Basic rule** If the tact time is short, work shall not be stopped until the ongoing cycle is completed. * The reasons shall be explained to workers and unions to ask for their understanding and agreement. **If the tact time is long:** ➡ "Work interruption rule" shall be standardized and followed by every worker. **Work interruption rule** Work Interruption Card storage place ⬆ Work Interruption Card Full name ○○○○ * The card storage space shall be installed for each worker. **Step 1** Place a "Work Interruption Card" at the interrupted point. **Step 2** At the time of restarting the work, confirm the position (and work) where the Work Interruption Card was placed and resume from the next work.	A worker stopped work for a while without using the Work Interruption Card because it is troublesome. ⬇ At the time of restart, the worker started from the wrong point, causing process skipping. Very frequently occurring mistakes "Keep workers following the rules." ⬇ A stern attitude shall be maintained against negligence of duty.
g Preventive maintenance for equipment	Among the preventive maintenance operations necessary for the machine to always run normally, the simplest one is carried out by the workers in the manufacturing department to reduce the burden on maintenance personnel. **Step 1** For each piece of machinery and equipment, preventive maintenance to be done by the manufacturing department shall be discussed with the maintenance personnel and determined. Examples: Greasing, oil-leak check, air leak check, filter cleaning, belt tension adjustment, etc. **Step 2** Create easily understandable inspection and adjustment procedure manuals, and educate and train the relevant workers.	Without any preventive maintenance system, various abnormalities are noticed only after the occurrence of defects or equipment trouble, resulting in various kinds of major waste. (Example) • Waste resulting from defective products • Waste resulting from production interruption due to equipment trouble

Item	Key points of standardization	Frequently occurring problems

g

Step 3	A preventive maintenance card is prepared and attached to each machine with a magnet for visualization.

Machine No. ○○   Preventive Maintenance Card   Operator name: □□□

No.	Preventive maintenance items	Frequency	Month 4	5	6	7	8	9	10	11	12	1	2	Month 3	Remarks
1	Filter cleaning	1/2 m	● 4/10SN	● 6/10SN		○		○			○		○		
2	Greasing	1/6 m	● 5/15SN					○							
3	Oil leakage check	1/6 m				● 7/15SN					○				
4	Belt tension	1/6 m						○					○		
5															
6															

Implemented   Plan

Month/ Day	Problems	Countermeasures	Person in charge

Step 4	When preventive maintenance is performed according to the plan, each open circle is blackened, with the date and signature filled in.

* If the open circle is not blackened even after the scheduled month, the TL shall immediately instruct the relevant staff to perform the maintenance.
* This is a simple and very effective system to quickly check whether the preventive maintenance is actually implemented or not.

h — Dies, jigs and tools inspection check sheet

An inspection check sheet shall be prepared for each die, jig and tool, important quality portions shall be periodically checked, and the results shall be visualized.
- Identify items and parts to be carefully inspected based on the past quality defect occurrence results.
  Examples: Wear, deformation and looseness of reference pin/surface, clamp, etc.
- Determine the frequency of inspection ... Once every three months, six months, etc.
- Determine acceptance criteria.
  Boundary samples shall be made for correct judgment.

If they continue to be used without checking:

↓

Abrasion on reference pins will be found only after a defect occurs.

It is too late after a defect has occurred.

Chapter 5

Standardization of material handling

The shape of parts will change in various ways in the process from material input to finished product. On the other hand, end materials, extra parts, etc. come out from the main flow. In order to completely eliminate quality trouble, it is very important to prepare a flow chart that visualizes the actual state of the company's material flow and to standardize the procedures for the handling each material, part or product.

The following is an example of material flow at a general parts manufacturer (Chart 5-1).

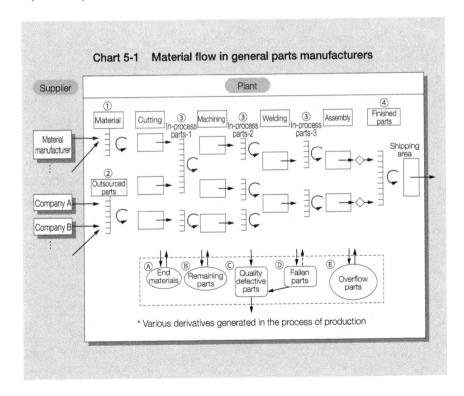

Chart 5-1　Material flow in general parts manufacturers

* Various derivatives generated in the process of production

1. Basics of material handling

Basics of material handling can be roughly classified into the separation of storage place from work process, First-in First-out (FIFO), and Pull System (requested by subsequent process) (Chart 5-2).

Chart 5-2 Basics of material handling

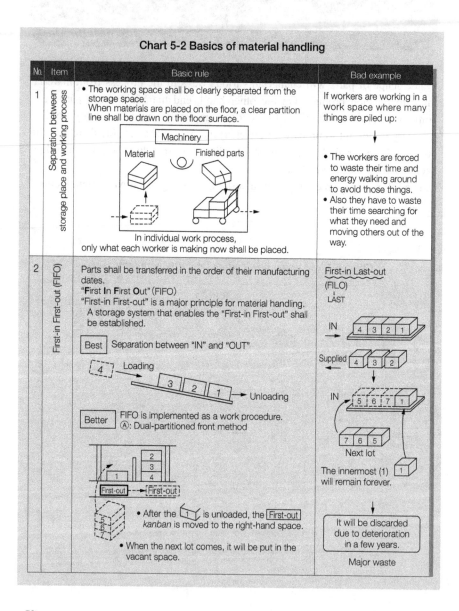

No.	Item	Basic rule	Bad example
1	Separation between storage place and working process	• The working space shall be clearly separated from the storage space. When materials are placed on the floor, a clear partition line shall be drawn on the floor surface. **Machinery** Material Finished parts In individual work process, only what each worker is making now shall be placed.	If workers are working in a work space where many things are piled up: • The workers are forced to waste their time and energy walking around to avoid those things. • Also they have to waste their time searching for what they need and moving others out of the way.
2	First-in First-out (FIFO)	Parts shall be transferred in the order of their manufacturing dates. "First In First Out" (FIFO) "First-in First-out" is a major principle for material handling. A storage system that enables the "First-in First-out" shall be established. **Best** Separation between "IN" and "OUT" 4 Loading 3 2 1 → Unloading **Better** FIFO is implemented as a work procedure. Ⓐ: Dual-partitioned front method 2 3 1 4 First-out ---→ First-out • After the 1 is unloaded, the First-out kanban is moved to the right-hand space. • When the next lot comes, it will be put in the vacant space.	First-in Last-out (FILO) LAST IN → 4 3 2 1 Supplied 4 3 2 IN 5 6 7 1 7 6 5 Next lot The innermost (1) will remain forever. It will be discarded due to deterioration in a few years. Major waste

72

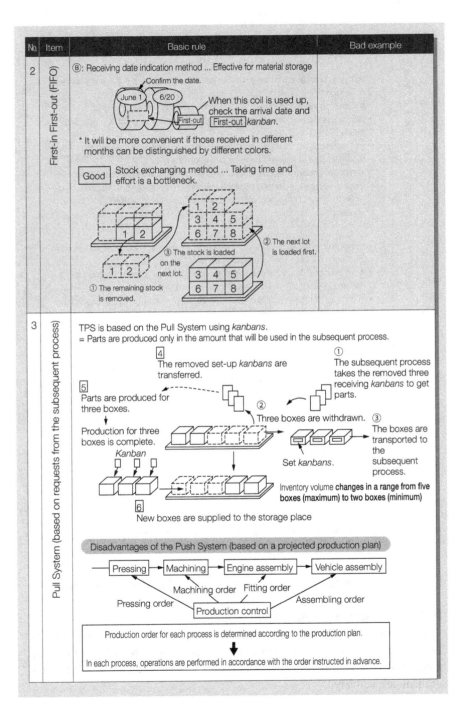

No.	Item	Basic rule	Bad example
2	First-in First-out (FIFO)	Ⓑ: Receiving date indication method ... Effective for material storage	

Confirm the date.

June 1 / 6/20

First-out

When this coil is used up, check the arrival date and First-out kanban.

* It will be more convenient if those received in different months can be distinguished by different colors.

Good | Stock exchanging method ... Taking time and effort is a bottleneck.

② The next lot is loaded first.
③ The stock is loaded on the next lot.
① The remaining stock is removed.

| 3 | Pull System (based on requests from the subsequent process) | | |

TPS is based on the Pull System using *kanbans*.
= Parts are produced only in the amount that will be used in the subsequent process.

4 The removed set-up *kanbans* are transferred.

① The subsequent process takes the removed three receiving *kanbans* to get parts.

5 Parts are produced for three boxes.

Production for three boxes is complete.
Kanban

② Three boxes are withdrawn. ③

Set *kanbans*.

The boxes are transported to the subsequent process.

Inventory volume **changes in a range from five boxes (maximum) to two boxes (minimum)**

6 New boxes are supplied to the storage place

Disadvantages of the Push System (based on a projected production plan)

Pressing → Machining → Engine assembly → Vehicle assembly

Machining order Fitting order
Pressing order Assembling order
Production control

Production order for each process is determined according to the production plan.
↓
In each process, operations are performed in accordance with the order instructed in advance.

73

No.	Item	Basic rule
3	Pull System (based on requests from the subsequent process)	1) The biggest problem with the Push System is that the plan and the reality are not the same in terms of production. • Vehicles cannot be produced as planned → The plan will be changed. • Defects, equipment failure, absenteeism, missing parts, etc. do not allow planned production. → Operations at individual processes become inharmonious, leading to a mountain of materials and parts formed in various places. • Therefore, leaders in each process try to secure extra workers or equipment, in order to ensure the planned production volume, no matter what happens. → Such excess equipment and personnel will deteriorate profitability ... the worst scenario. 2) Another problem with the Push System is that the planned quantity is not always consistent with the actually produced quantity. • If, for example, some material remains in the pressing process, the operation is performed until it is used up, resulting in excess parts. • In contrast, if the material is used up before the planned quantity is reached the operation ends at that time, resulting in a parts shortage. * As a result, the inventory amount data in the computer never matches the actual stock amount in storage. The chronic occurrence of parts shortages or excess stock is a major big waste! (* Toyota's *Kanban* system is designed to solve this problem.)

---

2. Standardization of "material handling" for individual forms

(1) Handling of main flow items

The main flow items (forms of materials) to be handled are classified into four categories: raw materials, outsourced parts, in-process parts, and finished products (Chart 5-3). It is important to properly determine how to handle each of them, respectively.

Chart 5-3 Handling of main flow items

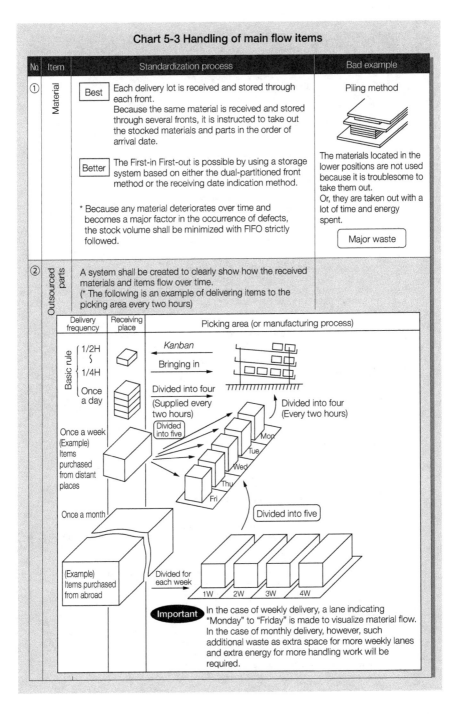

No.	Item	Standardization process	Bad example

| ② | | As the lot size gets bigger, extra space and work are required. Therefore, it is necessary to negotiate with suppliers to make deliveries in lots that are as small as possible. | |
| ③ | In-process parts | • In each process, a storage place for the parts to be transferred to the next process shall be secured and clearly indicated.
• It shall be strictly prohibited for the operator in the subsequent process to pick up parts from anywhere other than the specific storage place.
• Specific positions for individual items shall be determined as much as possible. If that is not possible, each container shall have an indication of its contents, which can be seen at a glance.
• Visualization shall be made to clearly indicate how far the process has been completed and when completed. | If the finished parts and in-process parts are mixed in a storage area:
↓
Workers will have to wander around looking for what they need every time they come. There will be many cases where they mistakenly take out similar but wrong items. |

| ④ | Finished parts | In order to completely eliminate incorrect parts delivery, it is important to properly arrange the finished part storage place. Necessary investments in storage space, racks, containers and others shall be properly made. | |

| | Store arrangement | 1) | Storage place | Storage space shall be secured to allow each part number to be located at each specific position.
Racks shall be installed to maximize the storage capacity. | Space shortage resulting materials being piled |

Store arrangement (1)

		Standardization process	Bad example
Storage place		Storage space shall be secured to allow each part number to be located at each specific position. Racks shall be installed to maximize the storage capacity.	Space shortage resulting materials being piled
Location number		An address (location number) shall be assigned to and indicated in each storage place. The address shall allow anyone to go to any specific positions.	
Part number sign		This shall be visible in each storage place. If a scanner is used, the barcodes are also required.	
Quantity sign		The maximum and minimum volumes shall be indicated. This is to prevent inventory shortage.	
Discrimination		Actual items or photographs for correct identification or judgment shall be attached. Key points shall be highlighted with arrow marks or colors	• Workers waste time in looking for what they need and moving others out of the way.
Illumination		The illumination shall enable all signs to be clearly seen even in the night or rainy days.	• They produced parts in a hurry because they cannot find it.

Shelf indicator (example)

Location	Part No.	Quantity	Identification point
A-4-3	61555-36010	MAX MIN 5 - 1	⊢–300–⊣ ◯――――◯ 30 φ

• What they finally found are wrong parts.

Chronic waste and mistakes

* Arranging appropriate storage areas for standard work is an important task for supervisors. Before blaming the worker who mixed up parts, the supervisors shall first arrange the area for an ideal material flow.

No.	Item		Standardization process	Bad example
④	2) Material receiving work	Work manuals	Creation of the standard work procedure manual for receiving work and implementation of training The document shall visualize the procedure and key points.	Done the worker's own way with procedure manuals unavailable
		Trouble-shooting	Standardization of troubleshooting method at the time of abnormality • The rack is full and cannot accommodate any more materials. • The actual item is different from what is written on the shelf indicator, etc.	(Example) ↓ Outflow of wrong parts to customers due to taking them from an incorrect shelf
	3) Parts taking-out work	Work manuals	Creation of the standard work procedure manual for taking out goods and implementation of training • The document shall visualize the procedure and key points. • The actual item check must be performed to prevent dispatching wrong items: "Hold one in hand and check it against its sample or photo," etc.	Disregarding the work manual despite the training based on it (Example) ↓ Outflow of wrong parts due to mistakenly taking another type placed in the next location when taking the parts after scanning
		Trouble-shooting	Standardization of troubleshooting method at the time of abnormality • Nothing on the rack, shortage, etc. • Rust, damage, incorrect items, etc. are found. • Lighting problem, torn sign, etc. are found. * Do not leave any problem unsolved.	Such a mistake tends to happen over and over again.

(2) Handling of derivatives

End materials, extra parts and others (derivatives) come out from the main flow for various reasons. Although these "materials" are prone to be missed, standardization of their handling is also indispensable for zero defects (Chart 5-4).

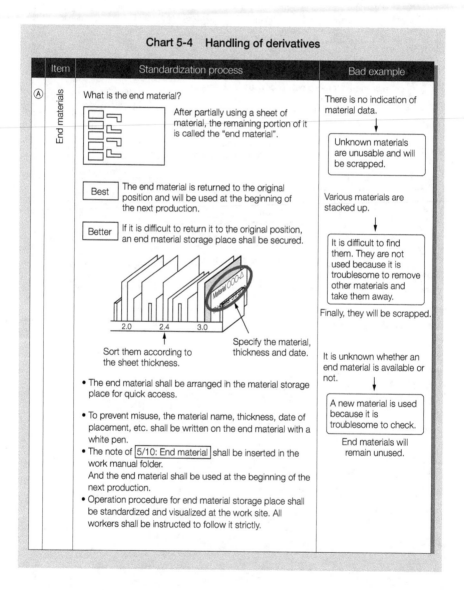

Chart 5-4 Handling of derivatives

Item	Standardization process	Bad example
Ⓐ End materials	**What is the end material?** After partially using a sheet of material, the remaining portion of it is called the "end material".	There is no indication of material data. ↓ Unknown materials are unusable and will be scrapped.
	Best The end material is returned to the original position and will be used at the beginning of the next production.	Various materials are stacked up.
	Better If it is difficult to return it to the original position, an end material storage place shall be secured.	↓ It is difficult to find them. They are not used because it is troublesome to remove other materials and take them away. Finally, they will be scrapped.
	2.0 2.4 3.0 — Sort them according to the sheet thickness. — Specify the material, thickness and date.	
	• The end material shall be arranged in the material storage place for quick access.	It is unknown whether an end material is available or not. ↓ A new material is used because it is troublesome to check. End materials will remain unused.
	• To prevent misuse, the material name, thickness, date of placement, etc. shall be written on the end material with a white pen.	
	• The note of |5/10: End material| shall be inserted in the work manual folder. And the end material shall be used at the beginning of the next production.	
	• Operation procedure for end material storage place shall be standardized and visualized at the work site. All workers shall be instructed to follow it strictly.	

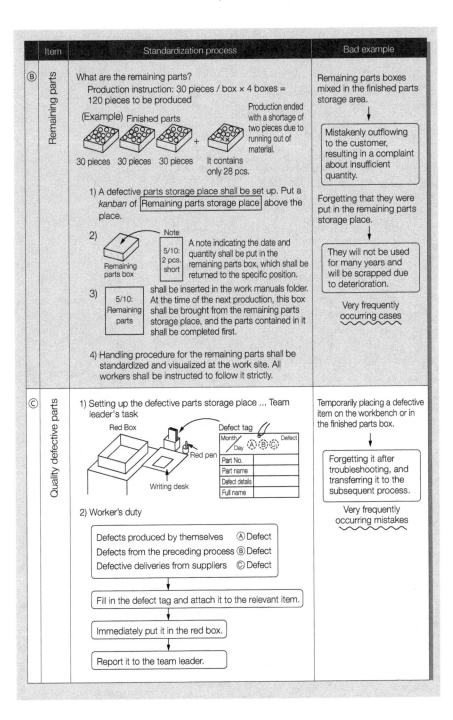

Item	Standardization process	Bad example
⑧ Remaining parts	What are the remaining parts? Production instruction: 30 pieces / box × 4 boxes = 120 pieces to be produced (Example) Finished parts / Production ended with a shortage of two pieces due to running out of material. 30 pieces 30 pieces 30 pieces It contains only 28 pcs. 1) A defective parts storage place shall be set up. Put a *kanban* of Remaining parts storage place above the place. 2) Note 5/10: 2 pcs. short Remaining parts box A note indicating the date and quantity shall be put in the remaining parts box, which shall be returned to the specific position. 3) 5/10: Remaining parts shall be inserted in the work manuals folder. At the time of the next production, this box shall be brought from the remaining parts storage place, and the parts contained in it shall be completed first. 4) Handling procedure for the remaining parts shall be standardized and visualized at the work site. All workers shall be instructed to follow it strictly.	Remaining parts boxes mixed in the finished parts storage area. ↓ Mistakenly outflowing to the customer, resulting in a complaint about insufficient quantity. Forgetting that they were put in the remaining parts storage place. ↓ They will not be used for many years and will be scrapped due to deterioration. Very frequently occurring cases
ⓒ Quality defective parts	1) Setting up the defective parts storage place … Team leader's task Red Box Defect tag Red pen Writing desk Month/Day ⒶⒷⒸ Defect Part No. Part name Defect details Full name 2) Worker's duty Defects produced by themselves Ⓐ Defect Defects from the preceding process Ⓑ Defect Defective deliveries from suppliers Ⓒ Defect ↓ Fill in the defect tag and attach it to the relevant item. ↓ Immediately put it in the red box. ↓ Report it to the team leader.	Temporarily placing a defective item on the workbench or in the finished parts box. ↓ Forgetting it after troubleshooting, and transferring it to the subsequent process. Very frequently occurring mistakes

	Item	Standardization process	Bad example

© 3) Team leader's tasks

Every four hours

Check and sort the actual items in the red box.

Ⓐ Defect → Check the work of the relevant worker and process that produced the defect. → Take temporary measures. Teach workers key points of work, adjust the relevant machine, etc.

Ⓑ © Defect → Immediately show the actual item to the QA department. → Explain the situation at the time of discovery and request measures.

4) Standardize the defective parts handling procedure and make it known to everyone.

Ⓓ Fallen parts

1) Setting up the fallen parts storage place ... Team leader

Fallen parts box — Set up a yellow box in the process.

2) Worker's duty

Pick it up quickly and put it in the yellow box.

Accidentally dropped a part.

3) Team leader's tasks

Every four hours

Check and sort the actual items in the yellow box.

Usable → Check them against the actual items located in the place. If they are the same ones, return them to the place

Not usable → Put them in the waste box.

4) Standardize the dropped parts handling procedure and make it known to everyone.

Bad example:

The worker picked it up and returned it to the box by himself.

↓

It was mistakenly put in an adjacent box containing a similar item.

↓

Occurrence of wrong assembly

Judged as acceptable and assembled as it was.

↓

A defect due to internal damage detected in the customer's inspection.

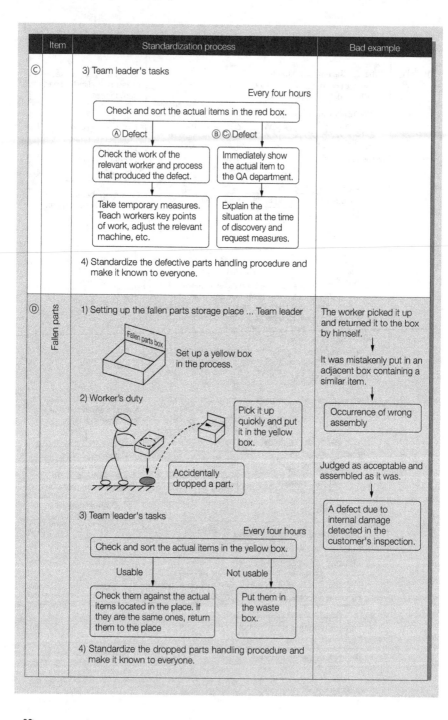

Item	Standardization process	Bad example
(E) Overflow parts	What are the overflow parts? Produced parts that cannot be stored due to fully-occupied shelves are called "overflow parts". 1) A temporary storage space for overflow parts shall be set up and used to accommodate the parts that cannot be put in the rack. A *kanban* of overflow parts shall be put on the rack. 2) At the time of the next supply, those in the overflow parts storage space shall be first put in the rack. 3) Standardize the overflow parts handling procedure, and make it known to everyone.	If boxes of overflow parts are left in the aisle or on the top of rack: **Those left in the aisle** intercept the traffic of hand carts. **Those left on the top of rack** will get forgotten and remain undone for a long time. Very common rule violation Leaving them shall be strictly forbidden.

The simplest way to handle them is to place them in fixed locations. However, if it is difficult to secure dedicated places for them even in the case of large-variety small-volume products or special models, it is also effective to set up "free-location storage" space, which allows for time saving in looking for and arranging a storage place. Operation of the free-location storage can be standardized as shown in Chart 5-5. It is important that anyone can place and pick out parts and materials without cohfusion.

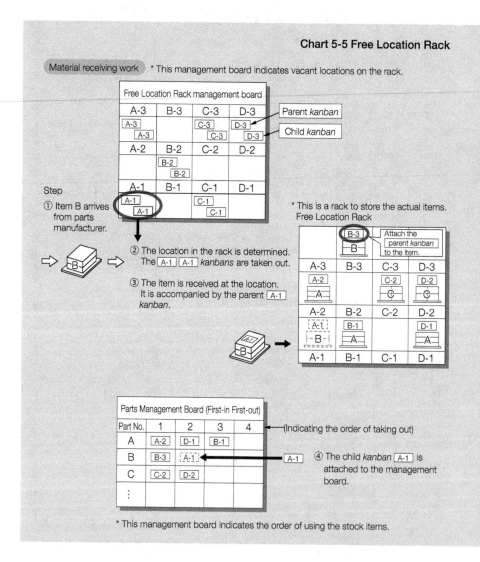

Chart 5-5 Free Location Rack

Management Method

Parts taking-out work

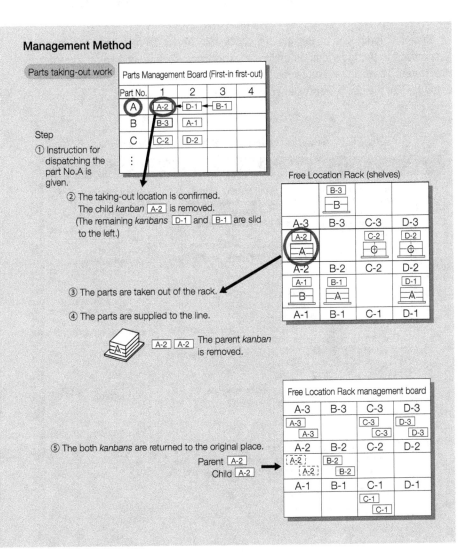

Parts Management Board (First-in first-out)

Part No.	1	2	3	4
A	A-2	D-1	B-1	
B	B-3	A-1		
C	C-2	D-2		
⋮				

Step

① Instruction for dispatching the part No.A is given.

② The taking-out location is confirmed. The child *kanban* A-2 is removed. (The remaining *kanbans* D-1 and B-1 are slid to the left.)

③ The parts are taken out of the rack.

④ The parts are supplied to the line.

A-2 A-2 The parent *kanban* is removed.

⑤ The both *kanbans* are returned to the original place.

Parent A-2
Child A-2 →

Free Location Rack (shelves)

	B-3		
	B		
A-3	B-3	C-3	D-3
A-2		C-2	D-2
A		C	C
A-2	B-2	C-2	D-2
A-1	B-1		D-1
B	A		A
A-1	B-1	C-1	D-1

Free Location Rack management board

A-3	B-3	C-3	D-3
A-3		C-3	D-3
A-3		C-3	D-3
A-2	B-2	C-2	D-2
A-2			
A-2	B-2		
A-1	B-1	C-1	D-1
		C-1	
		C-1	

83

Chapter 6

Standardization of quality check related items

Personal judgment in the quality check may differ from person to person according to the individual knowledge, experience, feeling, and so on. In order to minimize such variations and prevent defect outflow, it is important to standardize the check items shown in Chart 6-1.

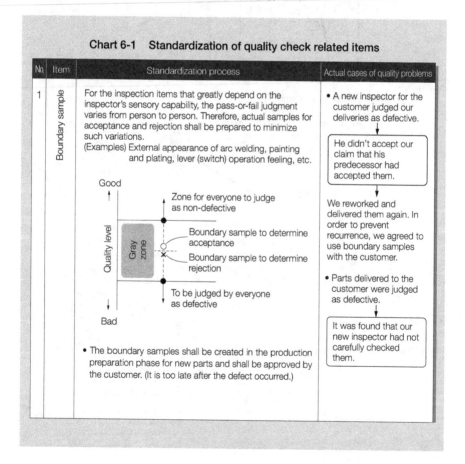

Chart 6-1 Standardization of quality check related items

No.	Item	Standardization process	Actual cases of quality problems
1	Boundary sample	For the inspection items that greatly depend on the inspector's sensory capability, the pass-or-fail judgment varies from person to person. Therefore, actual samples for acceptance and rejection shall be prepared to minimize such variations. (Examples) External appearance of arc welding, painting and plating, lever (switch) operation feeling, etc. Good ↑ Quality level Gray zone Zone for everyone to judge as non-defective Boundary sample to determine acceptance Boundary sample to determine rejection To be judged by everyone as defective Bad ↓ • The boundary samples shall be created in the production preparation phase for new parts and shall be approved by the customer. (It is too late after the defect occurred.)	• A new inspector for the customer judged our deliveries as defective. ↓ He didn't accept our claim that his predecessor had accepted them. ↓ We reworked and delivered them again. In order to prevent recurrence, we agreed to use boundary samples with the customer. • Parts delivered to the customer were judged as defective. ↓ It was found that our new inspector had not carefully checked them.

No.	Item	Standardization process	Actual cases of quality problems
2	Master sample	The die shape gradually changes due to wear. And when it exceeds the limit, a large scale quality defect occurs involving a whole lot. → For pressed parts, standardization was implemented to confirm the shape change on each lot by using the part produced in the early stage of mass production as a master sample for an overlapping check. The die is repaired to the original size. New die making 1 year Master sample creation 2 years Overlapping check The gap gets bigger. • The master samples with the designated color painted and with the part numbers indicated are stored with the corresponding dies.	The shape of pressed parts were checked against those of the same parts delivered last time. ↓ The customer informed us that they were rejected due to poor shape. As a result of our investigation, it turned out that the press dies, which had been made three years ago, wore out and deformed. It was the kind of defect that could not be detected through the shape check by using the parts delivered last time.
3	Stock check & sorting criteria	In order to cope with cases where any quality defects are found, the stock check and sorting criteria shall be standardized as an internal rule to eliminate misjudgment. (Example) Scope of 100% check and sorting after occurrence of a defect Our company Customer Ongoing-process storage Subsequent process Finished parts storage Deliveries storage Finished vehicle yard In-process inventory In-process inventory Type Ⓐ defects found in ongoing process Type Ⓑ defects found in subsequent process ? Type Ⓒ defects found by a customer Customer's instruction is followed. If any defect is found in the 100% check and sorting, the scope shall be expanded beyond that point (indicated by ..?) to completely eliminate defective products. * Depending on the customer, all their expenses required for 100% check and sorting and reworking finished cars are charged. They are very expensive! → This should be known to everyone as a case study showing "how major waste will be caused" by the occurrence and outflow of a defect.	The stock check and sorting was performed based on the independent judgment of team leaders. ↓ Misjudgment caused inconveniences to the customer a few times. ↓ After the same mistake occurring many times, an internal rule was finally established.

No.	Item	Standardization process	Actual cases of quality problems
4	Important safety inspection item	For important safety items in which a defect outflow will directly lead to serious trouble in the market, drawing-based instructions shall be given for important safety inspection items. Those items shall be absolutely free from defects, so the *pokayoke* (fool proof) functions designed to eliminate worker's mistakes shall be incorporated in the equipment planning stage and used properly to prevent occurrence of defects. (Example) Tightening of important safety bolts (1) Installation of a torque control gun with *pokayoke* functions for screw tightening. If the tightening torque is lower than the required value, the operator is warned by the buzzer and red lamp. If the tightening is completed with normal torque, the green lamp lights. In the case of the red lamp, the production line will not move. (2) Mechanical reliability check At the fixed time (twice a day), the operator measures the tightening torque of the relevant bolts with a torque wrench and records the measured values on the check sheet. Then, the operator shall check whether the measured values are within the specifications.	We fully relied on the torque check being performed by the operators without employing any *pokayoke* function. × There was a possibility of defect outflow due to the worker's neglecting the torque check. × There was a possibility of defect outflow due to a defective torque wrench that was unable to provide correct measurements. Defect outflow, if any, would lead to serious trouble and damage to the company.

<table>
<tr><td>5</td><td>Quality check after rework</td><td colspan="2">It is important to standardize not only the precautions when reworking defects, but also the check items and judgment criteria when checking the reworked states.</td></tr>
</table>

Weld defect reworking in a finished vehicle (example)

Weld defects are found in finished vehicle inspection → Points to pay attention to when reworking

Step	Work	Points to pay attention to
1	Removal of attached parts	• Minimize damage during removal. • Store all removed parts in a box to prevent them from being lost.
2	Removal of paint film and sealer	• Make the removal range as small as possible.
3	Correction of weld defect portion	• When using a grinder or sander, use covers to prevent dust from scattering in the room. • During re-welding, pay special attention not to cause a fire due to sparks. • Carefully and finely finish the appearance.
4	Sealer coating, spraying, and baking	• Before spraying, be sure to perform masking to protect unnecessary portions from the paint. • Be careful not to cause a fire with a baking lamp.
5	Reassembling	• Be careful not to cause damage to or scratch the parts.

No.	Item	Standardization process			Actual cases of quality problems
5	Quality check after rework	Step	Work		Points to pay attention to
		6	Recheck		Check for the following defects that are likely to occur at the time of rework, in addition to the usual check items. • Spattering • Paint blushing • Damage or scratches on assembled parts

* If such defects are found in the welding process, reworking can be done within 10 minutes. However, if they outflow to the finished vehicle inspection, a full day must be spent on reworking. Company-wide zero defect activities shall be promoted by repeatedly teaching all workers how major waste is caused by defect outflows.

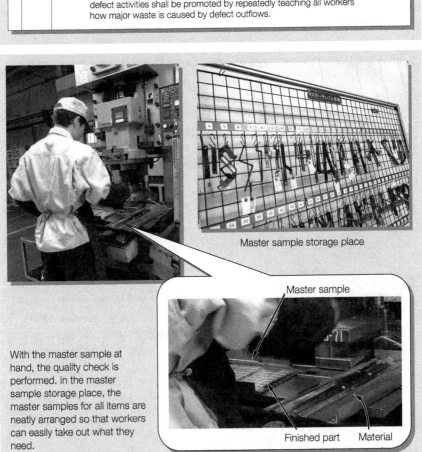

Master sample storage place

Master sample

With the master sample at hand, the quality check is performed. In the master sample storage place, the master samples for all items are neatly arranged so that workers can easily take out what they need.

Finished part   Material

The work standard is strictly followed at Kamizen Co., Ltd.

Chapter 7

Human development –
Education and training

Training of workers is an important task of managers and supervisors. This chapter describes how to educate and train workers who are directly involved in manufacturing.

First of all, let's think about what education and training mean, respectively.
- Education → Teaching things that workers do not know (to give knowledge)

  Example: Teaching a standardized procedure for making a certain item
- Training → Having workers repeat what they know until they can do it well

  Example: Having them repeat the procedure that they have learned until they can do it well

The both are very important.

1. Education of new employees

Questions

Imagine that a new employee has been transferred to your team. How can you educate and train the person who does not have manufacturing experience at all to become a reliable worker as soon as possible?

There may be various answers and it is difficult to tell what is correct, but the following are basically necessary.

(1) Preparing a text

Before new employees get into the manufacturing work, you should summarize what you want to teach them as basic matters in one booklet and hand it to each of them. When teaching them, you should tell them to take notes on it and review it whenever necessary. The content of the text should be as follows.

① Safety basics ... Personal protective equipment to be worn, safety rules to follow, etc.
② Important points of "standardized work" described in Chapter 4
③ Important points of "standardized material handling" described in Chapter 5
④ Important points of "quality check related items" standardized in Chapter 6
⑤ How to read drawings ... Basic and essential knowledge

(2) Education and training curriculum

Education and training period, order, subjects, etc. should be standardized in individual companies. (Chart 7-1).

In the long run, it is best to provide the appropriate education from the start, and it is too late to educate them after a serious trouble has occurred.

Chart 7-1   Education and training curriculum (example)

	8:00	9	10	11	13 12	14	15	16	17:00
Day 1	Opening speech	Classroom lecture	Plant (process) tour		Basic Skills Training - I		Basic Skills Training - II	
Day 2	Classroom lecture		Basic Skills Training - III		Basic Skills Training - IV		Classroom lecture	Ending speech

* Classroom lectures and basic skills training courses shall be efficiently arranged.

(3) Cultivation of instructors

It is necessary to systematically develop instructors or trainers who are familiar with the content to be taught. If they need more education, it is also important to prepare a system that allows them to devote full time to the education or training.

2. Training of new employees

(1) Training method

The best way to train is a two-step method: In the first step, new employees have "offline training" at a place different from the actual manufacturing line, and in the second step thereafter, they receive "online training" in the actual production lines while carrying out actual work (Charts 7-2 and 7-3).

Chart 7-2   Training of new employees

Best: Two-step training consisting of offline and online types				
Example of new employee training				
Step	Types of skills	Period	Type of training	Place for training
1	Basic skills	2 days	Offline training	Training *Dojo*
2	Individual skills*	3 to 5 days	Online training	Actual work process

* Individual skills training: Although the above chart indicates the "online training" for mastering individual skills of new workers, there are also many cases where further two-step training (offline training and then online training) is needed to master the individual skill depending on the type of required individual skills. (See the training method described later.)

Chart 7-3   Training and proficiency levels in vehicle assembly process (example)

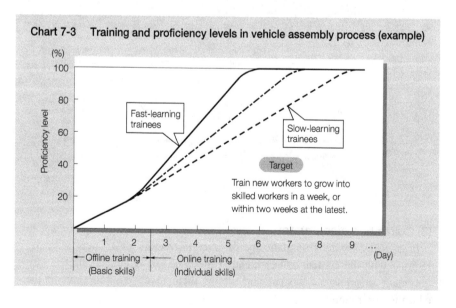

Through the basic skill training, the appropriateness of each worker is judged, so that individual workers can be assigned to the processes suitable to their individual skills and/or characteristics. In this way, new workers can get into work smoothly, and defects can be minimized.

(2) Offline training

As a place for offline training, a training place called a "training *dojo*" should be set up. Important points when establishing the training *dojo* are described below.

1) Make the *dojo* simple and efficient for each type of job training.

The training *dojo* should be established according to job type (Chart 7-4). It should be simple and efficient.

If you want to enable a single *dojo* to be used for training "various types of work" or "everything", its layout will become complicated, and training machinery, jigs and tools to be installed there will also become diverse. As a result, a complicated *dojo* is created. Even from the standpoint of both trainees and trainers, if people of various professions gather in one place and each performs or receives different training, they cannot concentrate on their own training.

Chart 7-4   Examples of basic skills by job category

Welding	Spot welding, Arc welding, Finishing, Assembling, and Quality Check
Painting	Spraying, Sanding, Sealing, Masking, and Quality Check
Assembly	Screw tightening, Piping, Wiring, Assembling, Adjustment, and Quality check
Machining	Programming, Workpiece setup, In-machine cleaning, and Quality check
Inspection	Handling of inspection tools, Pass-fail judgment criteria, and Reading of drawing

Assembly training *dojo* at CESAB (Italy)

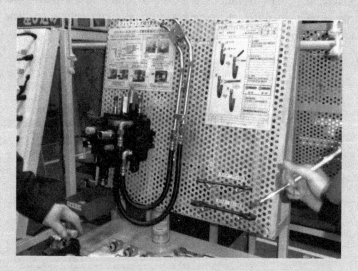

Piping connection training

Training for various skills

Bolt tightening training

2) Provide simple and efficient training tools designed for each individual skill.

The following is one of the training tools. Chart 7-5 shows a training tool that enables training for tightening bolts to the top and bottom, left and right sides. While the tool shown in the above photograph "Bolt tightening training" is used to practice bolt tightening in one direction, the tool shown in Chart 7-5 and the following photograph is specially designed for training for tightening bolts to the top, bottom, left and right holes with a single unit.

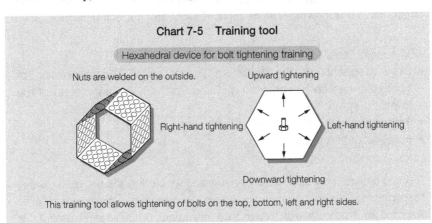

Chart 7-5   Training tool

Hexahedral device for bolt tightening training

Nuts are welded on the outside.   Upward tightening

Right-hand tightening   Left-hand tightening

Downward tightening

This training tool allows tightening of bolts on the top, bottom, left and right sides.

Hexahedral device for bolt tightening training

3) Set target times for each element work and test proficiency level.

"Targets" are indispensable for any training. In the case of bolt tightening training, for example, the target time should be set based on actual work at the site, such as "Tighten 30 bolts to the bottom holes within the target time of __ seconds", in order to measure the proficiency level.

At first, trainees are not used to it, so it may take two or three times longer than the target time. They may overtighten the bolts and cause bolt breakage or other defects. However, by learning "tips", most people will be able to clear the target time. The following is an example of such "tips" for bolt tightening.

«Example of "tips" for bolt tightening»
- How to distinguish the sound of impact guns: The completion of tightening can be judged from a change in the tightening sound of the impact gun.
- Tips to put a bolt into a socket in one shot.
- Force adjustment, etc.

Some trainees may have some operations at which they are not good, so that they cannot clear the target time. In such a case, those persons should be assigned to a process with fewer such operations. That is an indispensable consideration for stabilizing the whole process and reducing defects. In fact, there are many cases in which a worker produced a defect because of working hastily thinking, "I cannot make it in time". Even if you pressure new workers, they will not be able to master the work sooner. It is important to increase their proficiency level, without being impatient, through a proper combination of offline and online types of training until they can work reliably.

(3) Online training
1) Role and attitude of trainers (instructors)

The new worker training should be provided by a team leader or equivalent person of the team to which the new workers are assigned, who plays the role of trainer (instructor). That role is very important because proficiency of new worker skills and workplace quality greatly depend on the trainer's skill.

Before new workers are actually assigned, it is necessary to clearly identify the team leaders or equivalent persons as "trainers" and provide them with necessary lessons about the following roles and attitudes of the trainer in advance so that they can provide appropriate guidance to new workers.

[Roles of the trainer]
- Giving guidance to new workers on a "man-to-man" basis until they become 100% proficient
- Taking responsibility for overall quality, including work done by new workers during the training period

[Mental attitude of the trainer in training]
① Teaching with a strong will and enthusiasm for "developing newcomers to become skilled workers"
② Relaxing the trainees' feelings and trying to keep good human relations through the man-to-man guidance approach
③ Teaching tips for skills, as well as the importance of each operation and the standard work procedures in an easy-to-understand manner

2) How to teach practical operations (Chart 7-6)

Chart 7-6   Work training in multiple-model vehicle assembly process (example)

Step	Target portions for training	How to train	Important points
①	Parts common to all models	Show them what to do step by step and have them do it. Repeat that tenaciously. Teach them slowly but steadily.	• By using the standard work procedure manual, teach them the importance of observing the procedure. • Teach them how to read the assembly instructions and the meanings of various symbols.
②	Portions having the same structure and shape, but using different parts and mounting methods	For each operation, show them which parts to take and how to assemble them, and have them do it by themselves repeatedly.	• Explain the knacks and key points while showing them how to do it and have them do it by themselves. • Also, show and make them understand what will happen if the parts are forcibly assembled by using actual parts. • Sufficiently explain what will happen if any defect occurs and outflows.
③	Portions that vary from model to model	Explain the differences in the portion among models, show them how to assemble it, and let them do it.	• Teach them tenaciously until they can do it according to the procedure. • It is also good training to have them explain what to do from the beginning to the end.
④	Final follow-up check	Let them perform one-cycle operations and check their proficiency levels.	• Check the accuracy and quality more carefully than the speed and quantity. • Thoroughly instruct them to ask superiors when they do not know what to do or when they are delayed, and not to do things their own way. • Reduce the frequency of guidance gradually to have them do it by themselves. Every time → every 30 minutes → every hour → every half day → once a day

The best training steps, according to the actual circumstances of each company and individual process, should be standardized to help new comers grow into skilled workers as early and as properly as possible.

3. Multi-skill development

In order to avoid a situation where the absence of a worker in a team makes production impossible, it is necessary to have multi-skilled workers who can do other workers' operations. Expanding individual workers' range of work not only leads to the improvement in their skills and capabilities, but also enables manufacturing operations to continue without any problems, no matter what happens to team members. Multi-skill development is one of the important elements of TPS.

(1) Proficiency level

For each work process, the team leader evaluates the proficiency level of each worker according to the following standards (Chart 7-7).

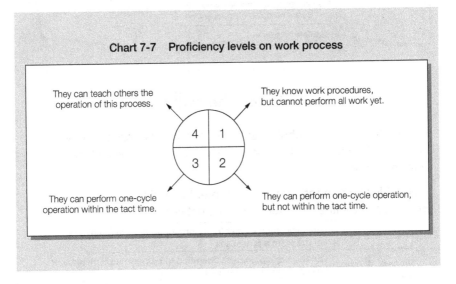

Chart 7-7   Proficiency levels on work process

They can teach others the operation of this process.

They know work procedures, but cannot perform all work yet.

They can perform one-cycle operation within the tact time.

They can perform one-cycle operation, but not within the tact time.

- For workers with proficiency levels 1 and 2, the trainer performs on-the-job training on a "man-to-man basis", while carrying out the quality check on products including the work done by the trainees.

(2) Skill map

A "skill map", which visualizes the skill proficiency level of all shop workers, is used for planning and implementation of staffing and training (Chart 7-8).

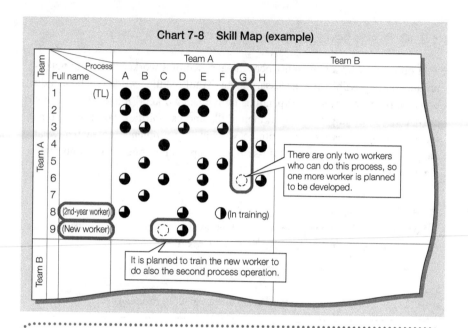

Chart 7-8   Skill Map (example)

There are only two workers who can do this process, so one more worker is planned to be developed.

(In training)

It is planned to train the new worker to do also the second process operation.

How to use the skill map

① Used to nominate substitutes when regular workers are absent

A substitute is nominated by confirming who can take charge of the process for the absent worker.

② Used for human resource development planning

[Examples of multi-skill development objectives]

Worker standard	Enabling each worker to perform operations in three or more of the team's processes
Process standard	Enabling each process operation to be performed by three or more members of the team

[Team leader's task]

- Creating and implementing a training plan for each worker who can work in less than three processes
- Creating and implementing a training plan for each process which can be handled by less than three workers

☞ Work training in a workplace with a limited number of workers is subject to time pressure and other restrictions, so careful planning and execution is important.

4. Education and training after countermeasures against defects

Every time a human-related failure or defect occurs, the team leader must conduct reeducation and retrain workers properly and manage daily care more carefully to prevent recurrence (Chart 7-9). If the team leader stimulates worker motivation with enthusiasm and continues careful watch and guidance on a daily basis, it is possible to completely eliminate human-related defects.

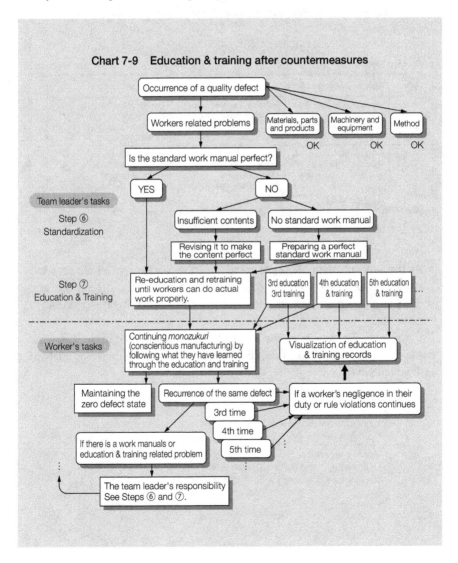

Chart 7-9   Education & training after countermeasures

☞ Visualization of worker education and training records

There may be workers who repeat work mistakes and/or rule violations, no matter how many times education and training are provided. In such cases, it is also important to visualize the individual worker's education and training records to raise consciousness in the workplace (Chart 7-10).

Chart 7-10   Individual Education & Training Record (example)

Individual Education & Training Record Table

Full name: ○○○○

Year/ Month/ Day	Reason for education & training	Details of education & training	Check item	Person in charge
'15 5/10	Skipped prescribed working steps. This is the second time. Non-use of Work Interruption Card	Retraining of how to use the Work Interruption Card	The worker promised to use the Work Interruption Card whenever necessary.	✒
'15 10/3	Skipped prescribed working steps. This is the third time. Loss of Work Interruption Card	Re-education about the importance of the Work Interruption Card Reissue of Work Interruption Card	Again, the worker promised to abide by the interruption rule from this point forward.	✒

- At the time of reeducation or retraining, the leader should discuss the relevant workers based on their education and training records, and specify their promises in the record sheet, with their signatures if possible.

In this way, by visualizing the fact that they have repeated excuses without doing what they promised to do, they will gradually feel a sense of crisis of losing their jobs.

If I don't make any improvement, my performance rating will go down, and...
· My salary may not rise.
· My bonus may become lower than my coworker's.
· My promotion may be affected.

It is often said: "People do not try to change seriously unless they feel a sense of crisis". Anyone will definitely change when recognizing it through conversation.

Part 3

Weak-Point Management and Quality Creation

Chapter 8

Weak-Point Management (WPM)
— Level-3 visualization

Weak-Point Management (abbreviated as WPM) is the name attached by members of overseas bases of Toyota Industries when we were implementing the activities to eradicate chronic and frequent defects.

Defect outflow will not go to zero unless chronic and frequent defects are eradicated. WPM features visualization of the transition of chronic defects with the record of countermeasures, allowing us to think about why the previous measures did not work after each recurrence and to consider new measures. By looking over the entire line and thinking about the cause by repeating "why?" questions, you can certainly advance towards zero defects, no matter how complicatedly entangled the factors are, so please try it.

1. Types of WPM

(1) WPM Type-1 ... Visualization of the transition of frequent defects with a record of countermeasures

Since there are many cases where quality defects are caused by various interweaving factors, such as manpower, materials, machinery and methods, it is necessary to take measures one by one against respective factors found (to prevent recurrence) (Chart 8-1).

- If the countermeasure is appropriate, defects will surely decrease.
  - → The result tells us whether the countermeasure was good or bad. Visualization enables everyone to understand it.
- If the countermeasure is inappropriate, the status of defects will not be improved.
  - → Find the remaining problems and take thorough measures.

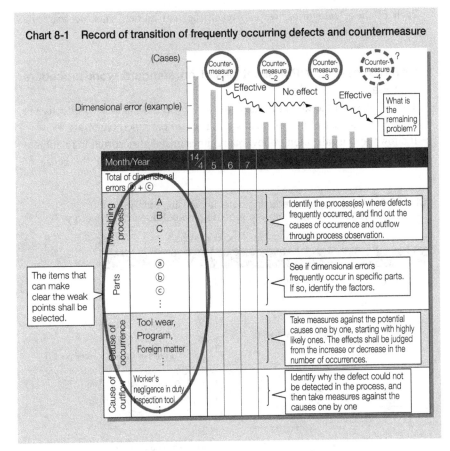

Chart 8-1 Record of transition of frequently occurring defects and countermeasure

- Explain the problems specified on the WPM sheet at "Quality *Asaichi* (morning) meeting" and receive advice or guidance from the meeting members (borrow wisdom).

The defects to be visualized on the WPM sheet should be divided as follows:
- Defects that continue to occur for many years on individual parts
- Major defects found at individual shops, such as:
  Dimensional errors in the machining shop
  Misalignment in the welding shop
  Oil leakage and tightening errors in the assembly shop
  Incorrect items or quantity shipments in the shipping area
  It is important to visualize them according to those individual categories. By locating various causes through the "why?" question-based investigation in

each of those categories, we can reach the real hidden cause to eradicate chronic defects.

(2) WPM Type-2 ... WPM sheet based on standard work procedure manual

The WPM sheet based on the standard work procedure manual is effective in reducing the number of mistakes caused during simple repetitive tasks.

It allows for visualization of how many times mistakes occurred in relation to which steps in the procedure specified in the manual, so that the cause of

Chart 8-2   An example of reducing defects by using standard work procedure manuals and recording defect occurrence history

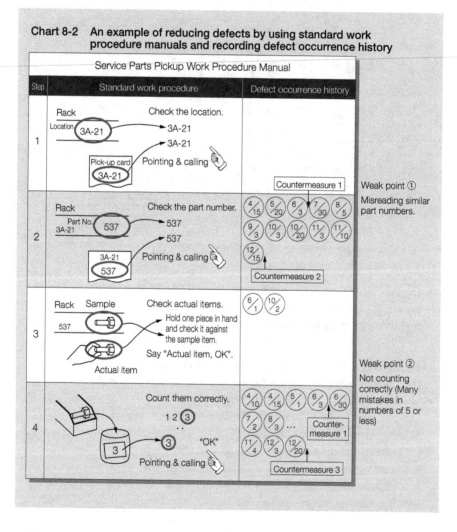

frequent defects occurring in the relevant procedure can be investigated and necessary countermeasures can be taken (Charts 8-2 and 8-3).

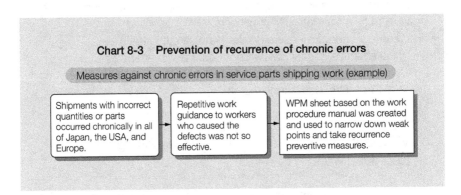

Chart 8-3   Prevention of recurrence of chronic errors

Measures against chronic errors in service parts shipping work (example)

| Shipments with incorrect quantities or parts occurred chronically in all of Japan, the USA, and Europe. | → | Repetitive work guidance to workers who caused the defects was not so effective. | → | WPM sheet based on the work procedure manual was created and used to narrow down weak points and take recurrence preventive measures. |

(3) WPM Type-3 ... Visualization of defective portions or processes based on the defect map

This is a technique used to visualize components and/or processes where defects occurred and to determine where to start from. When used in combination with the Type-1, it is an extremely effective technique to reduce chronic and frequent defects by starting to take countermeasures from the portion where the defects occurred most frequently (Chart 8-4).

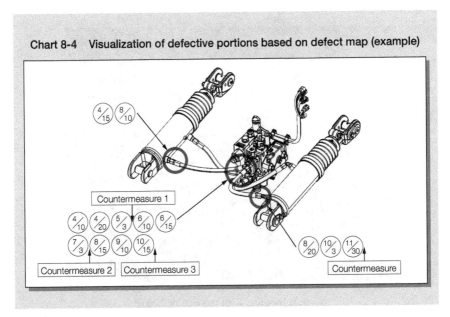

Chart 8-4   Visualization of defective portions based on defect map (example)

(Example) Oil leakage from a high-pressure hydraulic circuit
- Visualize the high pressure hydraulic circuit for each model.
- Every time an oil leak occurs, check the leaking portion, indicate it in the map, and fill in the date of occurrence.
- Each time a countermeasure is taken, indicate it in the map.
  - → If it is effective, the oil leak will not occur again after that.
  - → If it is ineffective, it will occur again, so try to find other causes and take necessary countermeasures.

2. Visualization of countermeasure records through "Plastic Board Activities"

To eradicate a deep-rooted chronic and frequent defect, long-term tenacious effort is necessary. Therefore, we started an activity of displaying the countermeasures and their results concerning each defect item on a commercially available plastic board, discussing and deciding what to do with all task force team members while looking at the board, and accomplishing it. We named it "Plastic Board Activity."

When observing problematic work, we brought the plastic board to the site, wrote out the problems we found on a "Problems and Measures" sheet,

Asaichi **meeting with the plastic board**

immediately decided on the deadline for a solution with the person in charge of the measures, and followed them up with all the team members until completion (Chart 8-5).

Chart 8-5 Plastic Board Activities (example)

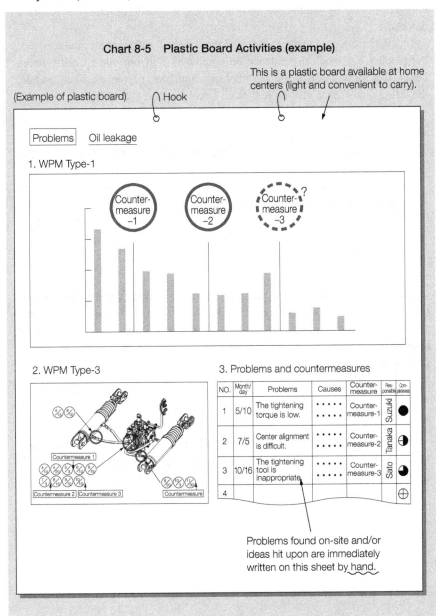

This is a plastic board available at home centers (light and convenient to carry).

(Example of plastic board)   Hook

Problems   Oil leakage

1. WPM Type-1

Counter-measure -1
Counter-measure -2
Counter-measure -3 ?

2. WPM Type-3

3. Problems and countermeasures

NO.	Month/day	Problems	Causes	Counter-measure	Responsible	Completeness
1	5/10	The tightening torque is low.	· · · · ·	Counter-measure-1	Suzuki	●
2	7/5	Center alignment is difficult.	· · · · ·	Counter-measure-2	Tanaka	⊕
3	10/16	The tightening tool is inappropriate.	· · · · ·	Counter-measure-3	Sato	◖
4						⊕

Problems found on-site and/or ideas hit upon are immediately written on this sheet by hand.

At the time of defect recurrence, we brought the plastic board to the "*Asaichi* Meeting" on the next morning and discussed reoccurrence prevention measures at the meeting, including the top management, until we discover the causes and eliminate them. By continuing such activities, we made progress toward zero defects.

Today, there are so many companies that store all information in computers, but placing too much dependence on computers will not make quality much better. If a lot of information is stored in computers, people are likely to take the following actions, making it difficult to solve quality problems.

- [Even if information is stored in computers ...]
① Because it takes time to get the necessary information from the computers,
  → there are many cases where inappropriate measures are taken without checking the information.
② When there are a lot of things to check, workers are likely to forget what they have checked, and take inappropriate measures based on incorrect memory.

Even if it is a complicated problem involving several departments or it is unclear which party should take responsibility, the parts manufacturer or the vehicle assembling plant, continuous and patient efforts through the plastic board-based visualization will surely allow chronic and frequent defect problems to be solved.

3. Examples of improvement based on WPM Types-1 and -2

Chronic and frequent defects of delivered service parts were found not only in Japan, but also in the United States and European companies, so we took drastic measures (Chart 8-6).

(1) Example of countermeasures based on WPM Type-1

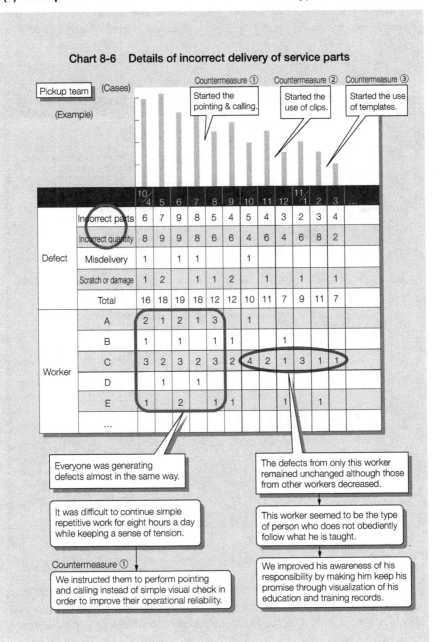

Chart 8-6   Details of incorrect delivery of service parts

Pickup team   (Cases)

(Example)

Countermeasure ① Started the pointing & calling.

Countermeasure ② Started the use of clips.

Countermeasure ③ Started the use of templates.

		10/4	5	6	7	8	9	10	11	12	11/1	2	3	...
Defect	Incorrect parts	6	7	9	8	5	4	5	4	3	2	3	4	
	Incorrect quantity	8	9	9	8	6	6	4	6	4	6	8	2	
	Misdelivery	1		1	1			1						
	Scratch or damage	1	2		1	1	2		1		1		1	
	Total	16	18	19	18	12	12	10	11	7	9	11	7	
Worker	A	2	1	2	1	3		1						
	B	1		1		1	1			1				
	C	3	2	3	2	3	2	4	2	1	3	1	1	
	D		1		1									
	E	1		2		1	1			1		1		
	...													

Everyone was generating defects almost in the same way.

The defects from only this worker remained unchanged although those from other workers decreased.

It was difficult to continue simple repetitive work for eight hours a day while keeping a sense of tension.

This worker seemed to be the type of person who does not obediently follow what he is taught.

Countermeasure ①

We instructed them to perform pointing and calling instead of simple visual check in order to improve their operational reliability.

We improved his awareness of his responsibility by making him keep his promise through visualization of his education and training records.

(2) Example of countermeasures based on WPM Type-2

Chart 8-7 shows an example of visualization and countermeasures taken against problems found according to the procedure described in 1-(2) of this chapter.

Chart 8-7   Countermeasures for service parts pickup work

No	Problems	Countermeasures
1	Although workers were told to take out parts after visually checking the location number, part number, etc., they did not carefully check them.	**Countermeasure 1** We instructed them to perform the pointing and calling instead of a simple visual check in order to enhance their attention.
2	After pointing to a target box, workers tended to mistakenly take out parts from the next box (due to the shape of the boxes being the same).	**Countermeasure 2** We instructed workers to attach a clip as a marker after pointing to the target box.
3	It was very hard for workers to count the quantity by saying "one, two, three ..." all day. They frequently counted wrong when the quantity was five or less. (Slacking off was unavoidable.)	**Countermeasure 3** We instructed workers to "check the number", instead of "counting", by putting items on the template and saying "3:3 OK". (pointing & calling)
4	It was hard for workers to continue the pointing and calling of the location and part numbers all day long (Slacking off was unavoidable).	**Countermeasure 4** We introduced a barcode reader system since workers had limitations in reliability. Barcode We instructed workers to pull out the target box forward and scan the barcode, instead of using a clip.

We honestly took countermeasures against the problem of incorrect items or quantities globally at all of the six plants consistently, taking a lot of time, and finally, we were able to reduce the incorrect contents of service parts shipments by more than 90%.

4. Examples of improvement based on WPM Types-1 and -3

As in the case of incorrect contents of service parts shipments, oil leakage in the high-pressure hydraulic circuit was also a chronic problem at each company, so complaints came frequently from customers. So we worked on eradicating oil leaks by using the WPM system.

(1) Example of WPM Type-1

Chart 8-8 shows a visualization of the trend of oil leaks detected in the finished vehicle inspection.

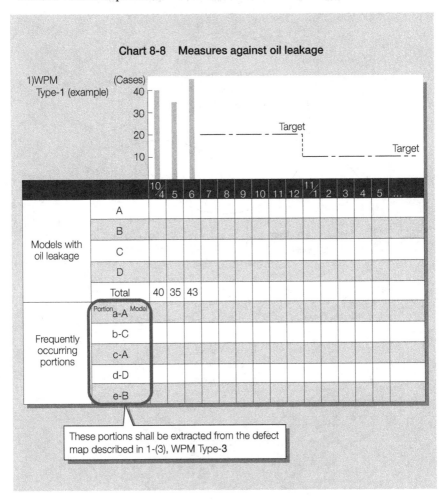

Chart 8-8   Measures against oil leakage

These portions shall be extracted from the defect map described in 1-(3), WPM Type-3

(2) Establishment of a task force team

Since oil leakage was a deep-rooted problem, we decided to establish a task force team to take thorough countermeasures, aiming at zero oil leakage (Chart 8-9). Since it also relates to the design structure, we appointed an engineer of the quality assurance department as the team leader. Every time an oil leak occurred, the team carried out *GENCHI GENBUTSU* check (on-site check of actual items) and identified potential causes.

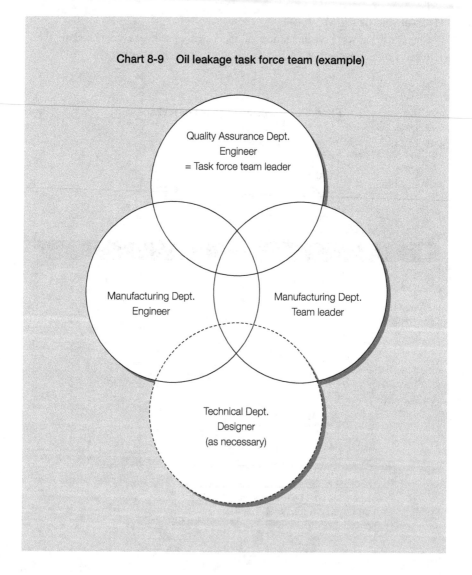

Chart 8-9   Oil leakage task force team (example)

Quality Assurance Dept.
Engineer
= Task force team leader

Manufacturing Dept.
Engineer

Manufacturing Dept.
Team leader

Technical Dept.
Designer
(as necessary)

(3) "Why?" questions to locate the cause of oil leakage

We conducted the cause investigation through the "why?" questions on individual oil leaking portions (Chart 8-10).

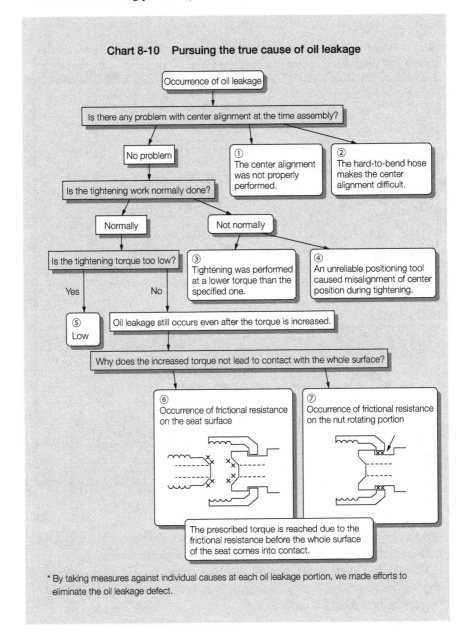

Chart 8-10   Pursuing the true cause of oil leakage

* By taking measures against individual causes at each oil leakage portion, we made efforts to eliminate the oil leakage defect.

(4) Countermeasures against each cause

We determined and implemented countermeasures at each oil leaking portion and against each cause of occurrence (Chart 8-11).

Chart 8-11   Countermeasures against individual possible causes of oil leakage

No.	Possible cause	Countermeasure	Responsible
①	The center alignment was not properly performed.	Education and retraining of workers will be implemented to make them understand the importance of center alignment and to teach the key points for center alignment.	Team leader
②	The hard-to-bend hose makes the center alignment difficult. High-pressure hose Hard and difficult to bend	It is difficult to cope with this problem only by work training, and also there was a strong desire for a "design change for easier assembling", so we will do so. * I had the designer experience the operation to know how difficult it was.	Design
③	The workers tightened screws at lower torque than the standard.	Retraining will be provided as in the case of ①.	Team leader
④	An unreliable positioning tool caused misalignment of center position during tightening.	The positioning tool is modified to have a more rigid structure that does not allow movement once it is set.	Engineer
⑤	The standard tightening torque was too low, causing oil leakage.	We increased the standard tightening torque.	Design
⑥	Occurrence of frictional resistance	The oil leakage problem was solved by applying oil to the relevant parts before assembly to reduce frictional resistance. "This is greatly effective."	Engineer

As a result of serious efforts made by all the team members while repeating trials and errors, oil leakage became almost zero in about one year.

Through horizontal deployment of this activity to overseas plants, we were able to eradicate oil leakage problems that had occurred chronically and frequently throughout the entire group.

5. Benefits of Weak-Point Management

There are famous words from Mr. Taiichi Ohno, who created TPS: "Observe the production floor without preconceptions and with a blank mind. Repeat 'why?' five times to every matter".

In fact, when a defect occurred, the workers repeated "why?" questions. However, it was not so easy for them to reach the root cause because there were too many possible causes. When they got stuck, they used to roughly determine a cause and finish the activity by taking uncertain measures. However, that was ineffective in reducing defects.

Therefore, by using the Weak-Point Management, I made them think about why the previous countermeasure did not work for the defects. And after they noticed the reason, I told them to take proper countermeasures. In this way, they narrowed down the causes of problems by repeating the "why?" questions.

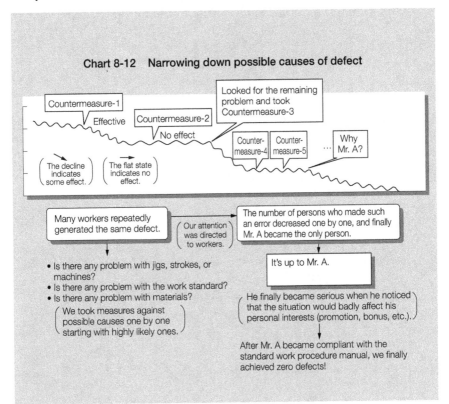

Chart 8-12   Narrowing down possible causes of defect

WPM is very effective in eliminating chronic and frequent defects because it is designed to investigate the cause by looking over the entire line and repeating the "why?" questions and take countermeasures step by step as shown in Chart 8-12.

In Toyota Industrial Equipment Manufacturing (TIEM), a direct U.S. subsidiary of Toyota Industries, the WPM was also deployed to the administrative department where it solved many chronic problems. Thus, WPM has proven to be widely effective for chronic problems occurring not only in the manufacturing field, but also office work and engineering development. Therefore, I strongly recommend repeating "why?" questions by looking over the entire line in your company.

Chapter 9

Reduction of in-process defects (Type Ⓐ defect)

1. What is an in-process defect (Type Ⓐ defect)?

The in-process defect (Type Ⓐ defect) was defined as a defect found by the worker who caused it or other workers in the same process and stopped there without flowing out to the subsequent process (Chart 9-1).

With the defective portion marked with a red pen, the Type Ⓐ defective item was attached with a tag indicating the date, reason, name, etc., and immediately put in a "red box".

2. Handling of defective items in a red box ... Team leader's task

Every day, the team leader sorted the defective items in the red box and recorded the number of defects by type (Chart 9-2). By the end of the day, the defective items were taken to what we called "cabbage field (defects visualization area)*".

At the same time, the team leader investigated the cause through careful observation of actual work and dialogue with workers to take immediate measures. For the defects that required time for preparing measures, the team leader took provisional measures, while planning for radical measures, and continued to follow up improvement actions until complete prevention of the recurrence was confirmed.

* For the "cabbage field", please refer to the next section of this book.

Chart 9-1　Example of in-process defects in a parts manufacturer

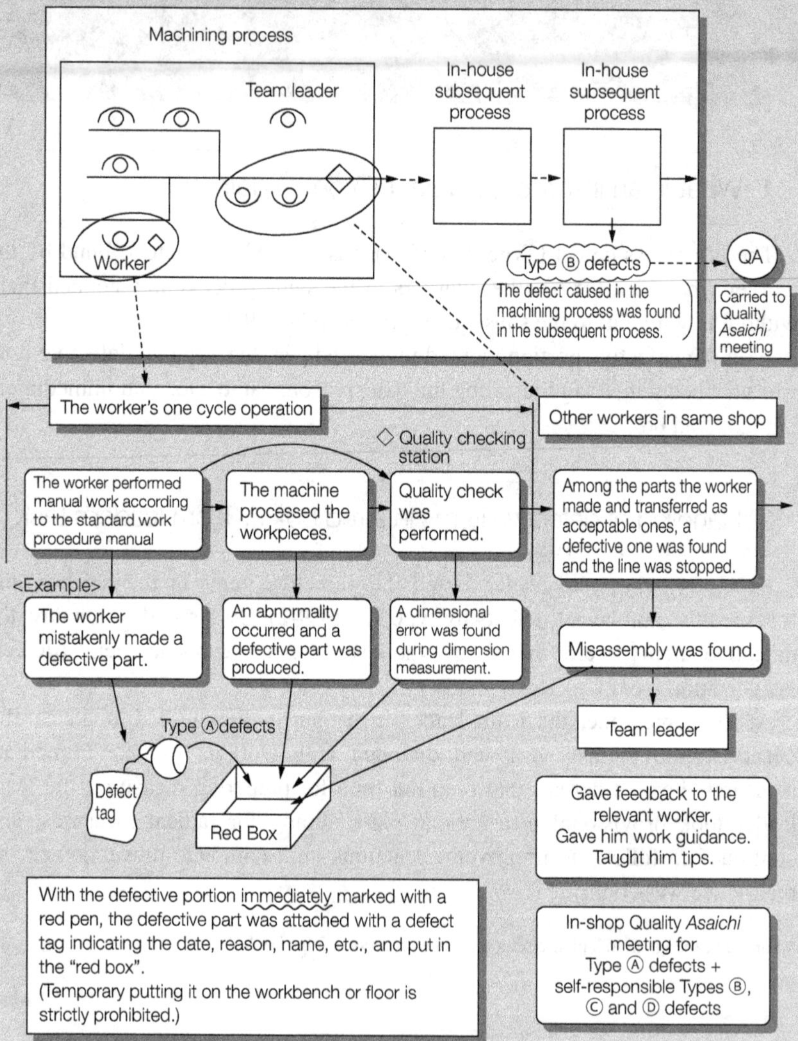

Machining process

Team leader

In-house subsequent process

In-house subsequent process

Worker

Type Ⓑ defects
The defect caused in the machining process was found in the subsequent process.

QA
Carried to Quality *Asaichi* meeting

The worker's one cycle operation

Other workers in same shop

◇ Quality checking station

The worker performed manual work according to the standard work procedure manual

The machine processed the workpieces.

Quality check was performed.

Among the parts the worker made and transferred as acceptable ones, a defective one was found and the line was stopped.

<Example>

The worker mistakenly made a defective part.

An abnormality occurred and a defective part was produced.

A dimensional error was found during dimension measurement.

Misassembly was found.

Team leader

Type Ⓐdefects

Defect tag

Red Box

Gave feedback to the relevant worker.
Gave him work guidance.
Taught him tips.

With the defective portion immediately marked with a red pen, the defective part was attached with a defect tag indicating the date, reason, name, etc., and put in the "red box".
(Temporary putting it on the workbench or floor is strictly prohibited.)

In-shop Quality *Asaichi* meeting for Type Ⓐ defects + self-responsible Types Ⓑ, Ⓒ and Ⓓ defects

Part 3 | Weak-Point Management and Quality Creation

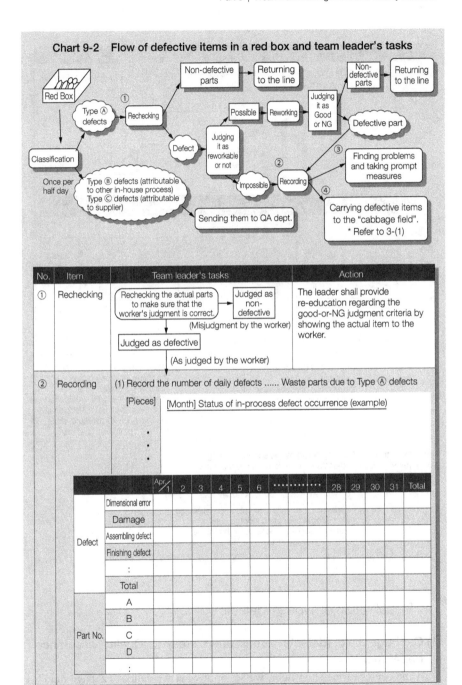

Chart 9-2   Flow of defective items in a red box and team leader's tasks

No.	Item	Team leader's tasks	Action
①	Rechecking	Rechecking the actual parts to make sure that the worker's judgment is correct. → Judged as non-defective (Misjudgment by the worker). Judged as defective (As judged by the worker)	The leader shall provide re-education regarding the good-or-NG judgment criteria by showing the actual item to the worker.
②	Recording	(1) Record the number of daily defects ...... Waste parts due to Type Ⓐ defects [Pieces] [Month] Status of in-process defect occurrence (example)	

		Apr/1	2	3	4	5	6	・・・・・・・・・・・	28	29	30	31	Total
Defect	Dimensional error												
	Damage												
	Assembling defect												
	Finishing defect												
	:												
	Total												
Part No.	A												
	B												
	C												
	D												
	:												

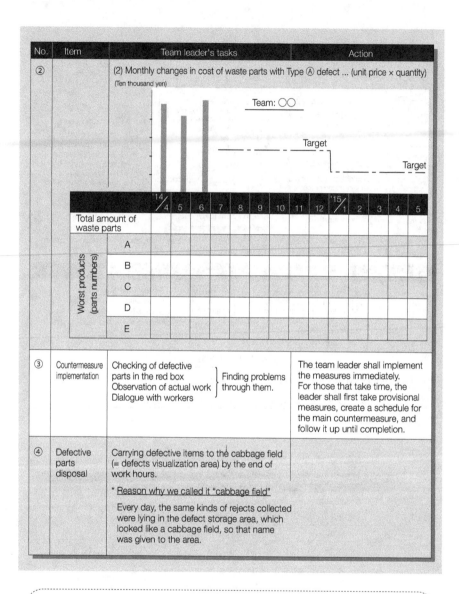

No.	Item	Team leader's tasks		Action
②		(2) Monthly changes in cost of waste parts with Type Ⓐ defect ... (unit price × quantity) (Ten thousand yen)		

Team: ○○

Target

Target

		'14/4	5	6	7	8	9	10	11	12	'15/1	2	3	4	5
Total amount of waste parts															
Worst products (parts numbers)	A														
	B														
	C														
	D														
	E														

No.	Item	Team leader's tasks		Action
③	Countermeasure implementation	Checking of defective parts in the red box Observation of actual work Dialogue with workers	Finding problems through them.	The team leader shall implement the measures immediately. For those that take time, the leader shall first take provisional measures, create a schedule for the main countermeasure, and follow it up until completion.
④	Defective parts disposal	Carrying defective items to the cabbage field (= defects visualization area) by the end of work hours. * Reason why we called it "cabbage field" Every day, the same kinds of rejects collected were lying in the defect storage area, which looked like a cabbage field, so that name was given to the area.		

3. Visualization of Type Ⓐ defects

(1) Cabbage field (defects visualization area) ... Quality assurance department

At the center of the shop floor, we set up a what we called "cabbage field", which was an area for visualization of actual defective items (Chart 9-3).

Chart 9-3   Visualization of Type Ⓐ defects

Cabbage field (defects visualization area) ... Quality assurance department
The cabbage field shall be set up as centrally as possible in the shop floor.

Asaichi meeting for Type Ⓐ defects: Points to be discussed

Day of week ╲ Team	Mon	Tue	Wed	Thu	Fri
Cutting	▱	⬭	⇠⬝	▤	▱
Machining	◖ ◖	◖	◖ ◖	◖ ◖ ◖	◖
Welding	◢	◷		⬗	
Assembling	◼				

Which processes cause many defects?

Which parts are likely to become defective?

What measures should be taken?

Who should do it?

If today is Wednesday, the team leader shall put the defective parts found last Wednesday in the disposal box and place today's defective parts in his lane.

Example of "cabbage field" (defects visualization area)

(2) Monthly transition of loss amount ... Quality assurance department

For each process, the loss amount due to Type Ⓐ defects was calculated to visualize the monthly changes. The quality assurance department set targets of a 50% reduction every six months based on actual results and allocated the target to each process (Chart 9-4).

Chart 9-4   Monthly transition of loss amount and reduction goals

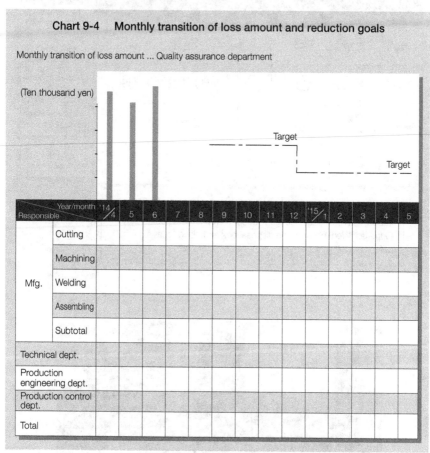

Monthly transition of loss amount ... Quality assurance department

(Ten thousand yen)

Target

Target

Year/month '14 Responsible		4	5	6	7	8	9	10	11	12	'15/1	2	3	4	5
Mfg.	Cutting														
	Machining														
	Welding														
	Assembling														
	Subtotal														
Technical dept.															
Production engineering dept.															
Production control dept.															
Total															

4. *Asaichi* for Type Ⓐ defects

When Types Ⓑ and Ⓒ defects diminished to some extent through implementation of the Quality *Asaichi*, full-scale efforts were made to reduce the Type Ⓐ defects (in-process defects) (Charts 9-5 and 9-6).

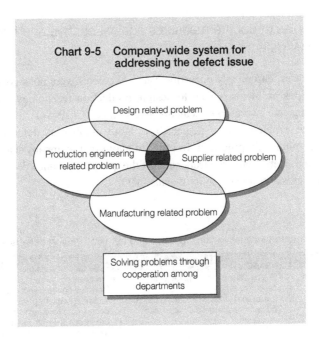

Chart 9-5   Company-wide system for addressing the defect issue

Design related problem

Production engineering related problem

Supplier related problem

Manufacturing related problem

Solving problems through cooperation among departments

Chart 9-6   Implementation of defect prevention measures

	Implementation Items	Key points
1) *Asaichi* meeting for Type Ⓐ defects	The members assemble in the cabbage field at a predetermined time every day in order to: • Check the Type Ⓐ defects found on the previous day. • Register the frequently occurring and/or costly defect items. • Determine a responsible person, goal, deadline, etc. for each problem through discussion. • Visualize and check the progress once a week. <Example> 	Mon	Tue	Wed	Thu	Fri
---	---	---	---	---
Machining Welding	Design	Assembling Painting	Production Engineering Production Control	Supplier		The meeting time shall be within 30 minutes. The moderator of the meeting shall be a manager of the QA department, who shall demonstrate leadership. The overall activities shall be visualized to enable everyone to know what is going on.
2) Task Force Team	The person appointed as the responsible person shall: • Designate the relevant departments and select the team members. Solve problems through teamwork. • Create SE manuals (see Chapter 14) as necessary, and find and deal with problems at the design and production preparation stages for new vehicles or parts.	Leadership of the responsible person is extremely important. The overall system shall be completed through a top-down approach.

5. Examples of countermeasures against chronic and frequent Type Ⓐ defects

In many cases, chronically occurring Type Ⓐ defects were not easy to solve because various problems related to design, production technology, suppliers, manufacturing, etc. were complicatedly intertwined (Chart 9-7). However, if such difficult problems were neglected, a large number of defects (waste) would be continuously produced. In order to avoid that, company-wide efforts were essential. Here again, the leadership of the quality assurance department is required for cross-sectional quality management.

Chart 9-7　Countermeasures against chronic and frequent Type Ⓐ defects (example)

No.	Defect	Problem	Countermeasure
(1)	Scratch/dent (Plated surface / Painted surface)	• Plating defects are irreparable and cause great loss. • It was hard to know where the damage occurred, making it difficult to take measures.	• Frequently occurring portions were identified on the defect map. • A damage checking station has been set up to identify the processes in which damage occurs to take quick countermeasures.

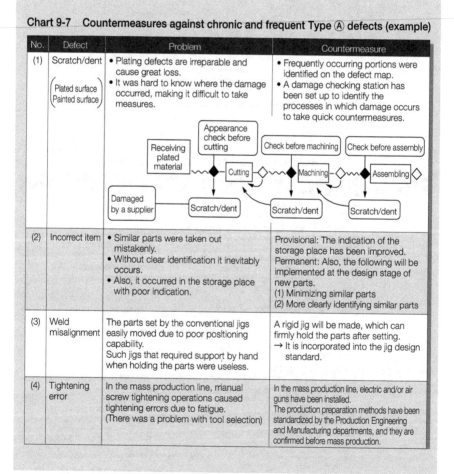

No.	Defect	Problem	Countermeasure
(2)	Incorrect item	• Similar parts were taken out mistakenly. • Without clear identification it inevitably occurs. • Also, it occurred in the storage place with poor indication.	Provisional: The indication of the storage place has been improved. Permanent: Also, the following will be implemented at the design stage of new parts. (1) Minimizing similar parts (2) More clearly identifying similar parts
(3)	Weld misalignment	The parts set by the conventional jigs easily moved due to poor positioning capability. Such jigs that required support by hand when holding the parts were useless.	A rigid jig will be made, which can firmly hold the parts after setting. → It is incorporated into the jig design standard.
(4)	Tightening error	In the mass production line, manual screw tightening operations caused tightening errors due to fatigue. (There was a problem with tool selection)	In the mass production line, electric and/or air guns have been installed. The production preparation methods have been standardized by the Production Engineering and Manufacturing departments, and they are confirmed before mass production.

No.	Defect	Problems	Countermeasures
(5)	Various defects caused by aging equipment	Old equipment caused accuracy problems, making it impossible to ensure 100% non-defective products (it is too late after failure).	An old equipment updating plan was created and has been steadily implemented with the necessary budget secured.
(6)	Various kinds of defects due to insufficient reliability of new technologies	At the time of introducing new technologies for productivity improvement, cost reduction, etc., various kinds of defects occurred frequently, bringing about confusion in production.	The conventional reliability confirmation methods for new technology development and production preparation stages have been reviewed. → We will create SE manuals to find problems and take necessary measures before mass production starts.
(7)	Various kinds of design related defects	Inappropriate designs not incorporating manufacturing requirements caused various kinds of defects. Any design change after occurrence of a problem will become very costly, requiring remaking of dies and jigs. And, if it is impossible, continuous occurrence of defects will also produce an extremely large amount of waste for many years. (It is too late after starting mass production)	The following system has been established to incorporate requirements from manufacturing and production engineering departments at the design stage. (Requirements have been standardized.*) ↓ (SE check is performed at the development stage.) See Chapter 14 - Very Important

* "SE manual" is the abbreviation of Simultaneous Engineering manual.

Chapter

10

Change-point control

In the field of manufacturing, some changes occur on a daily basis. The changes include, for example, replacement of workers due to annual holidays or sick leave, product changes due to design changes, and renewal of equipment due to aging. Such various changes sometimes drastically change the product quality, and if missed, serious defects will flow out to the market. In order to prevent the outflow of critical quality defects, it is important to standardize the procedure for controlling such change points and implement it honestly and consistently.

1. Standardization of change-point control

By referring to Chart 10-1, the change-point control method can be standardized suitably for your company. Since characteristics to be managed vary depending on the department and process, it is important to appoint responsible persons to create individual standards.

Chart 10-1   4M change-point control (example)

Change item	Change factor	Preparations for change points	What to do at each change point
Man	New workers	New employees Temporary employees Temporary workers / Novice workers	• Preparation of new employee education manual • Installation of a training *dojo* (training place) • Implementation of offline education and training • Development of instructors and trainers (see Chapter 7 "Education and Training")	• The online training shall be implemented on a one-to-one basis. Instructors and trainers shall teach new workers until they familiarize themselves with the basics of their work. • The instructors and trainers shall take responsibility for overall work quality, including the work done by new workers. • The process joined by the new workers shall be reported to the inspection section. It shall be carefully checked to prevent defect outflow.

Change item		Change factor	Preparations for change points	What to do at each change point
Man	Substitute workers (Relief Men)	Absentee relief Backup for workers leaving their posts (for training, poor physical condition, etc.)	• Development of relief men and promotion of multi-skill development • Securement of substitute workers • Periodic training for relief men (to remind them of other work)	• Relief men shall be determined based on the skill map. • Relief men shall check the standard work procedure manual again before starting the work. • The team leader shall check the relief men's operations for three cycles. • The process joined by the relief man shall be reported to the inspection section. It shall be carefully checked.
Material	Design change	Change of materials	• Trial production to check the quality and ease of manufacturing • Revision of the relevant work manuals. • Explanation to workers and training • Adjustment of timing of design change (to minimize the stock of old parts)	• The worker shall check three pieces of the first parts and record the results. • The first parts shall also be checked by the team leader. • In the case of a part's design change, the first parts shall be sent to QA dept. for quality judgment. • Initial problems, if any, shall be written down, and necessary measures shall be taken immediately.
	Change of supplier	Change in quality, price, delivery period, internal/ external production, etc.	• Evaluation of new supplier's process • Quality check through trial production • Adjustment of timing of supplier change • Notice to customers	• First part acceptance shall be checked by QA dept. • The worker shall check the first part in detail and record the result. • The first parts shall also be checked by the team leader. • The finished parts shall be sent to the QA dept. for quality judgment.
Machine	Dies and jigs	Repair/ remodeling	• Trial production to check the quality and ease of manufacturing • Explanation to the operators about how they have been repaired or remodeled • Notice to the customer about the details of remodeling (if it's to be done)	• The worker shall check three pieces of the first parts and record the results. • The first parts shall also be checked by the team leader. • The first parts quality judgment shall be made by the QA dept. depending on how the equipment has been repaired or remodeled.
		Replacement	• Trial production to check the quality and ease of manufacturing • Notice to the customer about the replacement	• The worker shall check three pieces of the first parts and record the results. • The first parts shall also be checked by the team leader. • After the quality check on the first parts by the QA dept., if passed, mass production can be started.
	Machine	Repair/ remodeling	• Pre-check of the quality and operability through trial operations after repair or remodeling • Notice to the customer about the details of remodeling (if to be done)	• The worker shall check three pieces of the first parts and record the results. • The first parts shall also be checked by the team leader. • The first parts quality judgment shall be made by the QA dept. depending on how the equipment has been repaired or remodeled.

Change item		Change factor	Preparations for change points	What to do at each change point
Machine	Machine	Replacement	• Trial production to check the quality, operability and safety after the installation • Notice to the customer about the equipment replacement	• The worker shall check three pieces of the first parts and record the results. • The first parts shall also be checked by the team leader. • After the quality check on the first parts by the QA dept., if passed, mass production can be started.
Method	Process	Change or addition to manufacturing process	• Trial production to check the quality and ease of manufacturing • Notice to the customer about the change or addition	• The worker shall check three pieces of the first parts and record the results. • The first parts shall also be checked by the team leader. • The first parts shall be sent to the QA dept. for quality judgment.
	Manufacturing method	Change in manufacturing method	• Trial production by a new manufacturing method to check the quality and ease of manufacturing • Notice to the customer about how the method has been changed	• The worker shall check three pieces of the first parts and record the results. • The first parts shall also be checked by the team leader. • The first parts shall be sent to the QA dept. for quality judgment.
	Standard work	Change of tact time/ change by *kaizen*	• Trial production to check the quality and ease of manufacturing • Revision of the relevant standard work manuals. • Implementation of work training	• The worker shall check three pieces of the first parts and record the results. • The first parts shall also be checked by the team leader. • The first parts quality judgment shall be made by the QA dept. depending on how the previous standard work procedure has been changed.
	Decision	System, rules, quality standards, etc.	• Standardization of changes and additions • Trial production to check for any problems • Education to make workers strictly follow the rules and standards	• The team leader shall observe the situation on the first day of introduction and correct if there is any problem. • If workers find any problem, they shall immediately contact the team leader.

* 4M: Man, Material, Machine, and Method

[Important points of 4M change-point control]
① Prepare the workplace to cope with any changes

For each change item, create a schedule plan, make advance preparations for possible changes to find problems, take countermeasures against those anticipated problems, and then start mass production. This makes it possible to minimize trouble. In each department, the general manager and/or section manager should check the progress once a week, and if delay occurs, it should be recovered within one week.

② Horizontally deploy the procedures not only to primary suppliers, but also to Tier 2 suppliers

To minimize the occurrence of trouble throughout the entire supply chain, the change-point control procedures established by your company should be horizontally deployed to your suppliers.

2. Visualization of "today's change point"

To make "today's change point" visible to every worker, a Change-Point Control Board should be installed at each shop floor or for each team leader (Chart 10-2). At the daily pre-operation meeting, the leader should inform everyone of "today's change point" and reconfirm what to do before starting the day's work.

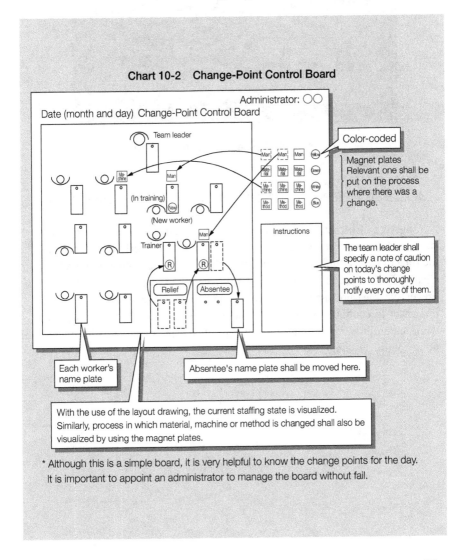

Chart 10-2   Change-Point Control Board

* Although this is a simple board, it is very helpful to know the change points for the day. It is important to appoint an administrator to manage the board without fail.

Example of Change-Point Control Board

3. Use and retention (one year) of Change-Point Control Sheet

We used a "Change-Point Control Sheet" to visualize the daily change-point status and check whether the things to do were done properly (Chart 10-3). At the time of defect outflow to a customer or market, we reconfirmed the relevant Change-Point Control Sheet to find out the cause and what is to be done as a preventive measure against recurrence, and implemented the measure. It is important to continue to honestly implement the zero defect outflow activities while carefully watching and remedying deficiencies of the existing change-point control system.

Chart 10-3   Change-Point Control Sheet

Date (month and day)   Change-Point Control Sheet   Prepared by ○○
Process: ○○○

Change factors		Implementation Items	Quality check results	Notify to customer
Man	☐ New worker New worker Trainer Process ☐☐☐ ☐☐☐ ☐ Relief Absentee Relief Process ☐☐☐ ☐☐☐			— —
Material	☐ Design change DC No. ☐ ☐ Change of supplier Supplier name ☐			— ☐
Machine	☐ Dies and jigs Re- Modi- Re- pairing fying placing Part number ☐ ☐ ☐ ☐ ☐ Machine Re- Modi- Re- pairing fying placing Equipment name ☐ ☐ ☐ ☐			☐ ☐
Method	☐ Process Process name ☐ ☐ Manufacturing method Process name ☐ ☐ Standard work ☐ Decision			☐ ☐ — —

4. Example of defect outflow to the market due to improper change-point control (reference)

In the process of investigating the reason for defect outflow to the market, I often noticed that it could have been prevented if the change-point control had been done more properly. The following are such examples.

[Example 1] Weld separation defects coming from high-skill required arc welding

Due to the absence of an experienced worker with a high degree of arc-welding skill, a substitute worker did that work. The product was shipped because there was no problem in the appearance after welding, but welding separation occurred later in the market due to insufficient weld penetration. At the supplier that produced it, the skill level of the substitute worker had not been confirmed because change-point control had not been implemented. As a result, the weld defect at an important portion caused serious trouble to the customer.

[Example 2] Failure to apply grease ... A massive defect outflow resulted in expensive market claims.

Due to many absentees, a helping hand was lent from another section. The worker who came to help had previously worked on the operation, but forgot to apply grease to a shaft and released the ungreased products to the market. (Lack or insufficient amount of grease is a typical cause of a defect directly flowed out to the market because it is not possible to detected it in the subsequent and inspection processes.)

[Example 3] Incorrect oil supply due to piping mistake in manufacturing process

Due to lubricator's piping deterioration, the piping renewal work was carried out on Saturday and Sunday. At that time, pipes for different types of oil were mistakenly connected. On Monday, the next day of the renewal work, incorrect oil was supplied through routine work. That was an unbelievable defect caused by an oil pipe misconnection.

In order to reduce such serious defects to zero, there is no way other than thoroughly performing change-point control. Since certain defects continuously occur without change-point control, companies that have not implemented it yet need to start as soon as possible.

Unless change-point control is performed thoroughly, outflow of serious defects to the market may continue to occur several times every year. Yet, change-point control is based on the accumulation of steady daily efforts, so it is difficult to maintain it thoroughly without top-down instruction and continuous guidance. Therefore, top management should strictly check whether change-point control is properly conducted in the company to prevent serious mistakes.

Part 4

Always Respect the Basics

Chapter

11

2S (*Seiri* and *Seiton*)

"*Seiri*" (sifting) and "*Seiton*" (sorting), which are often called "2S", are the basis of "*monozukuri*" (conscientious manufacturing).

Even though everyone is fully aware of this fact, the reality is that there are so many companies indicating poor 2S. Therefore, this chapter describes why poor 2S is a big problem and how it can be improved. By referring to it, please work on 2S improvement in your company.

1. Criteria for judging good or bad 2S

Judging whether the state of 2S is good or bad varies greatly depending on the people, the plant, and the country. This is because the generally used 2S evaluation standards are abstract, making it difficult to clearly judge whether the 2S state is acceptable or not. Therefore, in our Dantotsu Quality Activities, we adopted an evaluation standard that allows for quantitative judgment of whether the state of 2S is good or bad.

2S evaluation standard

Work site	Evaluation standard
In process	Whether you can pick up what you need or return it within **one second** without asking anyone where it is
On the shop floor	Whether you can pick up what you need or return it within **one minute** without asking anyone where it is

The new standard was easy to understand, enabling everyone to judge good or bad accurately, so it became very popular. In order to pick up what is needed or return it very quickly, such as within one second or minute, thorough sorting and shifting things are essential at every workplace. Since that was well understood by every worker, this standard made a big contribution to the 2S improvement.

2. Waste resulting from poor 2S

Improper 2S generates a lot of waste (Charts 11-1 and 11-2).

In a plant having 100 workers, if each worker spends an average of 30 minutes per day on such wasteful motion as "looking for" and/or "clearing distractions", the waste of time can be calculated as follows:

100 workers × 0.5 H × 250 days / year = 12,500 H / Year.

Thus, as many as 12,500 hours of waste continue to occur every year and forever as long as the 2S is not improved. If you leave this invisible major waste untouched, it can be a problem that affects your company's survival.

Chart 11-1   Waste resulting from poor 2S

State of 2S	Examples of unnecessary waste
Because things are not properly arranged and located, what is necessary cannot be found easily. What you need now is here. ① Searching ② Moving others	• Searching for what you need is a waste of time. • Moving others out of the way to take what you need is a waste of energy. And returning them to the original position is a waste of motion. • Producing defective products as follows is a major waste of time and money. After taking a lot of time to search for what is needed, the worker hurries production. The worker takes similar but wrong parts, resulting in production of incorrect parts. • Failing to find necessary items and urgently ordering them is a waste of time and money. Products cannot be produced until replacement items arrive, resulting in delivery delays. • Leaving necessary items and purchasing new ones due to failing to find them is a waste of money.
Various things are left on the floor of the workplace.	• Injury resulting from tripping on things on the floor • Injury due to leg being caught by a hose Preparing an accident report is a waste of time. Considering and taking countermeasures is an additional waste of time. • Bending over to pick up things on the floor is a waste of motion. • Damage or deformation of something caused by dropping when placing it on the floor is a waste of money. • Walking while avoiding things on the floor is a waste of energy. • Searching for what you need is a waste of time and energy.

Chart 11-2 What actually happens at work sites in poor 2S state (example)

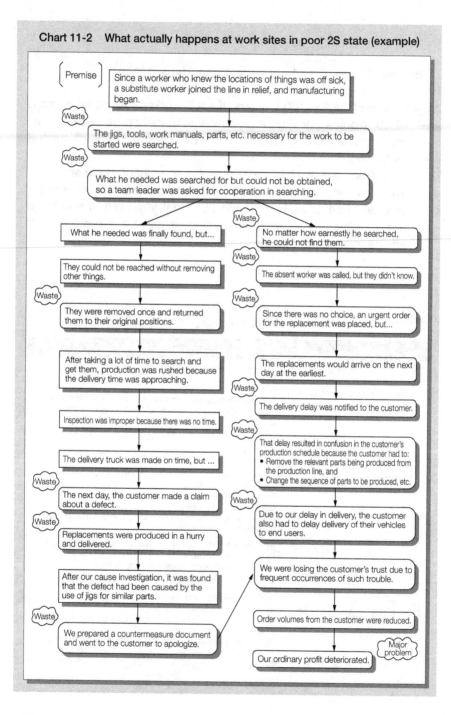

[Premise] Since a worker who knew the locations of things was off sick, a substitute worker joined the line in relief, and manufacturing began.

(Waste) The jigs, tools, work manuals, parts, etc. necessary for the work to be started were searched.

(Waste) What he needed was searched for but could not be obtained, so a team leader was asked for cooperation in searching.

What he needed was finally found, but...

They could not be reached without removing other things.

(Waste) They were removed once and returned them to their original positions.

After taking a lot of time to search and get them, production was rushed because the delivery time was approaching.

Inspection was improper because there was no time.

The delivery truck was made on time, but ...

(Waste) The next day, the customer made a claim about a defect.

(Waste) Replacements were produced in a hurry and delivered.

After our cause investigation, it was found that the defect had been caused by the use of jigs for similar parts.

(Waste) We prepared a countermeasure document and went to the customer to apologize.

(Waste) No matter how earnestly he searched, he could not find them.

(Waste) The absent worker was called, but they didn't know.

(Waste) Since there was no choice, an urgent order for the replacement was placed, but...

The replacements would arrive on the next day at the earliest.

(Waste) The delivery delay was notified to the customer.

(Waste) That delay resulted in confusion in the customer's production schedule because the customer had to:
• Remove the relevant parts being produced from the production line, and
• Change the sequence of parts to be produced, etc.

(Waste) Due to our delay in delivery, the customer also had to delay delivery of their vehicles to end users.

We were losing the customer's trust due to frequent occurrences of such trouble.

Order volumes from the customer were reduced.

Our ordinary profit deteriorated. *(Major problem)*

140

3. Improvement of 2S through top-down decision and implementation

Just saying "2S is bad" will go nowhere. To improve poor 2S, the time (= labor cost) and the equipment, such as a shelf, cabinet or other things for sorting and arranging things (= cost of equipment), are necessary. Because it is not an easy task that can be done between main operations, it is important for top management to decide to invest time and money to tackle thorough improvement of 2S, as well as to instruct the employees to implement it through to completion.

Improvement of 2S should be carried out by taking three steps as shown in Chart 11-3.

Chart 11-3   Top-down strategy for 2S improvement

	Step	What the top management should do
①	Proper understanding of the importance of 2S	As stated above, if you leave a poor 2S state as is (where only certain people know where something is located), the following will happen. • Continuous occurrence of wastes of time in "searching" and "moving other things out of the way" The workers may think that it is within the scope of their job, and such a waste of time will not lead to reduction of their salaries. However, it will become a big loss for a company in the long run. • Continuous occurrences of delays in delivery and quality defects The company will lose the customer's trust, and accordingly, order decreases will make the company's management more and more difficult. **It is important to have all employees recognize that it is an issue that affects the company's management.**
②	Current status check (By top management)	Check whether you can take what you need now under the following condition without asking anyone. • Target time in work process: 1 second • Target time in each shop: within 1 minute Example: Taking out a necessary jig If you take the following procedure, you can do it within one minute. That indicates an acceptable state of 2S. **Step ①** Check the relevant holder No. with the production sequence table. ➡ **Step ②** Remove the holder and confirm the location of the necessary jig on the setup condition table. ➡ **Step ③** Go to the jig storage place and take the necessary jig from the designated location. (1-(2) in Chapter 4) (1-(1)-① in Chapter 4) Without such a procedure, it is difficult for any third party to take out the correct one, indicating an improper state of 2S. **If the current state is in an improper 2S state, the following step ③ shall be executed immediately.**

	Step	What the top management should do
③	Taking leadership in 2S improvement campaign	• Decide to start the 2S improvement activity throughout the company and give the following instructions. Activity period: Six months | Target	To make the entire plant enable anyone to take out what is needed within one second in each process or within one minute in each shop | • Set up an "2S improvement team" and kick off the "2S improvement campaign". • Budget for the 2S improvement project... Labor costs, purchase costs, etc. • Check the progress by visiting every work site (*GENCHI GENBUTSU*) once a month and persistently follow up until the 2S state is improved.

4. Development of 2S improvement campaign

(1) Standardization of "the ideal state of 2S" for each work site

The first job of the 2S improvement team is to standardize the state of 2S best suited to each workplace. With reference to Chart 11-4, the "ideal state of 2S" for each work site is determined by the team.

Chart 11-4   Standardization of ideal 2S state for individual locations

No.	Place	Ideal state of 2S	Key points
(1)	Passage/ walking zone		• In the plant, the roadway shall be clearly separated from the sidewalk. • The walking zone shall be marked in green.
(2)	Parts storage area		• Each part's location shall be fixed and clearly indicated. (while considering separation from similar parts) • Importance shall be attached to FIFO. (For details, see Chapter 5.)

No.	Place	Ideal state of 2S	Key points
(3)	Workbench	Necessary items shall be placed at fixed positions. There shall be nothing left on the bench. Do not put personal belongings or unnecessary items on the lower shelf.	• A fixed position shall be assigned to each of what you need for work, allowing you to take it out or return it within one second.
(4)	Storage rack	Jig storage place (example) Partition line Indication Location 2-3 Part number ○○○○ It shall also be indicated on the relevant jigs.	• A fixed position shall be assigned to each item and clearly indicated. • The racks shall be arranged so that anyone can find the location (address number) and take out anything necessary within one minute.
(5)	Storage space	Storage space No. Indication I-1 6ø drill 5MAX-2MIN 4th row E-4 E-3 E-2 E-1	• The inside of the drawer shall be partitioned, with each location of tool parts indicated by: • Name of parts • MAX-MIN • When the MIN quantity is reached, the relevant parts shall be ordered with the use of kanban (2d-3 in Chapter 4).
(6)	Storage on the floor	In case where something is stored on the floor, the area shall be indicated by a compartment line. Hand cart White line width: 70 mm (Compartment line) Name of item to be stored	• If there is something in an area not indicated by any compartment line, it shall be removed immediately.

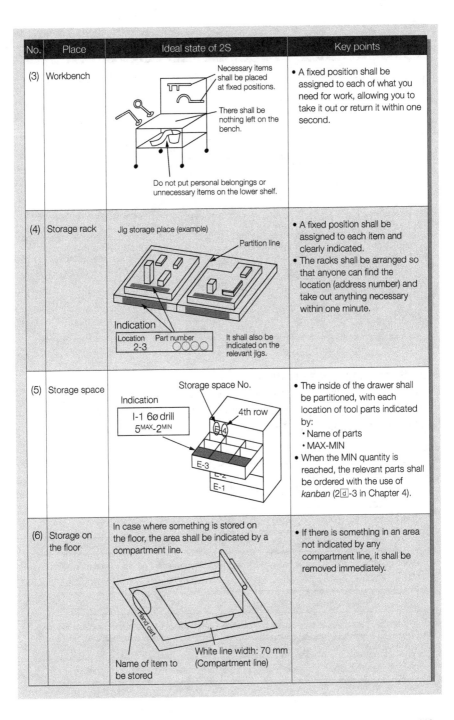

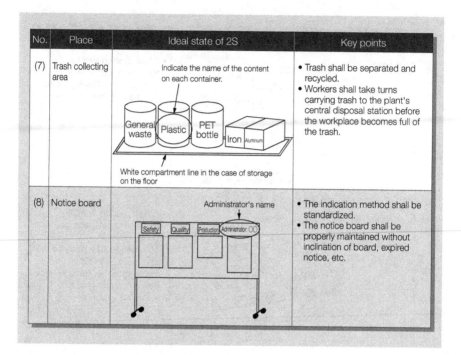

No.	Place	Ideal state of 2S	Key points
(7)	Trash collecting area	Indicate the name of the content on each container. General waste / Plastic / PET bottle / Iron / Aluminum. White compartment line in the case of storage on the floor	• Trash shall be separated and recycled. • Workers shall take turns carrying trash to the plant's central disposal station before the workplace becomes full of the trash.
(8)	Notice board	Administrator's name. Safety / Quality / Production / Administrator: ○○	• The indication method shall be standardized. • The notice board shall be properly maintained without inclination of board, expired notice, etc.

(2) 2S model process creation

The next job of the 2S improvement team is to create a model process for 2S. The team should pick up a work process with the worst state of 2S in the plant and improve it within four weeks or so.

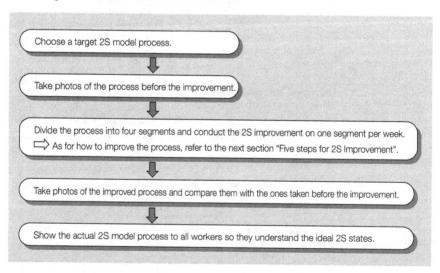

Choose a target 2S model process.

⬇

Take photos of the process before the improvement.

⬇

Divide the process into four segments and conduct the 2S improvement on one segment per week.
⇨ As for how to improve the process, refer to the next section "Five steps for 2S Improvement".

⬇

Take photos of the improved process and compare them with the ones taken before the improvement.

⬇

Show the actual 2S model process to all workers so they understand the ideal 2S states.

(3) Five steps for 2S improvement

I have standardized the method of drastically improving poor 2S states in a plant through "five steps" and taught it to a lot of plants not only in Japan, but also in many foreign countries. And I have confirmed at those many plants so far that the dramatic improvement of terrible 2S states was possible only at the plants where everyone seriously worked on it.

The method shown in Chart 11-5 is simple, easy to understand, and very effective, so please try it at your plant.

Chart 11-5   Five steps for 2S improvement

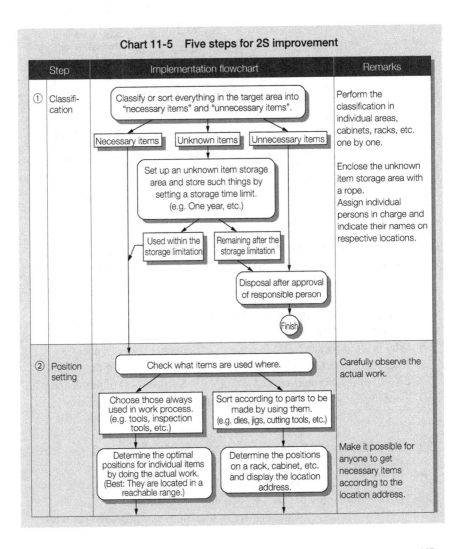

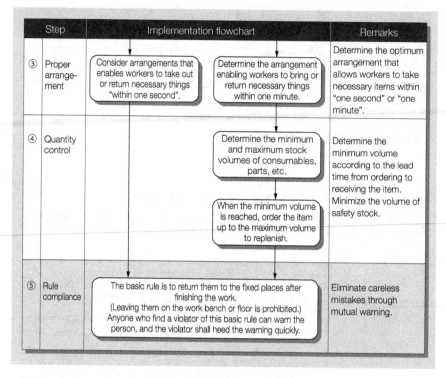

Step	Implementation flowchart		Remarks
③ Proper arrangement	Consider arrangements that enables workers to take out or return necessary things "within one second".	Determine the arrangement enabling workers to bring or return necessary things within one minute.	Determine the optimum arrangement that allows workers to take necessary items within "one second" or "one minute".
④ Quantity control		Determine the minimum and maximum stock volumes of consumables, parts, etc. When the minimum volume is reached, order the item up to the maximum volume to replenish.	Determine the minimum volume according to the lead time from ordering to receiving the item. Minimize the volume of safety stock.
⑤ Rule compliance	The basic rule is to return them to the fixed places after finishing the work. (Leaving them on the work bench or floor is prohibited.) Anyone who find a violator of this basic rule can warn the person, and the violator shall heed the warning quickly.		Eliminate careless mistakes through mutual warning.

(4) Implementation of 2S improvement campaign

1) The improvement team installed a 2S campaign board, allocated 2S improvement areas to individual team leaders, and made the activities visualized.

2) Education of 2S for team leaders at individual work sites ... Improvement team
   - Why is 2S important? .... Section 2 of this chapter
   - Ideal state of 2S for each work site .... Section 4-(1) of this chapter
   - Five steps for 2S improvement .... Section 4-(3) of this chapter
   - Confirmation of actual improvement results in the 2S model process
     .... Section 4-(2) of this chapter

3) Implementation of 2S improvement by individual teams
   - The team leader divided the responsible area into six sections.
     .... One section was improved per month.
   - The team leader divides each section into four segments.
     .... One segment (1/4 section) was improved per week.

- The six-month plan and achievements of the activity were visualized on each team's board.
- All team members tackled 2S improvement.

4) Monthly check of 2S improvement result ... Top management and 2S improvement team

① When 2S improvement was completed in each section (1/6) of the responsible area, the relevant team leaders declared it by a show of hands.

② The 2S improvement team evaluated the 2S state of the declared section. The evaluation was performed by checking whether everyone can get what they need within one second (or one minute).

③ In each case of passing the test, one Lego block was stacked.

④ In the case of failure, existing problems with the state of 2S were explained to the relevant team leader on the basis of *GENCHI GENBUTSU* (on-site check of actual items).

⑤ The progress status of each team was visualized (Chart 11-6).

Chart 11-6   Visualization of each team's progress status.

The goal was a status with six pieces of LEGO blocks stacked up.
→ The 2S improvement team competition was done to stimulate members' motivation and promote the activities.

5) Commendation ceremony for goal achieving teams ... To raise the morale of workers at each site

- Top management appreciated the efforts of the team by handing out a little prize. (Example: Free lunch tickets, etc.)
- The campaign was continued until all teams achieve the goals.

5. Evolution to 5S improvement

Only after the basic 2S (*Seiri* and *Seiton)* is done properly at the work site, the activity can be evolved to a more advanced "5S" improvement, with "*Seiso*" (sweeping), "*Seiketu*" (cleanliness), and "*Shitsuke*" (discipline) added.

In other words, emphasizing sweeping, cleanliness and discipline without doing *Seiri* (sifting) and *Seiton* (sorting) is like simply saving appearances. The "2S comes first" is the basis of "*monozukuri*" (conscientious manufacturing) (Chart 11-7).

Chart 11-7 5S based on 2S

	Category		Definition	Key points
5S	2S (basic factors)	① *Seiri* (sifting)	To sort "necessary items" from "unnecessary items" → Disposal	• Items that are no longer needed shall be disposed of at each change point time (model changes of vehicles, use of new parts, etc.).
		② *Seiton* (sorting)	To determine individual storage places. To make proper arrangement. To control the stock volume.	• Workers shall follow the basic rules when working. • If there is a problem, it shall be immediately improved.
	+ 3S (sustained & improved)	③ *Seiso* (sweeping)	To sweep and clean up the workplace	• Individual cleaning areas shall be assigned to respective workers so that they can clean their own positions. • The cleaning time shall be determined for each workplace. • Trash shall immediately be picked up by the person who finds it.
		④ *Seiketsu* (cleanliness)	To keep the workplace and personal appearance clean	• Workers shall do what they can do on site without saving their trouble. • What they cannot do by themselves on site shall be implemented according to a plan under the company's responsibility. (e.g. replacement of old equipment and repair of oil leaks)
		⑤ *Shitsuke* (discipline)	To follow the workplace rules, work standards and general disciplines when working; and as soon as a problem is found, improve it immediately	• The administrator shall decide rules and standards and properly educate and train workers. • Workers shall follow the rules and standards when working. • A teamwork culture shall be built, which allows workers to mutually point out violations or abnormalities.

Stabilization of production line

It is often said, **"Quality cannot be secured without stable production."** This is because good quality products can be produced when the production line is running stably and each worker is working with a certain rhythm leading to fewer mistakes. In other words, the probability of making a mistake increases and that of making a good product decreases in a situation where frequent work interruptions due to frequent occurrences of equipment failure, missing parts, and quality defects inevitably result in non-standard work. In such a case, the production line must be stabilized before speaking of quality. This chapter describes the points to be observed and measures for stabilization of production lines.

1. Definition of time in TPS

In TPS (Toyota Production System), the time is defined as shown in Chart 12-1.

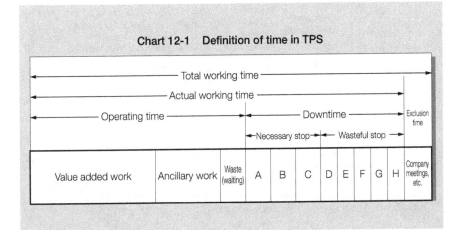

Chart 12-1   Definition of time in TPS

Classification			Definition
Operating time	Value added work		Work activities that create added value for products Example: Tightening bolts, arc welding, wiring, piping, etc.
	Ancillary work		Work activities that do not produce any added value but are necessary Example: Picking up parts, taking out and returning tools, walking to the next process, etc.
	Waste (waiting)		Waiting time due to shorter one-cycle operation time than tact time ⇨ Review of work allocation to make the waiting time close to zero
Downtime	Necessary downtime	A Machine setup time	Time necessary to set up the press machines and other machine tools ⇨ Time saving by changing in-line setup to off-line setup and reducing walking steps for setup work
		B Consumables replacement time	Time necessary for replacement of cutting tools, welding tips and nozzles used in processing machines ⇨ Time saving through adoption of simple and quick replacement systems
		C First and final parts quality check time	Time necessary for quality checks on the first and final parts in a continuous production Proper implementation of quality checks as determined
	Wasteful downtime	D Stoppages due to machine failure	Stoppages caused by machine failure, poor adjustment, etc. ⇨ Enhancement of preventive maintenance and/or renewal of old machinery
		E Stoppages due to defects in dies, jigs and tools	Stoppages caused by wear, breakage, deformation, or looseness ⇨ Elimination of such problems through regular or quantitative-based maintenance
		F Stoppages due to quality defects	Production stops due to occurrence of a quality defect, which requires significant time for corrective and preventive measures ⇨ Promotion of activities to reduce in-process defects
		G Stoppages due to missing or incorrect parts	Line stops caused by a shortage of necessary parts or inclusion of wrong parts ⇨ Enhancement of basic education about materials handling
		H Stoppages due to manufacturing problems	Exceeding the cycle time due to human failure, such as a work delays and operational mistakes ⇨ Enhancement of work training and improvement in difficult-to-do and tough (YK) work

* The downtime of A to G shall be recorded on the Production Control Board each time they happen. For the "H: manufacturing-related downtime", major stoppages can be recorded, but short ones in seconds cannot be fully covered, so they are calculated.

2. Terminology and calculation method

Definition of terms and calculation methods are shown in Chart 12-2.

Chart 12-2   Terminologies and their calculation methods

Terminologies	Definitions & calculation formulas	Results
Tact time (T.T)	Required time per unit when producing the required volume, with 100% operational availability in the regular time	$\dfrac{460\times1.00}{99} \approx 4.64$ minutes/unit
Execution tact time (Actual T.T)	Required time per unit when producing the required volume, with the target operational availability[1] applied in an actual working time (e.g. If the target operational availability is 95%)	$\dfrac{520\times0.95}{99} \approx 5.0$ minutes/unit
Operating time	Actual T. T × Production volume = (e.g. Today's production is 90 units.)	5.0 × 90 = 450 minutes
Total downtime	Actual working time - Operating time =	520 - 450 = 70 minutes
Manufacturing-related downtime	Total downtime - (Total time of A to G) = (e.g. 20 minutes according to Production Control Board)	70 - 20 = 50 minutes
Operational availability* (%)	$\dfrac{\text{Operating time}}{\text{Actual working time}} \times 100$	$\dfrac{450}{520} \times 100 \approx 86.5\%$

Premise: Producing 99 units during "regular time 460 minutes + overtime 60 minutes = actual working time 520 minutes"

* Although the ideal operational availability is 100%, in reality production actually stops for some reason. Therefore, it is common practice to set a target rate of operational availability for each process and calculate the execution tact time (e.g., 95% in assembly line, 85% in machining line, etc.).

3. Visualization of production by Production Control Board

A sheet of board called the "Production Control Board", shows the production schedule and production results for each production line and process, as well as various records, such as line stopping time and the reasons for the stoppage. The results are entered in the Productivity Control Chart, and necessary countermeasures are taken, starting with items that occur frequently and cause a long-time line stop. In this way, stable production is achieved, with both productivity and quality improved. To grasp what the existing problem is, accurately recording what is actually happening is required.

(1) Production Control Board for line operations

Chart 12-3 shows an example of a Production Control Board for line operations.

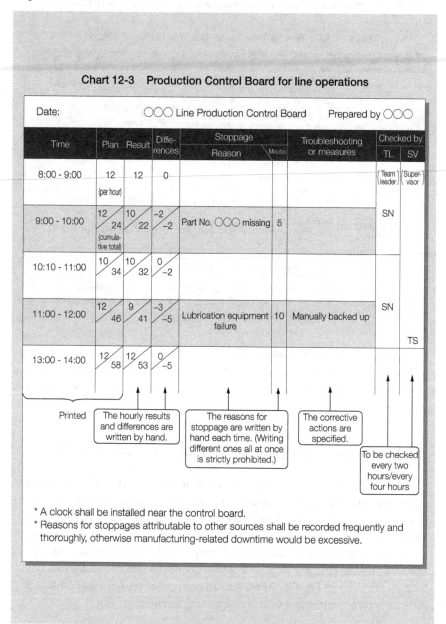

Chart 12-3　Production Control Board for line operations

Date:				○○○ Line Production Control Board				Prepared by ○○○	
Time	**Plan**	**Result**	**Diffe-rences**	**Stoppage** Reason	Minutes	**Troubleshooting or measures**	**Checked by**	TL	SV
8:00 - 9:00	12 (per hour)	12	0					(Team leader)	(Super-visor)
9:00 - 10:00	12 / 24 (cumula-tive total)	10 / 22	-2 / -2	Part No. ○○○ missing	5			SN	
10:10 - 11:00	10 / 34	10 / 32	0 / -2						
11:00 - 12:00	12 / 46	9 / 41	-3 / -5	Lubrication equipment failure	10	Manually backed up		SN	TS
13:00 - 14:00	12 / 58	12 / 53	0 / -5						

Printed

The hourly results and differences are written by hand.

The reasons for stoppage are written by hand each time. (Writing different ones all at once is strictly prohibited.)

The corrective actions are specified.

To be checked every two hours/every four hours

* A clock shall be installed near the control board.
* Reasons for stoppages attributable to other sources shall be recorded frequently and thoroughly, otherwise manufacturing-related downtime would be excessive.

152

(2) Production Control Board in a process for lot production of large-variety products

The following shows a Production Control Board for large-variety products manufacturing processes including the machining, pressing, and various welding operations (Chart 12-4).

Chart 12-4   Production Control Board in a process for lot production of large-variety products

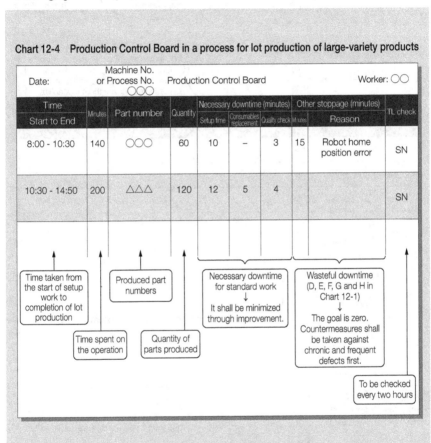

(3) Production Control Board (for each line, or each machinery/process)

For each month, the results of daily production are visualized, so that productivity can be improved by finding where the weaknesses in production are, locating the cause, and taking countermeasures, resulting in reductions in the total downtime. Thus, for quality improvement, it is extremely important to stabilize the production processes by reducing the downtime and the frequency of line stops (Chart 12-5).

Chart 12-5 Production Control Board (example)

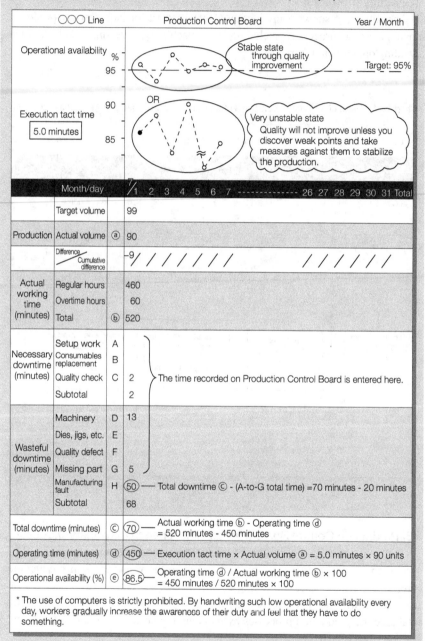

○○○ Line	Production Control Board	Year / Month

Operational availability %
95 — Stable state through quality improvement — Target: 95%

Execution tact time
5.0 minutes
90 — OR
85 — Very unstable state. Quality will not improve unless you discover weak points and take measures against them to stabilize the production.

Month/day		7/1	2	3	4	5	6	7	- - - - - - - - - -	26	27	28	29	30	31	Total
	Target volume	99														
Production	Actual volume ⓐ	90														
	Difference / Cumulative difference	-9	/	/	/	/	/	/			/	/	/	/	/	/
Actual working time (minutes)	Regular hours	460														
	Overtime hours	60														
	Total ⓑ	520														
Necessary downtime (minutes)	Setup work A															
	Consumables replacement B															
	Quality check C	2		The time recorded on Production Control Board is entered here.												
	Subtotal	2														
Wasteful downtime (minutes)	Machinery D	13														
	Dies, jigs, etc. E															
	Quality defect F															
	Missing part G	5														
	Manufacturing fault H	50	— Total downtime ⓒ - (A-to-G total time) =70 minutes - 20 minutes													
	Subtotal	68														

Total downtime (minutes) ⓒ	70	— Actual working time ⓑ - Operating time ⓓ = 520 minutes - 450 minutes
Operating time (minutes) ⓓ	450	— Execution tact time × Actual volume ⓐ = 5.0 minutes × 90 units
Operational availability (%) ⓔ	86.5	— Operating time ⓓ / Actual working time ⓑ × 100 = 450 minutes / 520 minutes × 100

* The use of computers is strictly prohibited. By handwriting such low operational availability every day, workers gradually increase the awareness of their duty and feel that they have to do something.

154

4. Problem writing and *Yuichi* meeting (= evening meeting for discussing countermeasures)

(1) Problem writing

Anyone can write out any problems occurred during production or found from the Production Control Board or Control Chart anytime on a large sheet of paper ("Problems and Measures" sheet). Effective use of illustrations and photographs allows other members to see at a glance what happened, leading to easier cause investigation and faster countermeasures.

(2) Implementation of *Yuichi* meeting

Every day we held a "*Yuichi* meeting" at a scheduled time in the following manner.

How to hold a *Yuichi* meeting

To be held at the predetermined time every afternoon within 30 minutes

Moderator	Team leader of the relevant process

Attendees	Manufacturing department's engineering staff and quality team leader

Maintenance team leader   Section manager (optional)

Manufacturing department's supervisor

Production engineering department's engineering staff (if requested by the manufacturing department in the case of an equipment-related problem)

Production control engineer (if requested by the manufacturing department in the case of parts and/or logistics-related problem)

Concerning the problems written on a large sheet of paper

New problems → The person who will take measures and the deadline for the measures are determined and specified.

At the time of deadline for the ongoing countermeasures → The results are verified.
If the results of the measures are satisfactory → The problem is considered as solved but will continue to be watched.
It the measures are considered insufficient → What further will be done and when will it be started are determined and recorded.

5. Points to observe to reduce downtime

(1) Reduction of manufacturing-related downtime

"Manufacturing-related downtime" means line stopping time attributable to a fault in the manufacturing department.

1) Visualization of delaying processes

We could find from the Production Control Chart that the sum of the line stopping time (the total waste time) was very surprising when all of the work delays that were too small to be written on the Production Control Board (one that takes only a few seconds) were combined. In such a case, the first thing to do is visualize how much work delay occurs in which process(es). For lines

Chart 12-6   Indication of work delay with the lamp system

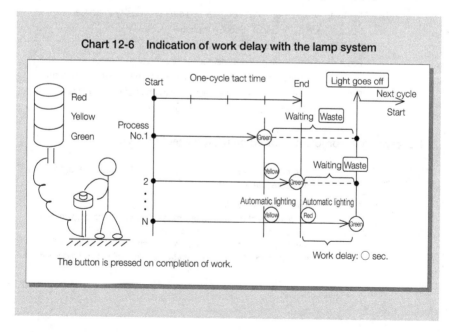

having no pacemaker, the lamp system as shown in Chart 12-6 is an effective methods.

2) Identification of "YK work" and measures at Work Observation Meeting

"YK" stands for the Japanese words "*Yarinikui* (difficult-to-do)" and "*Kitsui* (tough), *Kiken* (dangerous), *Kitanai* (dirty), or *Kizukai-ga-hitsuyou* (special attention-required)", so the "YK work" indicates such kinds of work.

All the team members go to the process where the red lamp lights up frequently, observe the actual work at the Work Observation Meeting based on the *GENCHI GENBUTSU* principle, and write down any problems found there. Examples of YK work and points to be observed are shown in Charts 12-7 to 12-9.

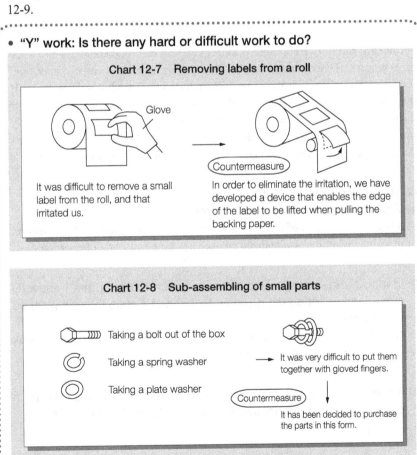

- **"Y" work: Is there any hard or difficult work to do?**

Chart 12-7   Removing labels from a roll

Glove

Countermeasure

It was difficult to remove a small label from the roll, and that irritated us.

In order to eliminate the irritation, we have developed a device that enables the edge of the label to be lifted when pulling the backing paper.

Chart 12-8   Sub-assembling of small parts

Taking a bolt out of the box

Taking a spring washer

Taking a plate washer

It was very difficult to put them together with gloved fingers.

Countermeasure

It has been decided to purchase the parts in this form.

- **"K" work: Is there any tough, dangerous, dirty, or special attention-required work?**

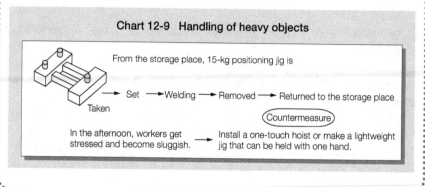

Chart 12-9   Handling of heavy objects

From the storage place, 15-kg positioning jig is

Taken → Set → Welding → Removed → Returned to the storage place

(Countermeasure)

In the afternoon, workers get stressed and become sluggish. → Install a one-touch hoist or make a lightweight jig that can be held with one hand.

Looking carefully from those perspectives, you may find countless YK work in a process. Those matters are written out on a large sheet of paper, and measures are taken with the responsible persons and deadlines determined. If the problems become clear, countermeasures come out one after another through discussion with the team members, and the next thing to do is steadily implement those measures. Accumulation of such efforts enables various slight delays to be eliminated, resulting in improvement in operational availability.

(2) Reduction of machine downtime
1) Visualizing each machine's downtime
Based on the record of the Production Control Board, the monthly transition of machine downtime is visualized on each machine and/or failure portion.

2) Identifying the cause of downtime on each machine that frequently stops, and restoring the machine to its normal state through planned repair work
Plans and schedules for updating aging parts, thorough cleaning, oil leak repairs etc. are made and implemented.

3) Reviewing preventive maintenance items and cycles, and creating a procedure to restore the machine to normal state before failure

4) 2S Improvement in maintenance spare parts warehouse ... Very Important!

There are many cases where it takes a lot of time to look for a replacement part, leading to longer line stop times. In such a company, it is necessary to implement the "five steps for 2S Improvement" described in Section 4-(3) of Chapter 11 in the spare parts warehouse to allow anyone to take out any necessary substitute parts within one minute (Chart 12-10).

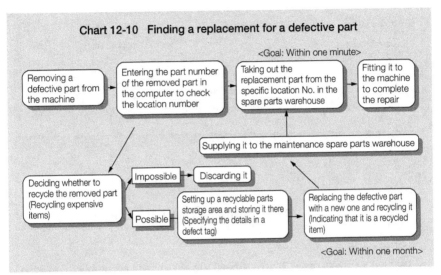

Chart 12-10 Finding a replacement for a defective part

<Goal: Within one minute>

Removing a defective part from the machine → Entering the part number of the removed part in the computer to check the location number → Taking out the replacement part from the specific location No. in the spare parts warehouse → Fitting it to the machine to complete the repair

Supplying it to the maintenance spare parts warehouse

Deciding whether to recycle the removed part (Recycling expensive items)

Impossible → Discarding it

Possible → Setting up a recyclable parts storage area and storing it there (Specifying the details in a defect tag)

Replacing the defective part with a new one and recycling it (Indicating that it is a recycled item)

<Goal: Within one month>

Such an improvement activity will not make any progress simply by relying on the maintenance department. To solve this kind of problem, it is important to first take up this issue as a subject for 2S improvement. Then, top management should instruct the maintenance department to prepare a schedule to be completed in six months and visit the site to check the progress on a monthly basis.

(3) Reduction of setup time

Setup work is an operation to change settings of production machines including stand-alone machines (e.g. stamping press, molding machine, etc.) and automated lines when changing models of products (or parts) to be produced. The setup work includes not only replacement of parts, molds, cushion pins, jigs, liquids and chemicals, but also machinery adjustment and quality checks as necessary.

Reduction in the setup time leads directly to reduction of line stopping time.

In addition, it also promotes heijunka and enhances the capability of producing large-variety products in small quantity (Chart 12-11).

Chart 12-11   Reduction of setup time (example)

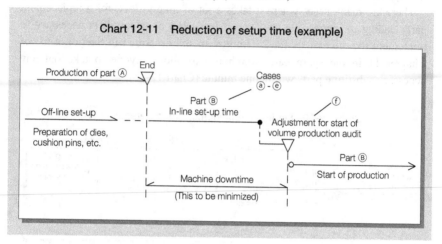

Examples of setup time reduction

ⓐ In-line setup → Off-line setup

ⓑ Walking → Creating a "Motion Sheet"* to minimize the number of walking steps

ⓒ Manual tightening work → Automatic tightening with electric guns or air impact guns

ⓓ Creating a "Quick Program Input Chart" to allow for short-time and accurate input

ⓔ Installing a positioning guide to allow for quick setting

ⓕ Standardizing the machine settings in the optimum state to ensure product quality from the first production and eliminate the need for frequent machine adjustment.

Through various kinds of efforts as described above, single setup time should be reduced (to less than 10 minutes in our case).

It is also effective to organize a voluntary setup work study group.

 Motion Sheet:

Illustrating worker's motion, this was used as a tool to locate waste in walking.

Chart 12-12 shows an example of improving the press die setup work with the use of the Motion Sheet.

Chart 12-12   Improvement of press die setup work

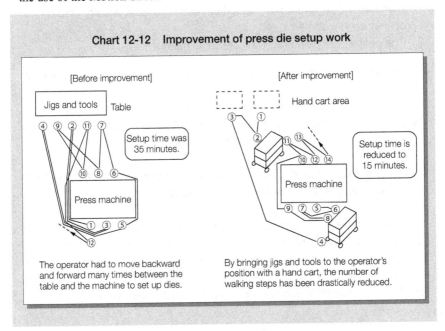

[Before improvement]

Jigs and tools | Table

Setup time was 35 minutes.

Press machine

The operator had to move backward and forward many times between the table and the machine to set up dies.

[After improvement]

Hand cart area

Setup time is reduced to 15 minutes.

Press machine

By bringing jigs and tools to the operator's position with a hand cart, the number of walking steps has been drastically reduced.

6. Improvement by Task Force Team

In the case of problems that were difficult to solve at the work site that involved two or more departments, or that were related to new equipment or new technologies, the relevant department that was in trouble immediately brought up the issue at the "Asaichi (morning meeting)" for discussion and determination of what to do. Thus, It is important to make efforts to solve problems through the teamwork of the entire plant.

<Example> Line stop due to missing parts

If a necessary part is not in the production line when needed, such unusual events as ceasing production to wait for it or incorporating it in the subsequent process will occur. If this happens frequently, productivity will decrease, and various quality defects will occur; therefore, "prevention of missing parts" is essential.

1) Formation of missing part prevention team (Task Force Team)

Team Leader: An engineer of the production control department

Members: Staff from manufacturing (each section), quality assurance, procurement departments, etc.

The goal should be achieved by the same members.

2) Visualization of the state of missing parts and recurrence prevention activities

In case of a missing part, it was visualized what part was missing and which section was responsible for it, and the responsible person took recurrence prevention measures within that day.

 The exact same countermeasures against the quality defects were applied to cases of missing parts.

The responsible section or department was determined consensually through *GENCHI GENBUTSU* check (on-site check of actual items) and discussion by the task force team members. When a missing part occurred, there was a tendency to press the responsibility on logistics. However, it was not so easy to specify the responsibility because various departments were involved.

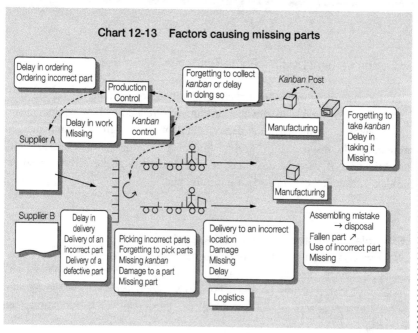

Chart 12-13   Factors causing missing parts

As shown in Chart 12-13, there were various factors causing that problem.

In the case of the Takahama Plant, the production control, logistics, and manufacturing departments voluntarily started going hand-in-hand together to completely prevent missing parts when the number of defects detected in the finished vehicle inspection was reduced to almost zero and the time required for Quality *Asaichi* meeting became short.

What we found out was that the manufacturing side also had many problems. By clarifying "who made the mistake in which process" and conducting reeducation and/or retraining of the relevant worker, the problems gradually declined. As a result of steady efforts by all team members over three years, we were able to drastically reduce the number of missing parts.

Part 5

Systems for Continuation and Deepening

Claim *Asaichi*

1. Reflecting on the results of Dantotsu Quality Activities and starting up Dantotsu-II

In March 2010, looking back on the three years of activities and results since the start of Dantotsu Quality Activities at the Industrial Vehicle Division of Toyota Industries, we found that the market claim cost was still far higher than our original goal and further countermeasures were necessary. Although the number of defects detected in the finished vehicle inspection, as well as the number of defects from suppliers, drastically decreased, we had a long way to go until we would reach the market claim reduction goal. So, we decided to implement "Dantotsu-II" in the following three years, mainly targeting market claims.

(1) Reducing the number of defects per vehicle in finished vehicle inspection

Based on the actual results in 2006, the six plants, except BT (Sweden), achieved the target (88% reduction through three times of annual 50% reduction), indicating almost similar curves (Chart 13 -1).

Those plants obediently implemented the "Visualization", "8-step procedure", "Standardization" that I had taught. They were strongly interested in the changing situation where failures steadily decreased by doing what they were taught, so they actively worked on the Dantotsu Quality Activities, resulting in the achievements.

In contrast, at BT, top management were not so enthusiastic and they simply passed what I had taught them to on-site workers, and time passed. Three years later, when BT took a big lag from other companies in terms of performance, and the top management could no longer make excuses about it, the company finally started doing what I had taught. However, it was too late, and top management was replaced. Then, it took another three years before the company caught up with other companies.

In order to motivate such plants that will not try to change, it is necessary to have perseverance to make them understand the current situation by visualizing the difference with other companies in the global quality improvement competition and continue to teach them tenaciously until they obtain favorable results.

Chart 13-1   Number of defects per vehicle found in finished vehicle inspection (Takahama Plant)

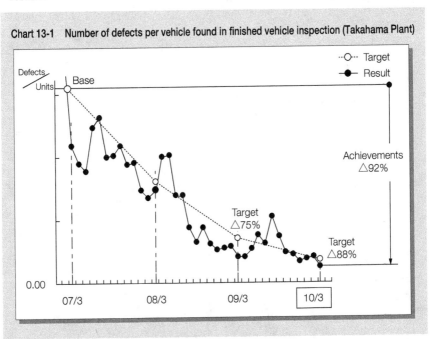

(2) Number of defective deliveries from suppliers

The achievements of the six companies were between -59% and -85%, which fell short of the target of 88% reduction (Chart 13-2). At the beginning of the Dantotsu Quality Activity, its effect was unknown, so there were not so many suppliers who actively participated in the activities. In addition, the ability of the Supplier Quality Improvement Support Team members was inadequate, and it was necessary to improve their leadership skills first.

However, the number of suppliers who actively participated in the activities began to increase in the latter half of the second year when they learned that the quality at the vehicle manufacturing plant was getting better and better in the first and second years due to the Dantotsu activities, and the favorable results also began to come out. Therefore, in Dantotsu-II, we were able to speedily implement our activities to reduce the number of defective deliveries from suppliers.

Chart 13-2 Number of defective deliveries from suppliers (CESAB ... Italy)

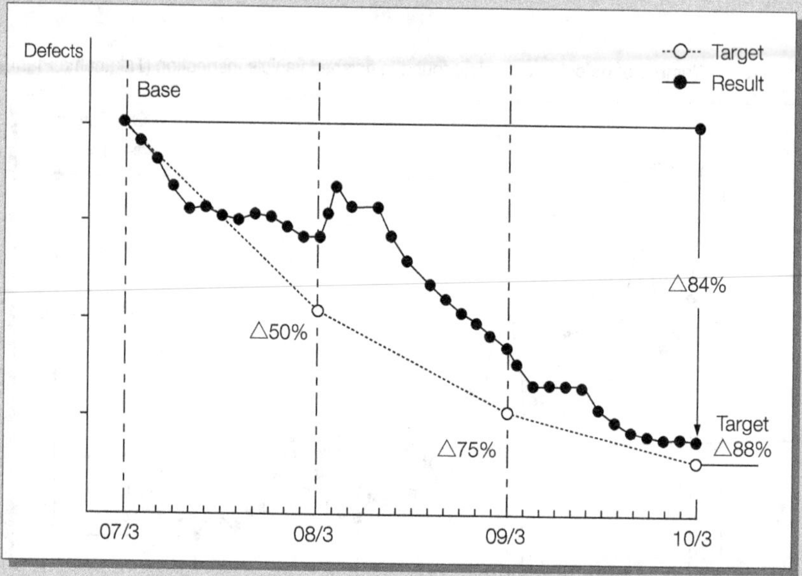

(3) Market claim cost

The annual reduction of "market claim cost", which is the most important indicator of customer satisfaction, remained at 38% or so on average, while the target was 50% (Chart 13-3). Especially, all of the three major plants in Japan, the United States and Europe failed to achieve the target, so quality differentiation from competitors was difficult.

Therefore, we decided to continue this global challenge with a three-year extension of this activity as Dantotsu-II, further setting the target of 50% defect reduction over the three years to a cumulative total of 75% reduction.

With the main goal set to reduce the market claim costs, we extended for three more years the period of activities for halving the both numbers of defects per vehicle in the finished vehicle inspection and defective deliveries from suppliers, with the target of a "50% reduction per year × 6 years = -98%". For that purpose, we decided to improve the quality of the parts from suppliers by strengthening the ability of Supplier Quality Improvement Support Team, as well as enhancing such activities as the "8-step procedure", WPM, and change-point control.

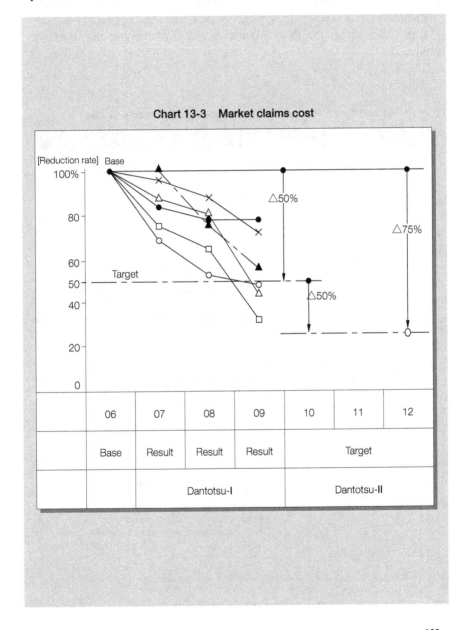

Chart 13-3　Market claims cost

2. Problems with market claim reduction activities

Through careful investigation of the current state and discussion with executives of each company about the reasons why they failed to achieve the market claim reduction target, we found the problems listed in Chart 13-4.

Chart 13-5 shows the flows of market claim information and defective products.

Chart 13-4 Problems with market claim reduction activities

	Problems	Reason
*1	Claimed items are not observed.	Claimed items returned from dealers are stacked in a warehouse, but few people come to check the defective condition. → Without seeing the defective condition, it is impossible to find the cause and take any measures.
*2	Without responsibility assigned, many claimed items are left unattended.	The vehicle manufacturing plant determines that the supplier has responsibility. After checking the actual defective item, the supplier judges that it has no responsibility and rejects the claim. → For many claimed items left unattended, the responsibilities and causes remain unknown.
*3	Low-cost frequent claims are left untouched.	Because high-cost claims receive a high priority in cause investigation and countermeasures, low-cost claims are left on the back-burner so they occur chronically. → Complaints from dealers are greatly increasing.
*4	Not all of the claimed items are collected. (Overseas plants)	They do not understand the necessity of collecting claimed items. Simply because the collection cost is high, they ask the dealers to keep those items in storage. → As in the case of *1, it is impossible to take any measures without observing the defective condition.

Chart 13-5 Flows of market claim information and claimed items

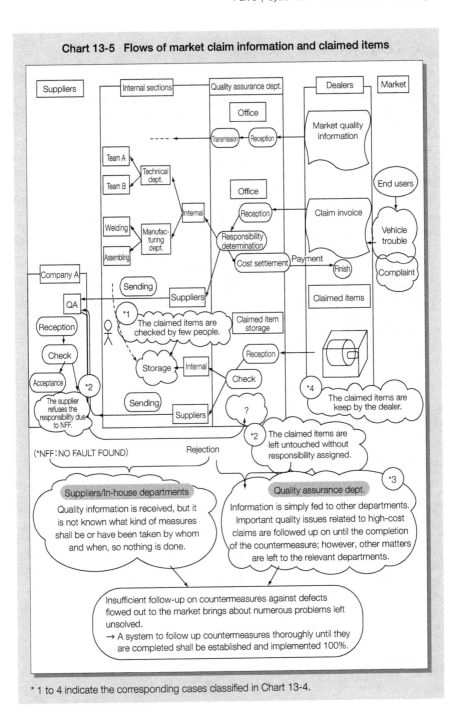

(*NFF: NO FAULT FOUND)

* 1 to 4 indicate the corresponding cases classified in Chart 13-4.

3. Launch of Claim *Asaichi*

We decided to launch "Claim *Asaichi* (morning meeting)", where all the claimed items returned from dealers were checked in the next morning after their return by all quality-related personnel, and where we determined who would be responsible for investigating the cause and taking countermeasures and followed them up until completion.

Initially, even at Toyota Industries, there were many complaints among workers due to so many returned parts, saying "It's impossible to respond to a problem that I hear today by tomorrow". While they were doing it, however, they learned the knack of what to do and how to do it, and finally they became able to do it. Sticking to the basics is important.

"Claim *Asaichi* Team" was organized in the quality assurance department, having a responsibility to see through from receipt of claimed items to verification of the effect of the recurrence prevention measure.

When there were too many defective items, a priority of countermeasures was given to the defects that occurred three or more times. Then, as the next step, necessary countermeasures were taken against all of other defects, as a matter of course.

(1) Flow of Claim *Asaichi*

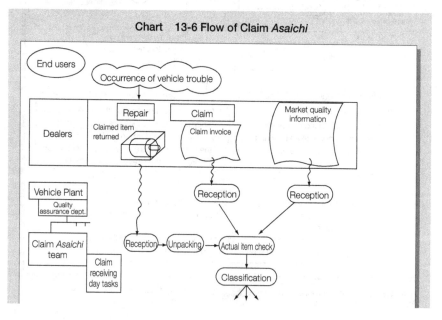

Chart   13-6 Flow of Claim *Asaichi*

172

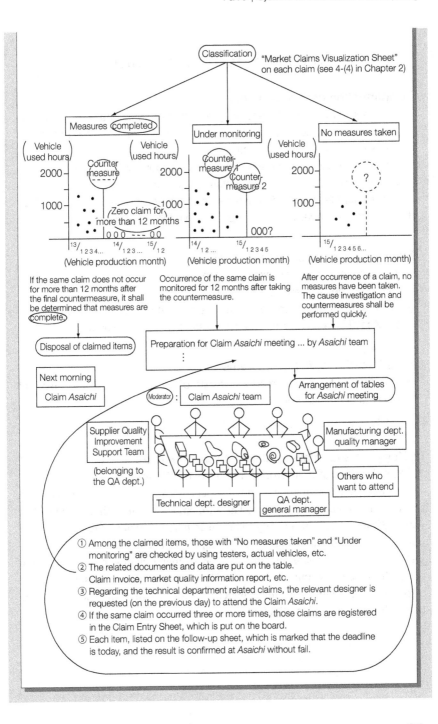

Classification "Market Claims Visualization Sheet" on each claim (see 4-(4) in Chapter 2)

Measures completed

Under monitoring

No measures taken

(Vehicle used hours)

Counter measure

Zero claim for more than 12 months

(Vehicle production month)

Counter measure 1
Counter measure 2

000?

(Vehicle production month)

?

(Vehicle production month)

If the same claim does not occur for more than 12 months after the final countermeasure, it shall be determined that measures are complete.

Occurrence of the same claim is monitored for 12 months after taking the countermeasure.

After occurrence of a claim, no measures have been taken. The cause investigation and countermeasures shall be performed quickly.

Disposal of claimed items

Preparation for Claim *Asaichi* meeting ... by *Asaichi* team

Next morning

Claim *Asaichi*

Moderator : Claim *Asaichi* team

Arrangement of tables for *Asaichi* meeting

Supplier Quality Improvement Support Team

(belonging to the QA dept.)

Manufacturing dept. quality manager

Others who want to attend

Technical dept. designer

QA dept. general manager

① Among the claimed items, those with "No measures taken" and "Under monitoring" are checked by using testers, actual vehicles, etc.
② The related documents and data are put on the table.
  Claim invoice, market quality information report, etc.
③ Regarding the technical department related claims, the relevant designer is requested (on the previous day) to attend the Claim *Asaichi*.
④ If the same claim occurred three or more times, those claims are registered in the Claim Entry Sheet, which is put on the board.
⑤ Each item, listed on the follow-up sheet, which is marked that the deadline is today, and the result is confirmed at *Asaichi* without fail.

Procedures for Claim *Asaichi*

① **Confirmation of claimed items**

- The Asaichi team members took up the claimed items one by one from the table and explained what had happened in the market and which portion of the actual part had been defective.
- They discussed the causes, measures, responsible persons, etc. and determined who should take countermeasures responsibly.

The *Asaichi* team recorded defects having three or more claims in a Claim Entry Sheet, and specified follow-up items in a follow-up sheet.

② **Verification of countermeasure effects**

- The responsible person explained the countermeasures taken each time, with questions and answers followed.
- For the items on which no report was submitted even after the deadline, the *Asaichi* team confirmed the progress of countermeasures.

③ **Confirmation of follow-up items**

- The *Asaichi* team confirmed the results of each of the follow-up items at the time of the deadline.

(2) Key points for making Claim *Asaichi* effective
1) Limit the time of all-member meetings to 30 minutes.

It should be avoided for key quality persons of individual departments to spend a lot of time on the meeting. The all-member meetings should be finished within 30 minutes, with priority given to important matters. Other individual issues should be discussed later among respective persons in charge. When we just launched the *Asaichi* meeting, we had so many claims that we could not finish the meeting within 30 minutes. However, as countermeasures became effective and the number of items under monitor increased, it became possible to end the meeting within 30 minutes.

Atmosphere of Claim *Asaichi*

2) Visualize the flow of claimed items.

The flow of claimed items should be visualized to prevent detention.

It is important to return the claimed items or parts to the responsible designer or supplier as soon as possible for immediate start of considering and taking countermeasures (more details are described in the following Section 4).

3) Confirm the progress of design-related claims at another weekly meeting.

It is often the case that claims attributable to product design take long to go through the following steps; cause investigation, measure determination, design change, and new parts manufacturing and replacement. Therefore, a different meeting from *Asaichi* should be held on a weekly basis to directly discuss with the responsible designer(s) and steadily take the above steps (more details are described in the following Section 5).

4) Assign supplier-related claims to "Supplier Quality Improvement Support Team".

The "Supplier Quality Improvement Support Team" should be organized in the quality assurance department, with persons in charge of individual suppliers appointed to take measures in concert with the respective suppliers.

Problems will not be solved simply by relying on the supplier's efforts (more details are described in the following Section 6).

4. Visualization of claimed parts flow

Claimed items are like a mountain of treasure! If you check the claimed parts thoroughly to find a problem and take countermeasures, the number of claims will surely decrease. However, in most cases, they are sleeping in a large warehouse, and many companies are "sitting on a gold mine", which is very disappointing.

In order not to leave the claimed parts unattended, but to utilize them for problem investigation and solution toward reducing the claim cost, the first thing to do is visualization of the flow of claimed parts as shown in Chart 13-7. Then, a system should be established to deliver them to the responsible person within a week, at the latest, and to make him/her start considering the necessary measures as soon as possible.

1) Example of standardization of handling claimed parts

Chart 13-7   Standardization of handling claimed parts (example)

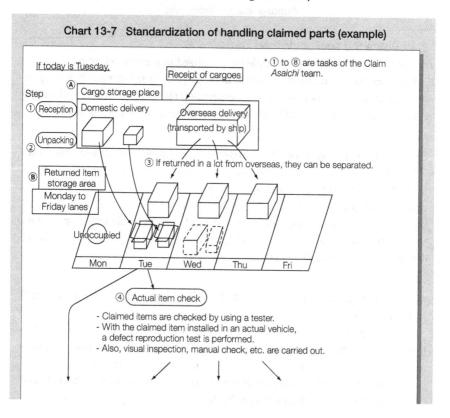

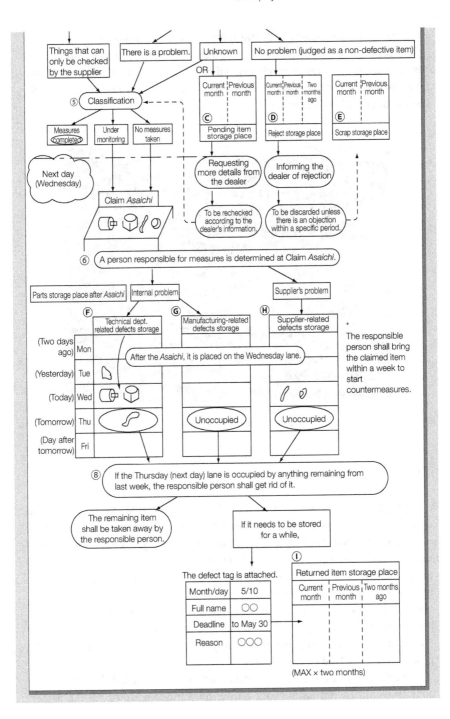

Things that can only be checked by the supplier

There is a problem.

Unknown

OR

No problem (judged as a non-defective item)

⑤ Classification

Current month	Previous month
©️	
Pending item storage place	

Current month	Previous month	Two months ago
⒟		
Reject storage place		

Current month	Previous month
⒠	
Scrap storage place	

Measures Completed

Under monitoring

No measures taken

Next day (Wednesday)

Claim *Asaichi*

Requesting more details from the dealer

Informing the dealer of rejection

To be rechecked according to the dealer's information.

To be discarded unless there is an objection within a specific period.

⑥ A person responsible for measures is determined at Claim *Asaichi*.

Parts storage place after *Asaichi*

Internal problem

Supplier's problem

⒡ Technical dept. related defects storage

⒢ Manufacturing-related defects storage

⒣ Supplier-related defects storage

* The responsible person shall bring the claimed item within a week to start countermeasures.

		Technical dept. related defects storage	Manufacturing-related defects storage	Supplier-related defects storage
(Two days ago)	Mon			
(Yesterday)	Tue			
(Today)	Wed			
(Tomorrow)	Thu		Unoccupied	Unoccupied
(Day after tomorrow)	Fri			

After the *Asaichi*, it is placed on the Wednesday lane.

⑧ If the Thursday (next day) lane is occupied by anything remaining from last week, the responsible person shall get rid of it.

The remaining item shall be taken away by the responsible person.

If it needs to be stored for a while,

⒤

The defect tag is attached.

Month/day	5/10
Full name	◯◯
Deadline	to May 30
Reason	◯◯◯

Returned item storage place

Current month	Previous month	Two months ago

(MAX × two months)

2) Ⓐ to Ⓘ: Arrangement of storage area ... *Asaichi* team

The positions of Ⓐ to Ⓘ were determined in the claimed parts storage and handling area, and they were clearly indicated by white marking lines on the floor for easy identification. When shelves are used, the optimum place for installation should be determined.

Claimed item storage area

5. Reduction of design related claims

"Design related claims" indicate claims attributable to the technical department, which is involved in product design. The design related defects were large in number and high in cost. Furthermore, they often required a lot of time to take measures. Therefore, Claim *Asaichi* was too short to conduct the follow-up activities on the design-related claims. For that reason, we decided to hold another meeting regarding the items registered as design-related market claims on a weekly basis for a joint progress check by the general manager of the quality assurance department and the head of the relevant quality section of the technical department, and persistently followed up the matters until the problems were solved (Chart 13-8).

If we fully relied on the efforts made only by the technical department, the activity would be left on the back-burner for various reasons. All the defects that flowed out to the market, including design-related ones, must be consistently followed up under the responsibility of the quality assurance department.

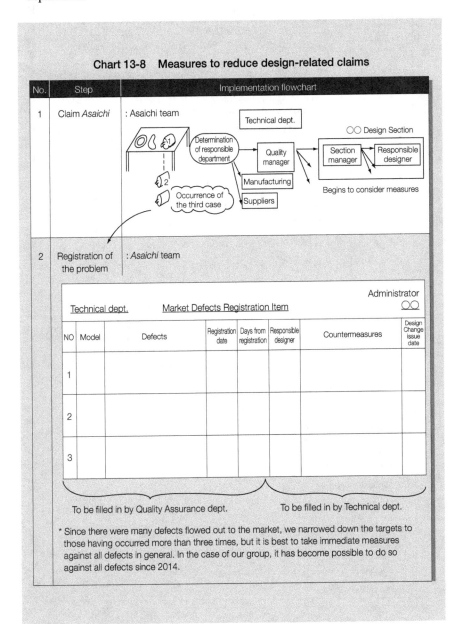

Chart 13-8   Measures to reduce design-related claims

* Since there were many defects flowed out to the market, we narrowed down the targets to those having occurred more than three times, but it is best to take immediate measures against all defects in general. In the case of our group, it has become possible to do so against all defects since 2014.

No.	Step	Implementation flowchart
3	Preparation of countermeasure schedule	: Individual responsible designer

General problem-solving procedure

No.	Implementation flowchart
	① Check of defective items ... Receiving claimed items at Claim *Asaichi*
	② Implementation of defect reproduction test By changing the test conditions, check under what conditions the same malfunction occurs in order to find the cause. Repeat the test under the following conditions until it is reproduced. More harsh test conditions Longer test time, etc.
	③ Analysis of the test results and identification of the cause of the malfunction Investigation by all team members including veteran engineers (This is very effective in finding something that the responsible designer has overlooked.)
	④ Consideration and determination of countermeasures against the possible causes Example: Increasing plate thickness, changing material, etc.
	⑤ Preparation of test samples
	⑥ Implementation of durability tests, on-vehicle tests, etc.
	⑦ Evaluation of test results
	(OK)　　　(NG) → Go back to ③
	⑧ Preparation and issue of Design Change Request form.

* For each problem, a schedule is prepared to cover the period until the countermeasure is completed.
(It is important to take time and consider the most appropriate measure, which can solve the problem with in one try.)

Market Defects Prevention Measure Schedule　　　Designer ○○
Defect: ○○○○○

NO. Step	Week Month/Day	1w 6/1 to 8	2w 15	3w 22	4w 29	5w 7/6	6w 13	7w 20	8w 	9w 27
① Registration date		6/3								
② Reproduction test (Cause investigation)		Plan / Result								
③ Consideration of measures										
④ Determination of measures										
⑤ Preparation of test sample										
⑥ Test										
⑦ Evaluation										
⑧ Issue of Design Change								7/15		

* Even if it takes time, necessary tests shall be performed to judge the quality.

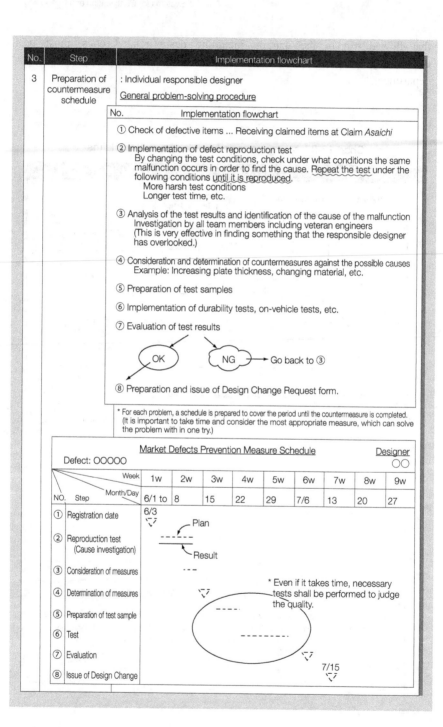

No.	Step	Implementation flowchart
4	Follow-up Meeting	This meeting is held on a specific day and time once a week. Moderator: Claim *Asaichi* team Confirmed by: General Manager of the Quality Assurance Dept., and Quality Manager of the Technical Department Explained by: Responsible designer for each problem 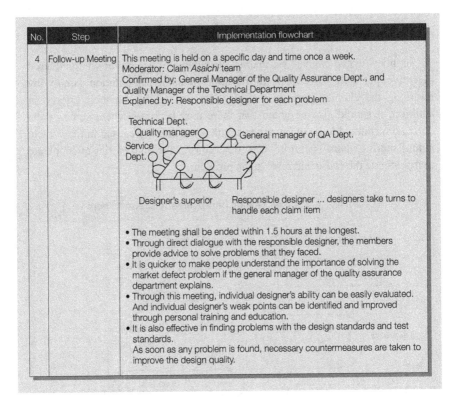 • The meeting shall be ended within 1.5 hours at the longest. • Through direct dialogue with the responsible designer, the members provide advice to solve problems that they faced. • It is quicker to make people understand the importance of solving the market defect problem if the general manager of the quality assurance department explains. • Through this meeting, individual designer's ability can be easily evaluated. And individual designer's weak points can be identified and improved through personal training and education. • It is also effective in finding problems with the design standards and test standards. As soon as any problem is found, necessary countermeasures are taken to improve the design quality.

Effectiveness of Claim *Asaichi* & weekly follow-up meeting

There were so many design-related defects flowed out to the market at each company that most of them were left untouched without any countermeasures. As a result, it took three years to take some measures for all of them.

By honestly continuing Claim *Asaichi* → Weekly follow-up meeting without fail, we became able to steadily reduce the claim amount.

Thus, Claim *Asaichi* and the weekly follow-up meeting proved to be very effective and important activities to reduce the cases of design-related defects outflow to the market.

6. Reduction of supplier-related claims

"Supplier-related claims" are claims attributable to a supplier who delivered defective parts. It is difficult to reach a fundamental solution simply by returning the claimed parts to the suppliers and relying on their efforts. In addition, it should also be noted that there may be cases where some of the defects considered to be the supplier's fault were actually caused in the vehicle manufacturing plant. Therefore, it is important for the both parties to cooperate to investigate the cause and resolve the problem.

Chart 13-9   Supplier Quality Improvement Support Team

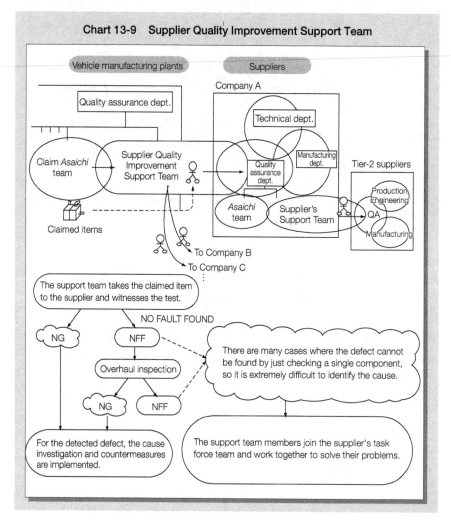

(1) Supplier Quality Improvement Support Team

We set up the "Supplier Quality Improvement Support Team" in the quality assurance department of the vehicle manufacturing plant to work on countermeasures against market claims with suppliers (Chart 13-9).

It tended to be considered that the claimed and returned parts were attributable to the fault of the supplier who had made them, but there were many cases where the cause existed in the vehicle manufacturing plant. In addition, there were cases, too, where a little change in work systems at the vehicle manufacturing plant greatly facilitated the supplier's operations. It is extremely important for both parties to cooperate with each other to investigate the cause.

(2) Case Study: Countermeasures against the worst problem (foreign material contamination)

1) The "worst problem"

A forklift incorporates high-pressure hydraulic units to move heavy cargo up and down, or right and left.

If contaminants (such as foreign matter) remain in the high-pressure hydraulic circuit, such failures as the flow rate drop due to clogging or internal oil leakage due to the damaged oil seal lip may occur, causing vibrations, noises, slow handling or other problems. Because a number of suppliers were involved in production of the high-pressure hydraulic circuit, it was difficult to identify what kind of contaminants entered in which part and which process, so the countermeasures were insufficient (Chart 13-10).

In order to reduce the claim amount, the most urgent matter was to solve the contamination problem. Therefore, we decided to address drastic measures.

[Types of contaminants]
- Chips and burrs (generated during machining)
- Spatters (generated during welding)
- Peeled coating film and paint residue (falling from paint jigs, spray guns, etc.)
- Waste textile (falling from working gloves and clothing)
- Hair, and other countless contaminants

Chart 13-10   High-pressure hydraulic circuit of forklift

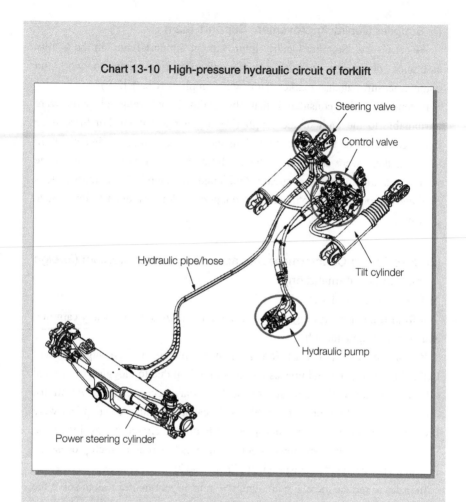

2) Contamination Prevention Handbook ... Prepared by the quality assurance department of Toyota Industries

In order to carry out "contamination-free manufacturing," the quality assurance department of Toyota Industries prepared a handbook illustrating and describing what to do and how to do it (Chart 13-11). Based on this handbook, we investigated the current state of each supplier company and vehicle manufacturing plant through a "Contamination Check Sheet" and thoroughly took corrective and preventive measures against the problems we found.

Chart 13-11 Major contents of Contamination Prevention Handbook

Classification	Item	Contamination problems	Countermeasures
Logistics	Parts box	Internal contaminants ... trash	• With the contamination limit defined, the box is washed before the limit. • A mesh plastic sheet is used inside. Some devices are used to avoid direct contact of parts with contaminants.
		Falling dust	• The box is covered with a lid to protect it from falling dust. Lid Washed items are always covered with a lid.
	Hand cart and parts rack	Falling dust (Dust falls on the parts during weekends and long holidays.)	Hand cart — Vinyl sheet — Parts rack The top and the sides are enclosed with vinyl sheets.
Work	Process	Falling dust	Vinyl roof Vinyl curtain The assembly process is fully enclosed.
	Glove	Dirty gloves Attached contaminants	Before every cycle of assembling operations, workers first remove the dust from their gloves. * The dust is removed with an adhesive sheet.
	Workbench	Dirty surface with contamination * It is difficult to recognize dust when the surface of the workbench is dark.	• A bright color as white or cream is used on the workbench surface. • During work, contaminants on the workbench are removed with a clean cloth.
Machining	Burrs and chips after cutting	A remaining burr at a corner radius Burrs - A burr generated during screw processing Remaining chips	• Design approach: Burr-free shapes are provided through the proper corner-radius design instruction. 3R • Burr-free and chip-free processing methods: Screw rolling process Use of burrless taps

Classification	Item	Contamination problems	Countermeasures
Machining	Cutting tools and blades	Burr generation and surface roughness failure due to worn cutting tool or blade	• Quantitative or periodic replacement of cutting tools or blades has been standardized. The cutting tools or blades are replaced before trouble occurs.
	Burr check	Burrs remaining inside	• The inside is checked visually or by using an endoscope. Any burrs found are removed with an appropriate tool. * A deburring tool is prepared.
	Air blow	Contaminants scattering on to various places during air-blowing in an open place	• The air-blow-dedicated simple ducts are used to prevent the scattering of contaminants.
Cleaning	Inside cleaning	Shower washing Outside is OK, but the inside is still dirty. 	• A nozzle is inserted inside the parts to clean up contaminants.
	Corner burr cleaning	Shower washing Fine burrs cannot be removed 	Washing with twin brushes. The two rotating brushes remove the corner burrs. * Very effective
	Washing pressure	Burrs unremoved at the usual washing machine's washing pressure of approximately 10 MPa	• A high-pressure washing machine is required. Burrs are blown off at the washing pressure of 20 MPa or more through high-pressure washing.
	Cleaning of washing machine	Occurrence of nozzle clogging and sludge formation due to accumulation of various contaminants	• Through regular cleaning, the inside of the machine is kept clean at all times. (The implementation of cleaning is checked with the cleaning record sheet.)
	Cleaning liquid management	Liquid replaced only periodically (Even if the liquid deteriorates due to an abnormality, it continues to be used.)	• Daily check of liquid sample. The cleaning liquid is sampled in a test tube for visual checking once a day. The liquid is replaced when the contamination exceeds the limit. New liquid Limit sample Today's sample * Although this is a simple method, it is effective.

186

Classification	Item	Contamination problems	Countermeasures
Cleaning	Cleaning status check	Invisibility of inside enclosed by iron plates Nozzle clogging, pressure drop and other abnormalities cannot be seen.	• The glass windows have been installed so that the interior is visible.
	Filter replacement	Replacement cycle not determined	• The degree of contamination of the filter is checked, an appropriate filter replacement cycle is standardized, and the results are recorded.
	Nozzle maintenance	Nozzle clogging and incorrect nozzle angle	• Nozzle clogging and angle are periodically checked, and the results are recorded.
Cleanliness	Air dust	Countless contaminants floating in a plant (even though the plant looks clean)	• Fixed-spot check of falling contaminants Fixed spots for observation are determined inside and outside of the work process, with a fixed-size blank paper placed in each spot. And the contamination state in each spot will be checked after a month. Whether or not the contamination has been reduced by the countermeasures is checked. The types of contaminants are identified, and measures are taken against their sources in the order from largest to smallest volume of contaminants.
	Cleaning liquid	Contamination of liquid due to removed contaminants during washing (Removed contaminants mixing in the liquid must be reduced.)	The types of contaminants caught by the periodically replaced filter are analyzed, and their sources are identified. Then, reduction measures are taken in the order from largest to smallest volume of contaminants.

3) Identification of problems and countermeasures using the Contamination Check Sheet

Based on the Contamination Prevention Handbook, we prepared the Contamination Check Sheet, and carried out contamination checks on all suppliers that manufacture high-pressure hydraulic unit parts and the related manufacturing processes in the vehicle manufacturing plant.

For each company, problems were found concerning about half of the check items, so we made improvements to them one after another. Although some measures are still in progress, full-scale efforts to combat contamination have enabled drastic reduction of market claims as described below.

4) Results of contamination reduction activities

As a result of continuing efforts towards ideal control of contamination, led by the engineers of the quality assurance department and in cooperation with in-house departments, suppliers, and overseas plants, a great achievement was made as shown in Chart 13-12.

This activity was horizontally deployed to also improve electronic parts contamination reduction and static electricity control, and remarkable achievements have already begun to appear, respectively.

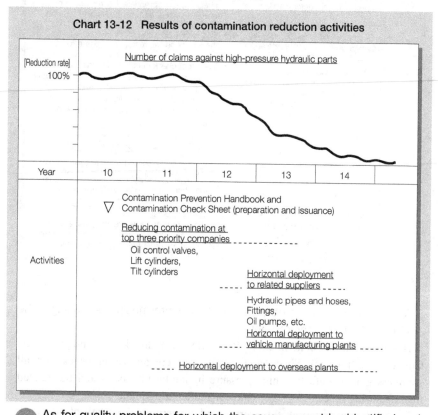

Chart 13-12   Results of contamination reduction activities

As for quality problems for which the cause cannot be identified and any responsible department cannot be determined for improvement, it is necessary for the quality assurance department to conduct cross-sectional quality management by leading all the related departments for quality improvement activities to achieve results. Therefore, engineering staff of the quality assurance department are required to have not only knowledge on quality, but also high levels of leadership to move internal and external organizations toward their goals.

7. Dealers' "information quality" improvement activities

Shortly after the start of Claim *Asaichi,* variations in dealers' "information quality" became obvious. Without detailed information, it was impossible for us to find the cause and take any measures (Chart 13-13).

Every time a problem occurred, we contacted a person in charge at the dealer to obtain detailed information, but it was very difficult to get useful information because his or her memory became ambiguous over time.

In order to take countermeasures against all defects and improve customer satisfaction, accurate information and cooperation from the dealers' mechanics who directly saw and repaired the defects at the forefront of the market are indispensable. The following describes our dealer's "information quality" improvement activities.

Chart 13-13　Information flow with dealers

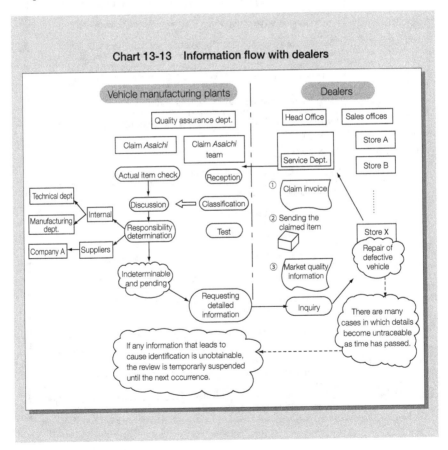

(1) Preparation of a manual concerning "information necessary to investigate the cause"

The engineers who led the Claim *Asaichi* concretely summarized the "information they want from dealers" in a sheet of paper (Chart 13-14).

Chart 13-14 Major points of request for improvement of information quality

NO.	Item	Information useful for identifying the cause of failure
1	General defects	Photos before and after repair of the defective portions ...(Required) The defective parts or portions shall be marked or pointed out with a pointer. Vehicle model, delivery date, failure date, and operating time ...(Required) Usage environment ... (Detailed information leads to cause identification.) Presence of any chemicals, temperature, humidity, altitude/elevation, static electricity, etc. Luggage type, weight, size, center of gravity, etc. and dust (paper, cotton, fiber, or wood) Road surface, angle of sloped road, distance, indoor, outdoor, etc. The results of the investigation shall be described quantitatively. Frequency of occurrence: "Always, twice per hour, several times a day, etc." Speed is slow → "It is so slow that it takes 10 seconds from ◯ to ◯" Hydraulic drift is large → "It indicates 120 mm of descent in 15 minutes with no load."
2	Insufficient tightening	Photos of the loosened state of bolts, nuts, and screws The relevant portions shall be marked. The loosened state means that they are so loosened that they can be rotated by hand, requiring two turns to retighten
3	Poor adjustment	"Since it was ◯ mm before repair, we adjusted it to ◯ mm."
4	Electrical system failure	Steps of checking to identify the defective part: "How did you identify the defective part?", "What did you check?", "Why did you think it was defective?", etc. and adjustments made. <Example> An engine did not start. ↓ The cell motor did not turn. ↓ Step 1: The battery voltage was checked: OK (no problem) Step 2: Neutral switch input voltage was checked: No problem Step 3: Neutral switch conduction was checked: Always open = No problem Repair: The engine started after replacement of the neutral switch.
5	Noise	Types of abnormal noises: "Rasping sound, whizzing sound, etc.?" Operation mode: "During acceleration, deceleration, or normal driving?"
6	Oil leakage	Photos of oil-leaking area: "Is that on the main body or joint portion of pipe or hose?" Leakage condition: "Does oil drop on the floor or just appear on the surface?"

(2) Improvement in communication with dealers

Through the implementation of Claim *Asaichi,* the relationship with dealers has been greatly improved (Chart 13-15). In order to solve pending problems as soon as possible, we put more emphasis on speeding up quality improvement activities throughout the entire group.

Chart 13-15 Improvement of communication with dealers

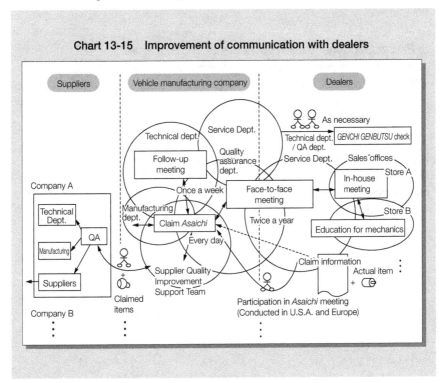

1) Face-to-face meeting ... Twice a year

By implementing the Claim *Asaichi,* it became possible to provide accurate explanations to dealers regarding all problems occurring in the market. At the face-to-face meetings twice a year, I explained to dealers about the details of "information necessary for investigating the cause" and asked them to educate all their mechanics.

Such efforts were also made enthusiastically in the United States and Europe, so that the number of "wait-and-see items with unknown causes" has steadily been on the decline.

2) *GENCHI GENBUTSU* check (on-site check of actual items)

When a problem frequently occurs on a specific user or in a specific area, there are some special factors to cause it in many cases. In such a case, the relevant designer and the engineer of the quality assurance department visited the site, and frequently conducted *GENCHI GENBUTSU* check to investigate the cause.

3) Participation by dealers' service staff in Claim *Asaichi*

We actively showed dealers in the United States and Europe how quality information and claimed items sent by the dealers were utilized at the vehicle manufacturing plant to solve problems.

When the dealers saw how seriously the information sent from them was handled at the plant to prevent defect reoccurrence, the trust relationship between the dealers and the plant was greatly improved. Involving dealers in our quality improvement activities, which developed into global-scale group-wide activities, was a big achievement and it became the strength of our group.

Chapter

14

Quality improvement of new model design and production preparation – For defect prevention and product value improvement

1. Reflecting on the result of Dantotsu Quality Activities-II and starting up Dantotsu-III

The results of the Dantotsu-II quality activities that were carried out at the six forklift manufacturing companies of Toyota Industries group in Japan, U.S.A., and Europe for "reducing claim costs" are shown below.

Chart 14-1　Market claim cost reduction rates

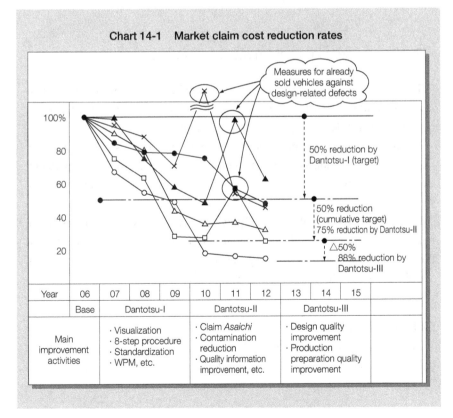

Although we did not reach the initial target of a 75% reduction after Dantotsu-II, we were able to reduce the claim costs by 52% on the annual average through implementation of the "Claim *Asaichi*" participated by all the relevant members to check all the claimed parts every morning, appoint a responsible person, and take necessary countermeasures.

However, as shown in Chart 14-1, the design quality was still very unstable, resulting in a large amount of claim costs spent on repairing the vehicles on the market that had design related defects, as well as occurrences of many market claims attributable to such defects.

Therefore, we decided to continue the Dantotsu Quality Activities for another three years as Dantotsu-III by setting a target of cumulative 88% reduction. As we had almost completed measures against existing market defects through the previous six years of activities, we shifted the focus of our activities to new models by making the utmost effort to prevent defect outflow.

2. New model's initial claim reduction target

There were many cases where a large number of claims occurred after launching a new model on the market due to outflow of defects that had been overlooked at the design or production preparation stage.

Therefore, aiming for improvements in working methods, which was the main theme of Dantotsu-III, we started with finding out where the problem existed in working methods or habits at the design and production preparation stages concerning each claim.

Based on the records of claims of previous new models, the goal was set to reduce the number of initial claims by 88% through 50% reduction on each of three models, of which design and production preparation had not been started yet (50% × 50% × 50% = 87.5% reduction) (Chart 14-2).

[Definition of initial claims]
Initial claims are defined as all of the claims that will occur in two years (24 months) after the launch of a new model.

Chart 14-2　New model's initial claim cost reduction targets (example)

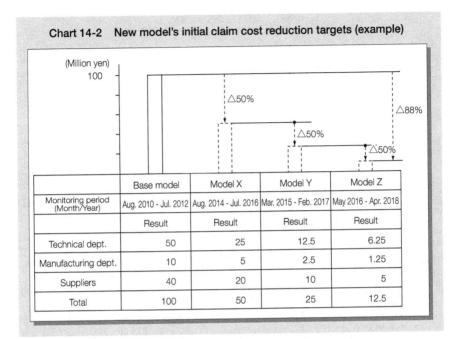

	Base model	Model X	Model Y	Model Z
Monitoring period (Month/Year)	Aug. 2010 - Jul. 2012	Aug. 2014 - Jul. 2016	Mar. 2015 - Feb. 2017	May 2016 - Apr. 2018
	Result	Result	Result	Result
Technical dept.	50	25	12.5	6.25
Manufacturing dept.	10	5	2.5	1.25
Suppliers	40	20	10	5
Total	100	50	25	12.5

[Key points of new model initial claims reduction activity]
① Selection of base vehicles and setting of target models and targets were carried out by the quality assurance department in each company.
② Although the activity period was long, it was important to go through it consistently. Under the strong leadership of the quality assurance department, the activity was carried out throughout the company.
③ With the activity clearly stated in the company's annual policy, the progress was followed up monthly by the top management until completion. Honest and consistent efforts bring about substantial results.

3. Visualization of initial claim results ... By quality assurance department

The Claim *Asaichi* team visualized the results in detail using a special form of paper for each target model and promoted early resolution of initial claim problems in collaboration with related departments. Not only the claim costs, but also the number of claims and causes & measures (for each claim) were visualized as three mandatory items (Chart 14-3).

Chart 14-3 Results of new model's initial claims

Results of new model's initial claim cost (example)

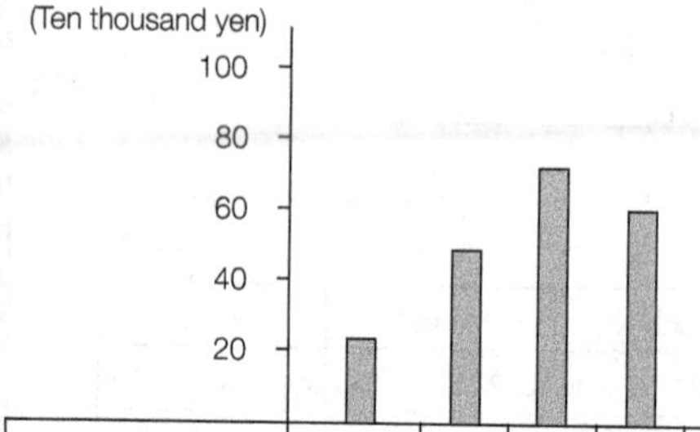

(Ten thousand yen)
100
80
60
40
20

Month/Year	Aug. 2014	9	10	11	....	16/5	6	Jul.
Technical dept.								
Manufacturing dept.								
Suppliers								
Total								
(cumulative total)	( )	( )	( )	( )		( )	( )	( )

Number of initial claims on new models (example)

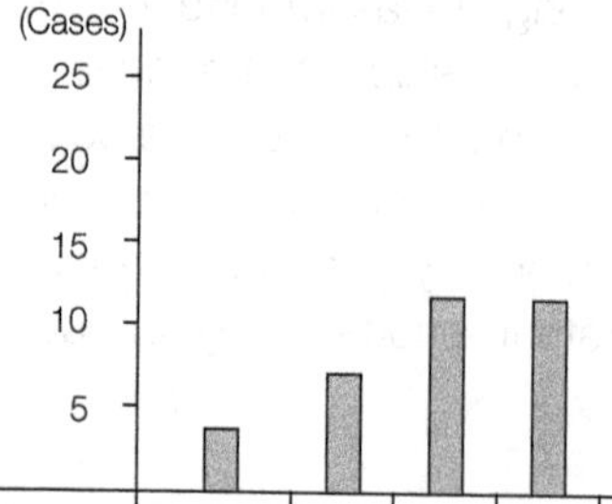

(Cases)
25
20
15
10
5

Month/Year	Aug. 2014	9	10	11	....	16/5	6	Jul.
Technical dept.								
Manufacturing dept.								
Suppliers								
Total								
(cumulative total)	( )	( )	( )	( )		( )	( )	( )

Chart 14-4　Claim Entry Sheet for each claim

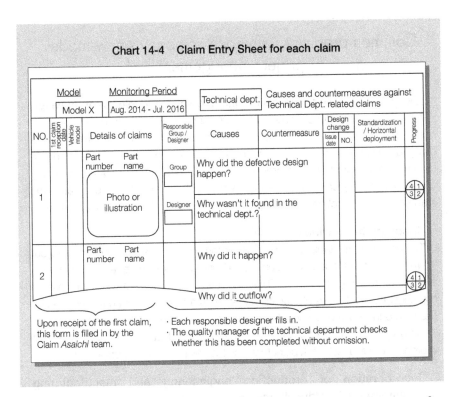

For the technical department related market claims, a countermeasure & progress meeting was held every week with the use of the sheet shown in Chart 14-4. We made it a rule to identify the responsible designer, start the cause investigation and take necessary countermeasures as soon as such the first claim occurred. Also, we registered such claims as soon as the first case occurred for new models, while we did it when the third case occurred concerning the vehicles already sold on the market.

4. Problems with new model project management

Each company's new model project management system seemed to be very good without any problems at first glance. However, during actual mass production of new models, trouble frequently occurred, causing a panic. My analysis of the current situation of each company showed that there were the following common problems.

Common problems with each company's new model project management

① Delay in production preparation due to delay in the release of drawings

Although an overall schedule table had been prepared for each project, the release of drawings from the technical department at the first process was delayed every time, causing delay in the subsequent processes and leading to a poorly prepared start of mass production. Due to insufficient process and quality assurance, quality defects and equipment trouble occurred frequently after the start of mass production, making it difficult to meet requirements (Chart 14-5).

② Incomplete drawings

The defects attributable to some faults in the product design process flowed out to the market without being detected during the design review or prototype evaluation, resulting in claims. That indicated low levels of completeness in drawings. For each case of market claims, we made a defect map related to each design group to visualize where the defect occurred in the design process and why it had gone through the quality check in the technical department. This is important in order to clarify a real weak point that was the key to recurrence prevention.

③ Incorporation of production engineering and manufacturing requirements into drawings

In order to produce quality products at low costs, it is required in the design phase not only to minimize the amount of investment by using existing facilities as much as possible, but also to take into consideration production engineering matters, such as product shapes that allow for the use of inexpensive molds and jigs. On the manufacturing side, however, the design needs to be simple so that 100% acceptable products can easily be made without disastrous mistakes simply by following the relevant drawing. When all designers are requested to incorporate both production engineering and manufacturing requirements in product design, it is sometimes difficult for them to do so due to insufficient knowledge and/or experience. In fact, it was often the case that a design problem was found after starting the design of molds and jigs, and a lot of time was spent on design change, causing delays in production preparation. Or, difficult work was found after the start of mass production, and a lot of time was spent on determining whether the design should be changed or not.

In order to avoid such trouble, it is necessary for the production engineering and manufacturing departments to standardize their requirements with the use of the SE manual and to work with the designers to incorporate those requirements into their drawings.

Chart 14-5   Problems of "baton-pass" type project management

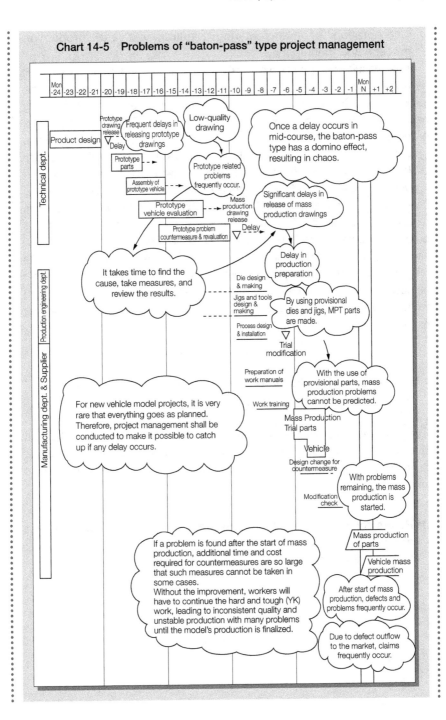

④ **Incorporation of manufacturing requirements into production process and machinery**

Once manufacturing processes designed for new parts and/or new models have been installed, they will continue to be used throughout the model life (usually five to ten years). If there is a problem with the mold and/or the jig design, workers will constantly be annoyed with such difficult-to-use molds/jigs or the resulting defects. Also, if the equipment layout makes it difficult to keep up with fluctuations in production volume, it will become impossible to increase or decrease the number of workers, resulting in a big waste of the workforce.

Even if you are aware of such a problem after starting mass production, you cannot easily change the layout due to such constraints as a large costs required and additional days for the layout change, resulting in continuous burden on workers or continuous occurrence of defects. That was often seen in each company. In order to solve such a problem, it is necessary to incorporate the manufacturing department requirements in advance into the relevant process design by standardizing the requirements in the SE manual and working with engineers of the production engineering department for designing molds, jigs, tools and the process.

5. <Measure-1> Standardization of time management and strict progress management

It is clear that the same level of time management is required throughout all phases from product development and design to mass production. Therefore, standardization of the way of time management and strict progress management must be carried out.

(1) Points for improvement in each step from product development and design to mass production

Chart 14-6 shows the case of a lead time of 24 months.

Chart 14-6   Major points of improvement in each step

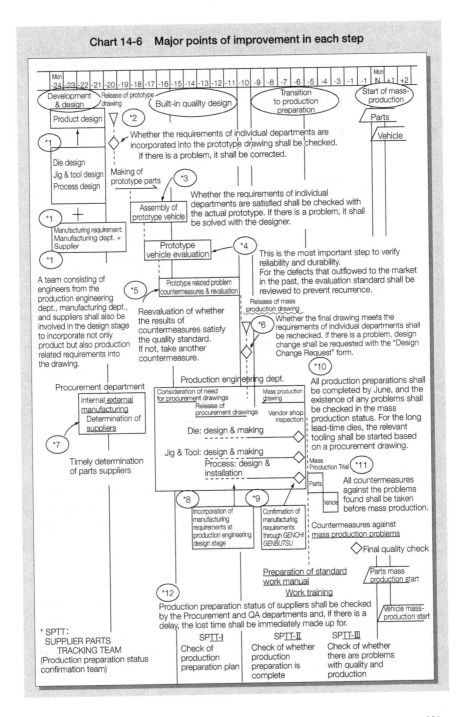

(2) Standardization of new model production overall schedule

We set up a new model project management improvement team, called "*Obeya* team" (operations command team), which worked under the direct control of the plant manager. The team's first task was to standardize the company's overall schedule (Chart 14-7).

Chart 14-7 New Model Project Management Improvement Team (*Obeya* team)

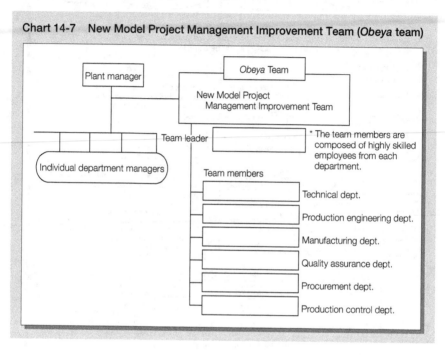

[Mission of *Obeya* team]

The team's mission was to achieve the start of trouble-free mass production within the limited lead time of 24 months through standardization and implementation of schedules through teamwork. First, the team standardized the plant's overall schedule as shown in Chart 14-6.

Then, it standardized the detailed schedules of individual departments on the overall schedule. The individual departments' schedules were properly incorporated into the overall schedule based on the opinions and advice of the members who had participated in the previous new model projects through discussion about the problems that had occurred in the past and how to prevent them from reoccurring.

(3) Strict progress management

It was not allowed to delay the new car launch time promised to dealers due to the plant's circumstances. Therefore, even if there is a delay in production preparation, we had to start mass production as scheduled, so that various problems occurred, such as outflow of many quality defects, production delays due to various trouble, and delayed dispatch of vehicles, resulting in major waste.

In order to put an end to such major waste, it is imperative for management to seriously work on drastic improvement of the operation of the new model car project.

Key points for strict progress management

(1) Individual department's progress management
- The plan and actual results were visualized, with a red mark put on the items that were behind schedule.
- The progress was checked by the general manager at least for an hour once a week.

  For delayed items, the general manager discussed with the subordinates the countermeasures to make up for lost time within a week and instruct them to take them.

② Overall progress management
The overall and individual department's progresses was checked by top management once a month based on the overall schedule and detailed schedules of individual departments, which had been visualized by the *Obeya* team. The general managers who were responsible for behind-schedule items (red marked) explained some catch-up measures, which implementation was led by them.

 Even if they explained it in a makeshift manner, that would be soon exposed because some problems would surely occur due to the delay. It is important to conduct progress management honestly without sweeping things under the carpet.

6. <Measure-2> Improvement of design drawing completeness

Problems related to new technologies are sometimes inevitable, but we have to make efforts not to cause recurrence of problems experienced in the past.

(1) Visualization of weak points by creating a design process defect map

After the launch of Claim *Asaichi*, more than three cases of similar claims occurred, so we performed visualization of problems by using a defect map showing all design-related defect items registered and countermeasures for vehicles sold on the market in order to find out a real weakness (Chart 14-8).

 For manufacturing related quality defects occurring day by day in the plants, the cause was investigated and countermeasures were taken within that day, and they were reported at the next morning's Asaichi meeting. If the defect was attributable to the fault of a worker who had not followed the standard work procedure, re-education and/or retraining was provided to the worker immediately. Thus, ceaseless efforts for zero defects were

Chart 14-8   Defect Map of design process

Base of design work

What was the problem?
?

*1 Design standard

Why was it overlooked?
?

Base of design quality

Evaluation standard

What was insufficient?
?

Why was it overlooked?
?

Why was it overlooked?
?

*3 Design Review   Prototype drawing release

Prototype evaluation

Product design

Prototype vehicle Assembling

Mass production drawing creation   Design review   Release of drawing

Production preparation

Mass Production Trial vehicle Assembling

Defective design

Prototype related problem + Rejection

*2 Designer

What was the design error?
?

Evaluator

Why was the defect judged as OK?

For all defects that caused three or more cases of market claims individually and against which measures have been taken in the market, the sources of occurrence and outflow shall be visualized on the defect map.
(It shall be created on each design group.) → Real weak points shall be found, and thorough measures for recurrence prevention shall be taken.

204

made through daily routine. On the other hand, concerning market defects, sufficient countermeasures had not been taken, except those against serious defects, because the relevant information did not reach the person who had caused or flowed out the defect or the information was insufficient. That situation was greatly improved after implementation of the Claim *Asaichi*, which enabled us to take recurrence prevention measures against all market defects as those against the manufacturing related quality defects. By doing it thoroughly as a main activity of Dantotsu-III, we were approaching the target of 88% reduction in claim costs.

(2) Countermeasures against design faults by creating the Design SE Manual

The SE Manual stands for Simultaneous Engineering Manual. In order to prevent problems that had occurred in the past from recurring, we created this manual for incorporation and accumulation of our past knowledge and knowhow, which should be regarded as an asset of the organization (Chart 14-9).

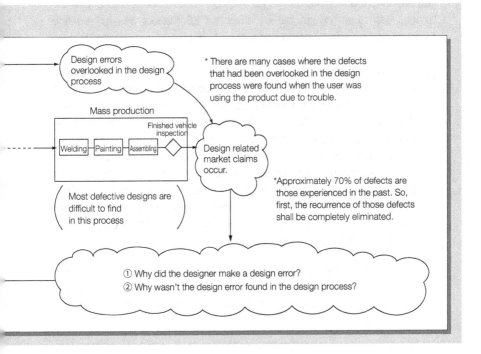

Background and concept of creating Design SE Manual

- **Problems with the current system ... (See Chart 14-8)**

  (*1) Because the design standard alone is not enough to clarify what should be or should not be done in product design, it is difficult to detect incorrect or inappropriate design for market needs.

  (*2) Design mistakes were also attributable to faults of inexperienced design engineers due to a high turnover rate of designers at overseas plants and a lot of temporary technical staff at domestic plants.

  (*3) In addition, drawing check items and judgment criteria were abstractly described, so that design defects were sometimes overlooked due to differences in ability and experience of checkers.

- **Countermeasure**

  - In order to cope with the above situation, we created an SE Manual that enabled comparison between the design which had caused the defect in the past and the required design for each part or each vehicle (one item per sheet). Each time any trouble occurred, an SE Manual was revised and retained as the property of individual departments.

    It is not possible to create and complete the SE Manual without decisions and strong follow-up by the top management. This is because it cannot so easily be prepared simply by instructing design staff to make it in their spare time. The manual is an indispensable tool for preventing quality defects or production trouble from occurring at the time of the launch of a new model, so it is strongly recommended to complete it by investing in lots of talented staff members and spending sufficient time. That depends on the decision by respective general managers of not only the technical department, but also production engineering and manufacturing departments.

  - When designing, the design staff checked both the design standard and the SE Manual corresponding to the part or vehicle to be designed, and created a drawing while comparing the ideal design with the previous defective design.

Chart 14-9   Design SE Manual (example)

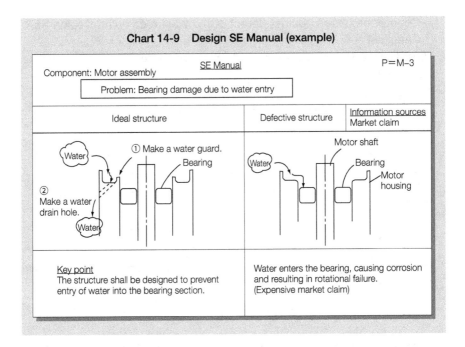

SE Manual

Component: Motor assembly

P=M–3

Problem: Bearing damage due to water entry

Ideal structure	Defective structure	Information sources Market claim

Key point
The structure shall be designed to prevent entry of water into the bearing section.

Water enters the bearing, causing corrosion and resulting in rotational failure.
(Expensive market claim)

 A claim attributable to entry of water or dust was a weak point common to each company.

When a negative pressure developed in a part, water or dust was sucked inside through a small hole or gap, causing malfunction after a certain period of time. Since it was difficult to detect such a defect in the conventional way of reading drawings, we created the SE Manual for each part on which water or dust related defects previously occurred for the purpose of preventing the recurrence of the same defect.

[Claims attributable to entry of water and/or dust]
- Inoperative switch, sensor, etc. due to entry of water
- Short-circuiting due to entry of water into a wiring connector
- Braking failure or abnormal noise due to entry of water into a brake
- Inoperative parking brake due to entry of water into a parking brake cable area
- Horn failure due to entry of dust into a horn

(3) Countermeasures against defect outflow sources using Design SE Checklist

Based on the SE Manual, we created an SE Checklist for each part or vehicle (Chart 14-10).

Chart 14-10 SE Checklist (example)

Parts   SE Checklist

Motor Assembly

NO.	Description	SE Manual page	① Designer	② Prototype drawing	③ Prototype vehicle	④ Mass production drawing
1			☐	☐	☐	☐
2.	Water entry into motor	M-3	☑	☑	☑	☑
3.			☐	☐	☐	☐

According to the SE Checklist, we checked the quality of each drawing at the steps ① through ④ shown in Chart 14-11 to ensure defect-free drawings before making the relevant molds, jigs, and tools.

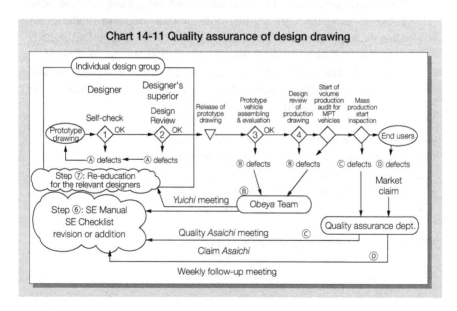

Chart 14-11 Quality assurance of design drawing

The quality assurance department, which is responsible for feedback on quality defect information, not only provided the quality information on design-related Type ⒟ defects and confirmed the preventive measures, but also followed up the implementation of the recurrence prevention steps ⑥ "Standardization and Horizontal deployment" and ⑦ "Education & training", among the eight steps, as in the case of the manufacturing related defects.

(4) Countermeasures against overlooking during prototype vehicle evaluation

As it was not possible for us to confirm whether the vehicle's reliability and durability conformed to the market needs simply by reading drawings, we conducted evaluation tests using a prototype vehicle to confirm it. Despite the fact that our vehicles had passed all the rigorous tests and were launched on the market with confidence, various problems arose due to lack of reliability and durability in reality. In those cases, we clarified the cause of defect outflows for each market claim and implemented thorough recurrence prevention measures (Chart 14-12).

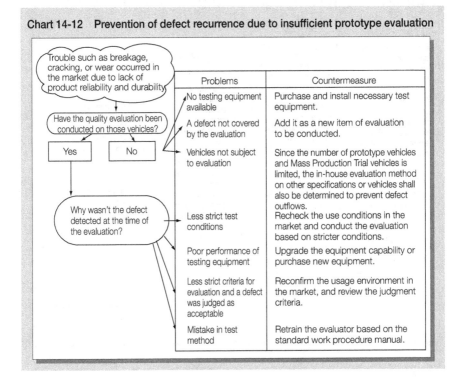

Chart 14-12　Prevention of defect recurrence due to insufficient prototype evaluation

7. <Measure-3> SE activities to incorporate production engineering and manufacturing requirements into drawings

Even if you finally notice a design problem due to occurrence of quality defects or trouble after launch of mass production, that is too late. Even a small problem takes major time and money to solve it. If it cannot be solved, plant workers will have to continue to do difficult-to-handle work or inevitably continue to produce defects for five to ten years until next model change is made. Therefore, production engineering and manufacturing supervisors at vehicle manufacturing plants, as well as suppliers, must establish and implement an appropriate system for SE activities that will completely prevent the recurrence of any quality and productivity related problems experienced so far.

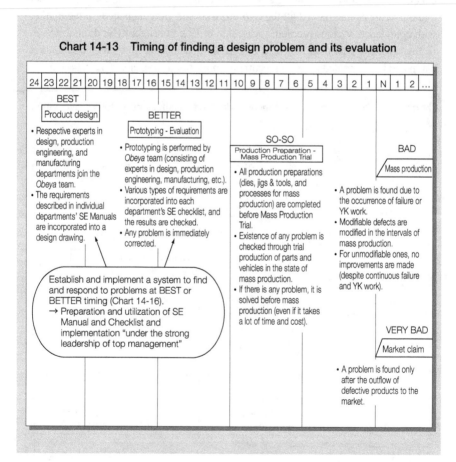

Chart 14-13   Timing of finding a design problem and its evaluation

(1) Timing of finding a design problem and its evaluation

Most preferable (evaluated as "Best") is to find a design related problem at the time of designing and solving it quickly. If it is found in the prototype phase, then the timing of problem finding is evaluated as "Better". If a problem is found at the production preparation stage, the evaluation of the timing is "So-so". If it is discovered after the start of mass production, it is "Bad", and if it is found on the market, it is evaluated as "Very bad" (Chart 14-13).

1) What kind of waste will occur if the discovery of the design problem is delayed?

<Example> Protrusion of a weld nut due to improper hole position for the nut

The weld nuts are fed automatically by feeders. If a nut is fed as shown in the figure, the protrusion defect will occur at the corner (even though the operation is correctly performed according to the drawing).

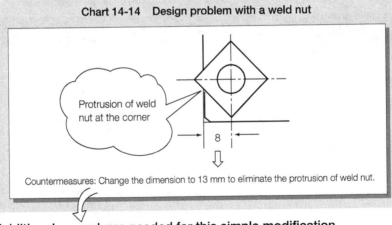

Chart 14-14　Design problem with a weld nut

Protrusion of weld nut at the corner

8

Countermeasures: Change the dimension to 13 mm to eliminate the protrusion of weld nut.

Additional procedures needed for this simple modification

① Creation and issuance of "Design Change Request" ... Manufacturing department
② Creation and issuance of "Design Change Instructions" ... Technical department
③ Creation and issuance of "Press Die Modification Instruction" ... Production engineering department
④ Implementation of press die modification ..."Laborious work"

Only "changing the punching position by 5 mm" requires the following operations: Disassembling the dies → Filling the existing hole → Punching another hole (at a 5-mm-deeper position) → Reassembling the dies → Trial pressing for check.

⑤ Final check with the relevant machine and start of new parts production
⑥ Check for elimination of the nut protrusion defect

If the manufacturing department's requirement of "weld nut hole position" is incorporated from the beginning in the design phase, there will not be such wasteful additional work as described above.

2) Estimated time required to complete countermeasures after problem finding

Depending on the timing of problem finding, the time required for the countermeasures against design problems greatly varies as shown in Chart 14-15. Therefore, it is necessary to establish and implement a system that enables the problems experienced in the past to be detected without omissions in the "Best" or "Better" timing and to be quickly solved.

Chart 14-15   Estimated time required to complete countermeasures after problem finding

Evaluation	Timing	Period required MIN~MAX	Description
BEST	Product design stage	1 hour to 1 day	Any problem can be easily corrected with a computer.
BETTER	Prototyping - Evaluation	1 week to 1 month	It takes some time to consider countermeasures, re-prototype the product and recheck it.
SO-SO	Production preparation - Mass Production Trial	1 month to 3 months	Time is required to modify dies, jigs, tools and processes that have been made or established.
BAD	During mass-production	3 months to 1 year	It takes a lot of time because the measures are taken in the intervals of mass production, or on weekends. Taking measures will become impossible if the cost is too high.
VERY BAD	Market claim	1 year to 3 years	Generally, it takes about three years until the claim ends because a lot of defective vehicles have flowed out to the market.

(2) Design problem prevention by using production engineering and manufacturing SE Manuals

It is ideal that high quality products can be easily produced 100% without trouble only by strictly following design drawings and the standard work procedure. Chart 14-16 indicates a system to realize it.

Chart 14-16 Prevention of design problems based on the SE Manual of the manufacturing or production engineering dept.

Step	Implementation flowchart	Key point
1	Design problems that have occurred at the start of mass production of new model vehicles so far are identified. • Quality defects, • YK work, etc.	Problems shall be classified and listed in individual departments and processes. Not only the opinions of the staff who conducted production preparations, but also the opinions and requests of other workers shall be incorporated into the manual.
2	Creation of SE Manual	To be created to describe one case per sheet

Example of Manufacturing department's SE Manual

Weld nut: Hole position	SE Manual: Page = N-01
Ideal structure	Problematic design

Nut size	Dimension "K"
M4~M12	13 or more

Standard or limit value

Nut size	Feeder	Manual setting
M6	9 mm	7 mm
M8	10	7
M10	11	8
M12	13	9

* In case of manual setting, work time of four seconds per piece is required.

Nut protrusion defect — M8 weld nut — 8 mm (too small)

* It is impossible to control the orientation of the nut in accordance with the part's shape through automatic feed by the nut feeder.

* This can solve the problem, but the nut cannot be controlled as intended.

Information source

In-process defects	Defects in finished vehicle inspection	Market claim

3	Creation of SE Checklist	To be created for each process or design group

Welding: SE Checklist

Part number   Part name   Checker

NO.	Check item	Ref. page in Manual	Month/day	/	/	Comment
			Prototype drawing	Prototype vehicle	Mass production drawing	
1	Weld nut: Hole position	N-01	☐	☐	☐	
2	Spot welding: Welding point	N-02	☐	☐	☐	
3	Arc welding: Torch access	N-10	☐	☐	☐	

Step	Implementation flowchart	Key point
4	Prior explanation to designers. The created SE manual is explained to individual designers to have them understand and use it in their design work.	Even if designers do not know past failure cases, they can see the requirements of the subsequent process by referring to the SE Manual, and can incorporate them into their drawings. (The manual shall be used in conjunction with the design standards.)
5	SE Manual & Checklist based new vehicle project management. • An *Obeya* team is organized for each new car project. • Production engineering and manufacturing departments incorporate their respective requirements into the design drawing based on their own SE Manuals and Checklists. • The required design quality is built in through the Prototyping to Mass production trial phases.	Aiming for the start of trouble-free mass production, the members of *Obeya* team selected from each department shall make concerted and united efforts to progress the project. "The key to success is effective cross-departmental team management"
6	Review of mass production results After three months from the start of mass production, a review meeting is held and a list of problems that occurred is made to prevent recurrence.	For each problem, clarify whether it was a problem with the SE Manual or the way of conducting the SE Review and, whenever necessary, add or revise the SE Manual.

Implement the following for each problem that occurred in the first three months after the start of mass production of this new vehicle model.

Is it described in the SE Manual & Checklist?

NO

YES

Add to SE manual. Add to Checklist.

Why did it recur?

There is a problem with the description of the SE Manual.

Judgment error by a checker (SE Manual has no problem.)

Revise the SE Manual. Revise the Checklist.

Reeducation and retraining for the checker

Completion of revised SE Manual & Checklist

It shall be fully used for the next new model project.

Examples of manufacturing problems caused by design

① **Defects occurred even if products were made strictly according to the drawing ... 100% quality assurance was impossible**
- A corner radius was too tight, causing press cracking.
- A spot welding position was too close to the end face, causing spot burr.
- Plating was impossible due to air in the surface of part, requiring an air vent hole.
- A gap between the pipe and accessories was too narrow to secure a sufficient angle for a torch.

② **"YK" work (difficult-to-do, dangerous, tough, and/or special attention-required work)**
- Vertical use of a tool was impossible, leading to insufficient tightening of bolts and nuts at an angle and causing a tightening failure.
- A thick and hard high-pressure hose made centering with the pipe difficult, causing oil leakage.
- Loctite liquid applied to the bolt thread part dripped down on hands.
- Setting washers on small bolts was difficult with gloved hands.
- Identifying similar parts only from the appearance was difficult, causing wrong assembly.

③ **Cost increase factors**
- Special, difficult-to-obtain materials were required, taking long lead time.
- Designed structures required special cutting blades and tools.
- There were many similar products with slight differences in dimension and shape.
  etc

8. <Measure-4> SE activities to incorporate manufacturing requirements into production process and equipment

As in the case of design problems, it is not easy to take countermeasures against any problem after you have made dies/molds, jigs/tools, and machines/processes that are necessary for production. If there is any unsolvable problem, heavy burden on workers and various kinds of waste will continue to occur for many years resulting from the problem as long as the relevant model exists in the market.

To avoid such a situation, what is needed is the SE activity to incorporate manufacturing requirements and defect recurrence prevention measures into the design drawings and equipment specifications before the production engineering department starts production. The manufacturing department's requirements for production engineering were standardized in the SE Manual and also incorporated into the equipment design and process plan at the SE meeting with the production engineering department to prevent the recurrence of trouble (Chart 14-7).

Chart 14-17 Prevention of production engineering related problems by using the SE Manual & Checklist

NO.	Item	Implementation Items
1	Creation of production engineering related SE Manual & Checklist	1) The production equipment and process related safety, quality, production, and cost problems that have occurred so far after the start of mass production of new vehicles are identified according to each process (pressing, welding, assembling, etc.). 2) An SE Manual is created for each process to illustrate the previous production engineering related problems and their recurrence prevention measures, with each problem described on each sheet.

Press die: Material positioning Page = Die-03

Countermeasure	Defect occurred
LH material cannot be set. Setting of incorrect materials can be prevented with the setting guides.	Erroneous set of similar materials. RH — LH material can also be set. Locating pins
Check	Checked by setting a similar material.	Information source	In-process defects

3) Creation of SE Checklist

Press Die SE Checklist   Checker: ○○

Check item	Page	① Design	② Vendor shop inspection	③ MPT	Comment
1 Setting of incorrect material	Die-03	✓	✓	✓	OK
2					

NO.	Item	Implementation Items
2	Production preparation overall schedule	Possible problems in mass production are predicted in the Mass Production Trial phase, and the full-scale mass production is started after taking all preventive measures. For that purpose, an overall schedule is prepared to enable all production preparations to be completed before the Mass Production Trial, and all departments work in accordance with the schedule.

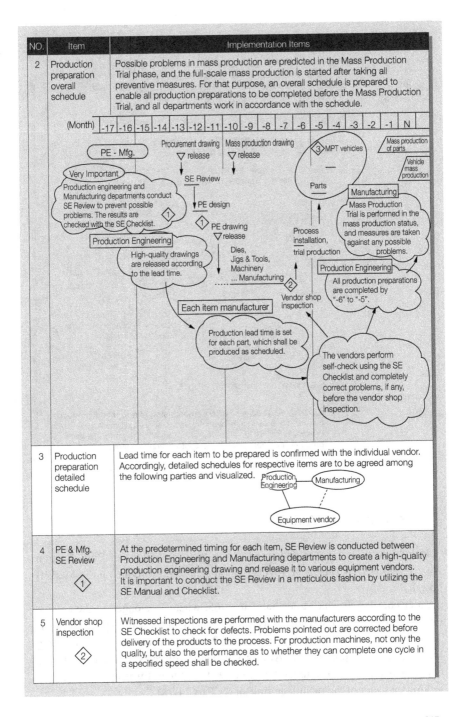

3	Production preparation detailed schedule	Lead time for each item to be prepared is confirmed with the individual vendor. Accordingly, detailed schedules for respective items are to be agreed among the following parties and visualized.
4	PE & Mfg. SE Review	At the predetermined timing for each item, SE Review is conducted between Production Engineering and Manufacturing departments to create a high-quality production engineering drawing and release it to various equipment vendors. It is important to conduct the SE Review in a meticulous fashion by utilizing the SE Manual and Checklist.
5	Vendor shop inspection	Witnessed inspections are performed with the manufacturers according to the SE Checklist to check for defects. Problems pointed out are corrected before delivery of the products to the process. For production machines, not only the quality, but also the performance as to whether they can complete one cycle in a specified speed shall be checked.

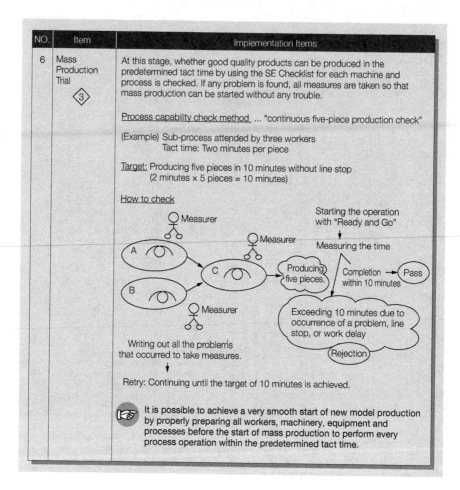

NO.	Item	Implementation Items
6	Mass Production Trial ③	At this stage, whether good quality products can be produced in the predetermined tact time by using the SE Checklist for each machine and process is checked. If any problem is found, all measures are taken so that mass production can be started without any trouble.

Process capability check method ... "continuous five-piece production check"

(Example) Sub-process attended by three workers
Tact time: Two minutes per piece

Target: Producing five pieces in 10 minutes without line stop
(2 minutes × 5 pieces = 10 minutes)

How to check

Measurer

Starting the operation with "Ready and Go"

Measuring the time

A

Measurer

C

Producing five pieces.

Completion within 10 minutes → Pass

B

Measurer

Exceeding 10 minutes due to occurrence of a problem, line stop, or work delay

Rejection

Writing out all the problems that occurred to take measures.

Retry: Continuing until the target of 10 minutes is achieved.

It is possible to achieve a very smooth start of new model production by properly preparing all workers, machinery, equipment and processes before the start of mass production to perform every process operation within the predetermined tact time.

9. Benefits of SE Manual

In February 1985, I was appointed as the section manager of Body Section No.2 of Body Department of Toyota Motomachi Plant (producing the Mark II body).

After entering Toyota Motor Sales in 1965, where I belonged to the service department and then the overseas assembly department, I was dispatched to PT. Toyota-Astra Motor in Indonesia in 1979 as an instructor in assembling knocked down imported cars. After a big merger of sales and manufacturing departments in 1982, I returned home in 1984, and then I was appointed as the section manager of the manufacturing site (Chart 14-18).

Chart 14-18   Author's history

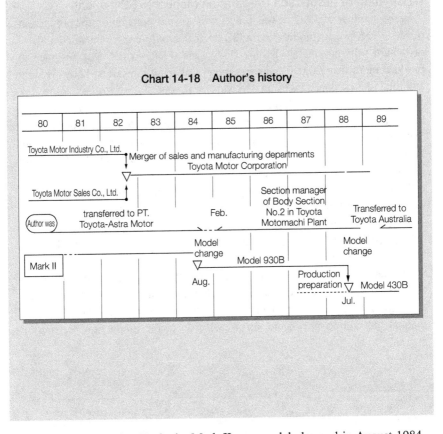

In the Body Section No.2, the Mark II was model-changed in August 1984, and a new model code 930B was being mass-produced. However, during five months of production, quality and production related trouble constantly occurred, and everybody had to work overtime for many hours to achieve the target production volume. Even after each day's production activities, the group leaders and team leaders had to rework quality defects and were too busy to talk with other members. Such a busy situation lasted about one year, and finally the production came under control after the year 1986.

In those days, such a hectic time after the start of mass production was not a rare case at Toyota, so most workers said "This is something usual". In fact, I was impressed by Toyota's hard workers reworking quality defects for many hours even after long-time daily production to respond to the new car demand. However, frankly, I thought it would be difficult for them to keep up such hard working conditions.

(1) Creation of Production Preparation Manual (= SE manual)

In the summer of 1987, it was time for us to start preparation for production of the next Mark II (model code 430B). For that purpose, we installed a state-of-the-art, fully-automatic Flexible Body Line (FBL), which was designed to produce more than 20,000 units per month, offering the fastest body welding tact time of 54 seconds by using 216 welding robots.

However, if we had such problems as those with the previous model 930B at the time of launching, we would cause a lot of trouble to the sales department and dealers, with the large planned volume taken into consideration. Furthermore, I was strongly requested to prevent the same failures from occurring during production preparation.

Therefore, I decided to devote myself to the production preparation work for the model 430B for one year, while entrusting daily production work to a deputy section manager.

The first thing I had to do was to create a "Production Preparation Manual". To get previous information, I asked a person who had worked as a leader for the model 930B production preparation to recall and tell me his experience in those days, and we worked in a room all day long. Then, in order to not repeat the same mistake in the next model production, I requested him to create a manual that allows anyone to see what to do at the production preparation stage.

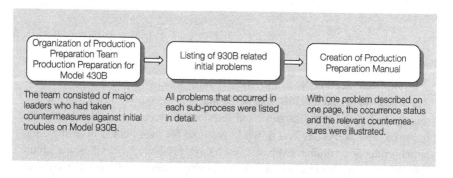

Organization of Production Preparation Team Production Preparation for Model 430B	Listing of 930B related initial problems	Creation of Production Preparation Manual
The team consisted of major leaders who had taken countermeasures against initial troubles on Model 930B.	All problems that occurred in each sub-process were listed in detail.	With one problem described on one page, the occurrence status and the relevant countermeasures were illustrated.

Although creating a manual in the room for three months seemed to be very painful for the man usually working on production lines, the completed manual was very practical one because it was based on the facts and his experience.

Based on this manual, we have modified and revised its contents for every subsequent model change, and named the manual the "SE Manual", which is still used now.

(2) 430B production preparation activity

Chart 14-19 shows what was implemented during the 430B production preparation period by using the production preparation manual and checklist.

Chart 14-19   Major implementation items for 430B production preparation

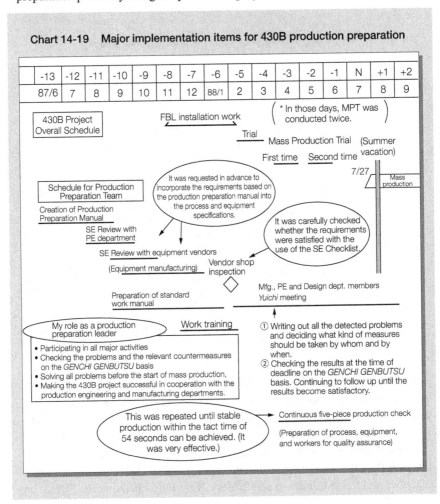

(3) Result of 430B mass-production start

Although I felt that almost all preventive measures against the problems experienced in production of the previous model 930B had been taken, nobody knew what would happen at the time of launching a new model. Therefore, I prepared for unexpected quality defects by organizing a reworking team consisting of five veteran team leaders so that rework can be done quickly during production hours. And finally, we started the mass production. It was planned that the production volume would be increased step by step, shifting to full production in four weeks (Chart 14-20).

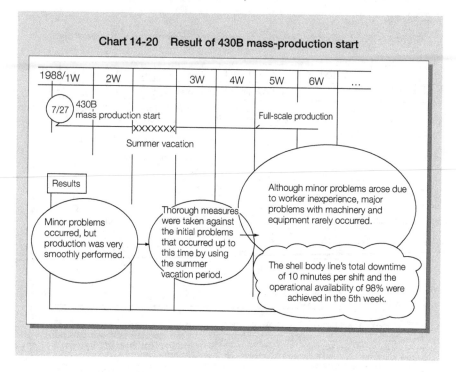

Chart 14-20   Result of 430B mass-production start

The first Production Preparation Manual was very rudimentary, but the result was far above our expectation as shown above. While it took more than a year to stabilize the production of the previous model 930B, it took only one month until the 430B production became stable enough to meet the market demand.

Coupled with the "bubble economy" in Japan, this new Mark II was a huge hit, with the sales exceeding 30,000 units per month. I still remember the days when we were able to mass-produce Mark II by fully operating the FBL at as fast as 54 seconds.

(4) Benefits of Production Preparation Manual (= SE Manual)

From my experience at Toyota Motor, and from the results of the Dantotsu-III activities at Toyota Industries later, I believe that the SE Manual will surely bring about some great effects.

Benefits of SE manual

① **Enabling problem finding at the "Best" (design stage) or the "Better" (prototype evaluation stage) timing.**

Since it visualizes what will happen from certain types of design based on past findings, it is easy to discover design problems and obtain consent of design and production engineering departments, allowing for quick countermeasures.

② **Minimizing variations in worker's performance.**

Even people who have never experienced any trouble or who have never done production preparation can make it without a mistake if they follow the manual and do "what they should do". Especially, it is very effective in overseas plants where employee turnover is high.

③ **Minimizing waste of time and money.**

If you notice a problem through trouble or market claims after the start of mass production and try to take necessary countermeasures, enormous cost and time will be necessary. To avoid such unnecessarily large waste, design and review based on SE Manual is indispensable.

As mentioned above, the SE Manual and SE Checklist, which visualizes past wisdom, are powerful tools to dramatically improve the work quality at the stages from new product development to production preparation. It is recommended that the top management consider creating the manual as an asset of the company and utilize it for better results. Without strong will from top management, it is impossible to make this system work satisfactorily.

Quality defects inevitably occur sooner or later unless all the 4M factors (Man, Material, Machine and Method) are perfect. Therefore, it can be said that "quality is a barometer of a company's strength" (Chart 15-1).

So far I have mainly described the ways to make Materials, Machines and Methods perfect through such methods as visualization, the 8-step procedure, standardization, and Claim *Asaichi*, from the viewpoint of managers and supervisors. However, it is the Men (individual workers) who actually make things one by one. Unless all the workers, who are directly involved with manufacturing, make up their minds to improve, it is impossible to achieve the zero quality defects.

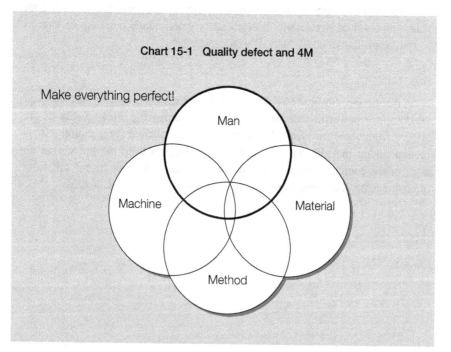

Chart 15-1   Quality defect and 4M

Make everything perfect!

Man

Machine

Material

Method

Then, how can you motivate those workers, who had just happened to work in the same company, to become enthusiastic workers about achieving the zero defects? One of the solutions is to create a teamwork culture based on the "QC circle".

The following describes an example of the QC circle activities that I joined and worked with the local staff at Toyota South Africa for five-and-a-half years from 1997. Although the notorious Apartheid (a system of institutionalized racial segregation and discrimination) was abolished in 1991, and President Mandela took office in 1994, color discrimination still remained remarkable in South Africa. In that country, it was the QC circle activities that made the oppressed people open up their minds.

The data shown below are those used at "All Toyota TQM Competition in 2004", which is an annual QC event held by Toyota Group.

QC circle-based quality improvement activities at Toyota South Africa

The Republic of South Africa is a beautiful lush country located at the southern tip of the African continent. Although it is the largest country in Africa, blessed with precious material resources such as diamonds, gold and platinum, it has a long history of difficult going as a European colony. It had been isolated from the world because of the Apartheid (a system of institutionalized racial segregation and discrimination) since 1948, but finally joined the world in 1991 with the abolition of the notorious system.

Chart 15-2   Outline of the Republic of South Africa

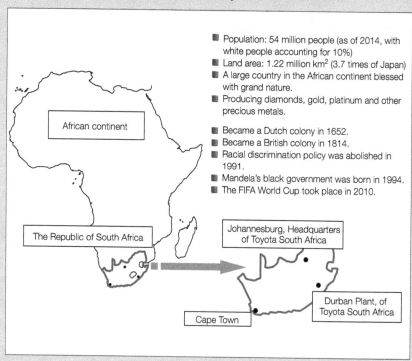

- Population: 54 million people (as of 2014, with white people accounting for 10%)
- Land area: 1.22 million km² (3.7 times of Japan)
- A large country in the African continent blessed with grand nature.
- Producing diamonds, gold, platinum and other precious metals.

- Became a Dutch colony in 1652.
- Became a British colony in 1814.
- Racial discrimination policy was abolished in 1991.
- Mandela's black government was born in 1994.
- The FIFA World Cup took place in 2010.

African continent

The Republic of South Africa

Johannesburg, Headquarters of Toyota South Africa

Durban Plant, of Toyota South Africa

Cape Town

It was in 1962 when Toyota Motor entered the South African market. In those days, most roads except main highways were not paved in that country, so the market share of Toyota vehicles that were strong against rough roads steadily increased, and in 1980, Toyota gained the largest share there by defeating its European and American competitors. Since then, the company has maintained the top position for 35 years or more. Until 1984, Fiat and Volvo vehicles were also produced at the same plant, but in 1985 it was rebuilt as a dedicated Toyota plant to respond to the increased demand for Toyota cars, and has been working only for Toyota since then.

Chart   15-3 History of Toyota South Africa
- Friendly relationship with Toyota for 53 years -

1962	Started CKD production of Toyota Stout.
1971	Constructed a new factory in Durban.
1972	Established Toyota Motor Industry FRO.
1980	Achieved the largest share in the South African market. (Continuing for 35 years since then)
1985	Became a 100% Toyota vehicle dedicated plant.
1996	Toyota acquired 27.8% of the stock.
1997	Three production-related experts (including the author) were transferred.
2002	Toyota acquired 75% of the stock.
2003	Started exporting Corolla to Australia.
2005	Started exporting IMV to Europe

Historically, such European car manufacturers as VW, BMW and Mercedes Benz, were strong in South Africa's automobile industry by taking advantage of the government's export promotion program to increase the exports of South African-made cars and by using those profits to lower the selling price of domestic cars and expand their market shares.

Under such circumstances, Toyota South Africa, which gained few benefits from the export-incentive program at that time, was losing its market share little by little, with the profitability sharply declining. Therefore, the South African subsidiary asked the Toyota headquarters for assistance, and three persons including me were dispatched there temporarily.

Chart 15-4   South African automotive industry

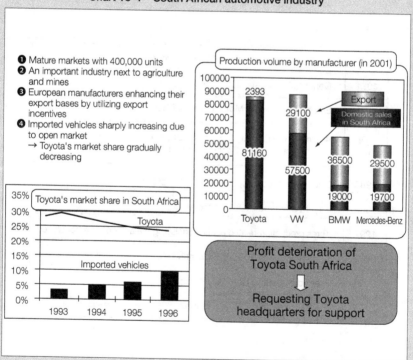

❶ Mature markets with 400,000 units
❷ An important industry next to agriculture and mines
❸ European manufacturers enhancing their export bases by utilizing export incentives
❹ Imported vehicles sharply increasing due to open market
 → Toyota's market share gradually decreasing

Production volume by manufacturer (in 2001)

Export
Domestic sales in South Africa

Toyota 2393 / 81160
VW 29100 / 57500
BMW 36500 / 19000
Mercedes-Benz 29500 / 19700

Toyota's market share in South Africa
Toyota
Imported vehicles
1993 1994 1995 1996

Profit deterioration of Toyota South Africa
⬇
Requesting Toyota headquarters for support

The mission given to us was "to change Toyota South Africa into a profitable company by enabling them to produce export quality cars". That means we had to make the quality of the locally produced vehicles equal to that of Japanese-made ones. However, according to the results of the quality audit conducted by a quality audit team sent from the Quality Assurance Department of Japan's headquarters, the quality of vehicles produced by Toyota South Africa was the worst among Toyota's overseas plants, as shown in the graph. Every day, I was thinking about how to improve the product quality in the plant where the white-vs.-black racial problem still remained remarkable.

Chart 15-5   A mission given to the author

> **To make it a profitable company by realizing export through achievement of world-class quality and stable production**

Results of quality assurance audit
on vehicles produced abroad

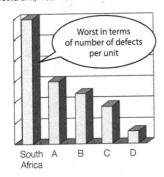

(Defects/unit) Year 1996

Worst in terms
of number of defects
per unit

South Africa   A   B   C   D

Other problems (1997)

(1) Frequent occurrence of strikes
· Strong power of British-style labor union
· White vs. black racial problem

(2) Large-variety, small-volume production of as many as eight models

(3) Crowded plant and office
9,000 employees producing 90,000 units a year

(4) Sharp deterioration in earnings
Restrictions on selling price increases due to competition with imported cars

To start with grasping the current situation, I walked around the plant, carefully looking at each process. The plant was overflowing with workers. As they flocked around a car for assembling, I couldn't find the person in charge for each operation. Since the cars flowed out to the subsequent processes without proper quality checks, innumerable quality defects were outflowing. For that reason, many defects were detected in the finished vehicle inspection, where a special reworking group consisting of as many as 200 workers corrected those defects before delivery to the market. However, there were many defects that were difficult to correct in the state of the finished car. In addition, defects that were overlooked in the inspection also outflowed to the market in large quantities. Therefore, I wondered what I would have to do first.

Chart 15-6   State of manufacturing at South Africa Toyota in 1997

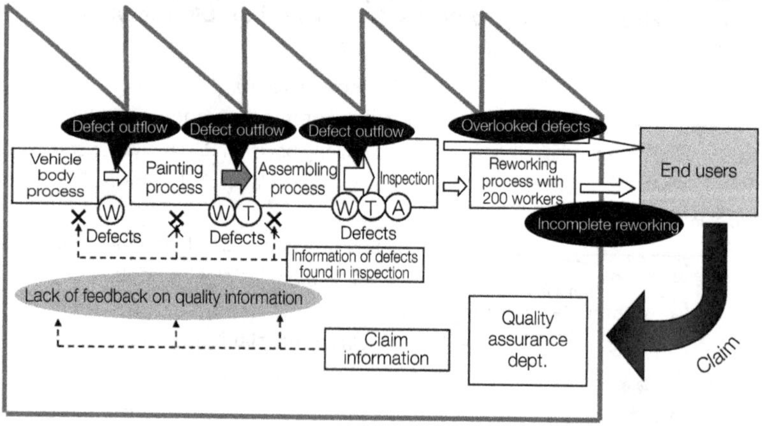

A large number of defective parts passed through every process and outflowed to the market without completely correcting the defects to.

(W) Vehicle body process   (T) Painting process   (A) Assembling process

The first step of improvement is the visualization of bad things. So we began to hold the Quality *Asaichi* (morning meeting) every morning, where the defects found in the finished vehicle inspection on the previous day were visualized, with responsible departments identified, and the results were checked by the president, plant manager, and each department's general manager. Next, I requested individual department's general managers to record the defects frequently found in each department, locate the relevant causes, and take necessary measures under their own responsibilities. Then, I taught the ways to locate the cause and take countermeasures day after day at the work site to management, such as section managers, general managers and plant manager, who were not willing to see the work site and tended to stay in individual rooms.

Chart 15-7   Improvement activities starting with "Quality visualization"

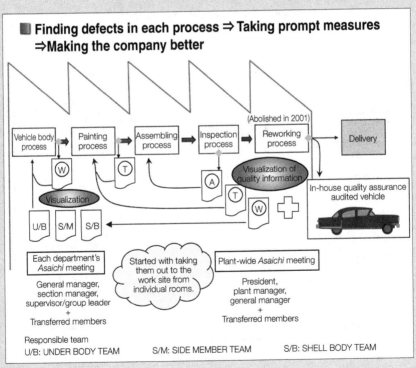

The following chart indicates major improvement activities for the first three years. Regarding the education about work site management for management people and supervisors who did not fully understand the fundamentals, I requested the Tahara Plant in Japan to accept 150 persons in total (seven times) including general managers and other managing staff and give them the *GENCHI GENBUTSU* (on-site check of actual items) training for two weeks. After the training, I asked the trainers to come to South Africa for two months and to conduct process improvement activities together with the trainees in the South African plant. Ill-reputed toilets, eating places, etc, in the South African plant were greatly improved after such study visits to Toyota U.S.A. and U.K. plants. In addition, a resting place was newly set up for each team, allowing team members to take seats and have meetings or do writing work. Three years passed as we implemented those things.

Chart 15-8   Major activities from 1997 to 1999

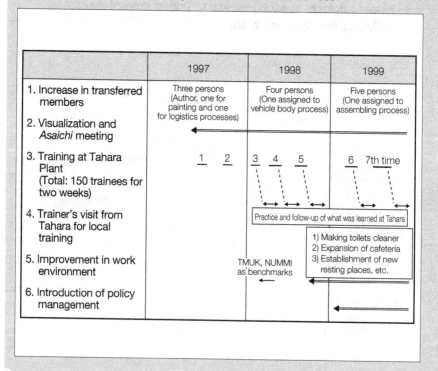

Although I actively promoted quality improvement activities in the plant, gaining the cooperation of local top management, the quality defects reduction rate was very small and still far from the initial goal. Major racial distrust could not be resolved overnight. Such a sense of distrust made it difficult for workers even to follow simple or ordinary instructions like "When a quality defect occurs, the section manager/supervisor (a white person) and the group/team leader (a black person) should listen to what the worker (a black person) wants to say, identify the cause, and take countermeasures through teamwork". In addition to that, there still remained a thick wall between the company and the labor union, which followed the instructions from the external union headquarters.

Chart 15-9   Improvement results from 1997 to 1999:
A foundation was established, but the results were not so acceptable.

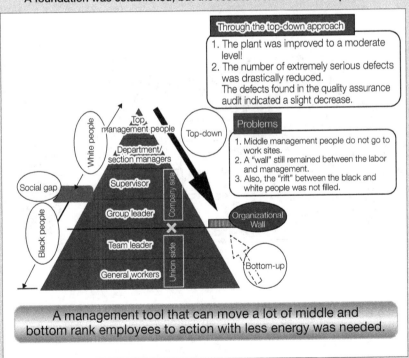

Through the top-down approach
1. The plant was improved to a moderate level!
2. The number of extremely serious defects was drastically reduced.
The defects found in the quality assurance audit indicated a slight decrease.

Problems
1. Middle management people do not go to work sites.
2. A "wall" still remained between the labor and management.
3. Also, the "rift" between the black and white people was not filled.

White people

Black people

Social gap

Top management people

Department/section managers

Supervisor

Group leader

Team leader

General workers

Company side

Union side

Top-down

Organizational Wall

Bottom-up

A management tool that can move a lot of middle and bottom rank employees to action with less energy was needed.

I really wanted something to make them get along with each other by crossing the racial barriers. Just at that time, a plan for the "introduction of QC circle activity" came up. For the purpose of successfully managing the growing overseas business, the plan to introduce QC circle activities in overseas plants was determined by the top management of Toyota, and Toyota South Africa, struggling with quality improvement activities, was chosen as its model company. It was an attractive proposal because the cost would be borne by Toyota headquarters and the guidance would be directly provided by the TQM Promotion Division if agreed on by Toyota South Africa.

Chart 15-10 Overseas advance of TQM Promotion Division (in 2000)

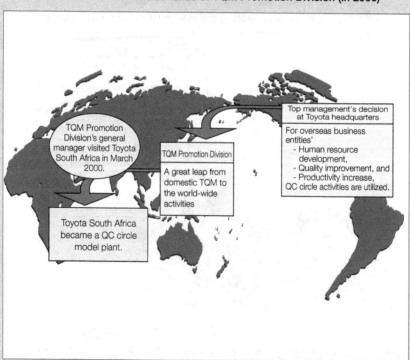

As a matter of fact, this was not the first QC circle to Toyota South Africa. In 1982, a plant manager at the time enthusiastically worked to introduce the QC circle activity, and the number of circles increased to as many as 150 in 1988. However, those QC circles were forcibly directed by the superiors (white people), and the circle members (black people) simply followed their orders. As they had no place to hold a circle meeting and no money necessary for improvement, it was a casual and half-hearted QC circle activity and disappeared after the change of the plant manager, with only a mental allergy to the QC circle remaining.

Chart 15-11   History of QC circle activity at Toyota South Africa

In 1982, it was first introduced by a plant manager at that time, who enthusiastically promoted it.

In 1988, the number of QC circles increased to 150.

The activity was forcibly conducted via a top-down approach.

(The black circle members were forced to follow orders from their white superiors.)

(1) It was a voluntary activity outside of work hours.

(2) The theme of each activity was determined by the head of each department or section according to individual needs.

(3) No consideration for the improvement budget or meeting place was made.

In the 1990's, the activity died a natural death as the top management changed.

(Everyone became happy because they were free from the strict plant manager.)

In March 2000, a general manager of the TQM Promotion Division of Toyota headquarters visited us and made a proposal for "Reintroduction of QC circle" to the top management of Toyota South Africa. However, not only the top management, but also workers still had the bad image of the previous QC circle, and most opinions in the company were "No more QC circle!". Nevertheless, we enthusiastically explained the necessity for QC circle by saying, "It will be helpful to improve the relationship between white and black people," "Without improvements in human relations, the quality will not be improved and exporting will be impossible forever," or "We will conduct it in a different way from the previous one". And finally, the reintroduction was determined by the chairman.

Chart 15-12   Persuasion for reintroduction of QC circle activity

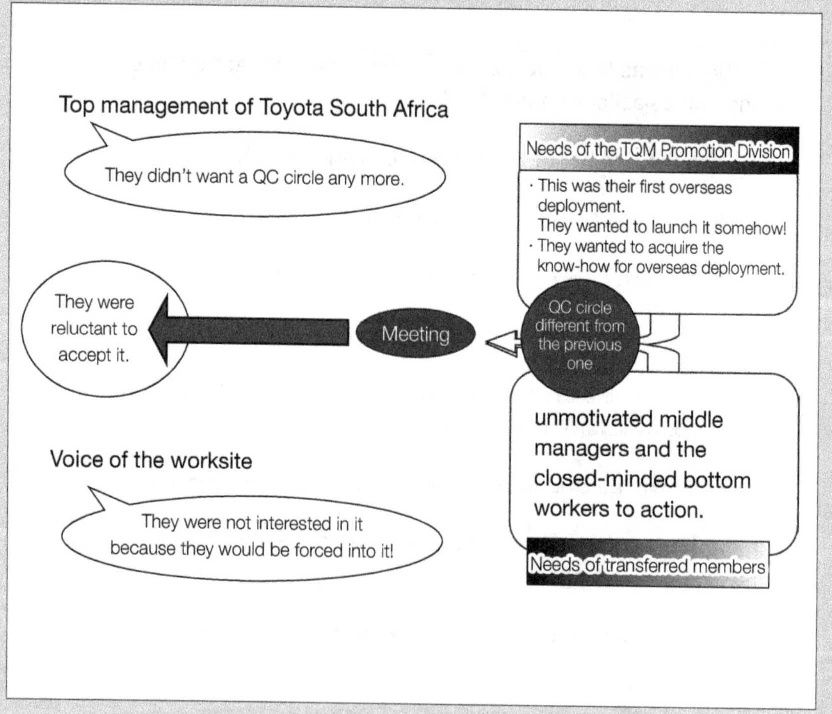

In order to avoid again discontinuing the QC circle to be reintroduced, it was important to make the QC circle activity enjoyable for the participants. Therefore, it was decided that the QC circle would be voluntarily participated in by the workers who wanted to improve their own problems in the workplaces, and I wanted to make them feel happy by solving those problems through their teamwork. By positioning that activity as the main event of the company, we aimed for an ideal QC circle, where members would attract lots of attention in the company, motivating others to join it. The QC teams were allowed to spend money on improvement of their problems if approved by the section manager.

Chart 15-13   What are the differences between the new QC circle and the previous one?

Fun, happy and worthwhile QC circle activity

Item	Last time	This time	Aims
1. Participants	Compulsory	To be participated in by only those who want to	Lively QC circle activities to be conducted by motivated persons. Motivation of participants will be emphasized over a number of them.
2. Themes	Accomplishment-oriented theme	Voluntary selection of themes that will make workers happy (The size of the accomplishment does not matter.)	Accomplishments will come even without requesting them. (Mandatory themes will lead to extinguishment again.)
3. Management people's interest	Less interested	Incorporation into company events as a task	The management people will realize the effectiveness of the QC circle and use it as a management tool.
4. Workers' interest	Less interested	Company-wide festival event	The QC circle members who look happy make others feel like doing the activity.

It is often said that people can feel very happy after working on difficult challenges, improving them by themselves, and getting a compliment from others. Therefore, I tried to make them happy through the experience of discussing with team members of QC circle the problems that could not be solved by individual persons, solving them through the teamwork, improving their workplaces and processes, increasing product quality, and getting a compliment from the management people. I encouraged general managers and section managers to proactively support the QC circle activities and increase opportunities to congratulate them on results.

Chart 15-14   Realization of "joy of working" through the QC circle activities

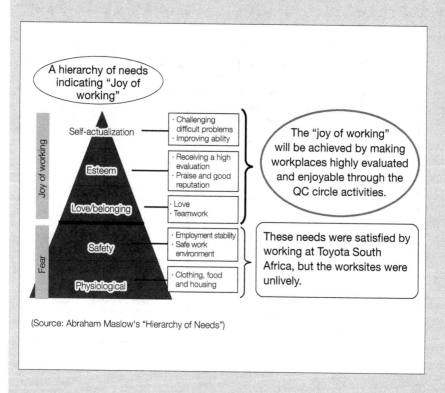

(Source: Abraham Maslow's "Hierarchy of Needs")

In order to make the QC circle activity successful, it was important to organize a strong promoting committee that supports the company-wide QC activities, and in that respect, the TQM Promotion Division's know-how was fully utilized. I also asked the TQM Promotion Division not only to provide education to the key persons, such as promoting committee administrator and trainers, but also to prepare easy-to-understand manuals and "QC Flags" which indicate details of individual QC teams' activities and progress. As the top of the QC promoting committee, we dared to appoint a black person, defying the opposition of the white people. Also, I requested representatives of the labor union to become members of the QC promoting committee from the beginning to improve labor-management relations.

Chart 15-15   Major considerations for successful QC

1) Appointing a black person as the top of the QC Promoting Committee

· 95% of workers were black people
· Personality was emphasized over experience.
(against the opposition of a lot of white people)

2) Labor union's representatives participated in the committee from the beginning.

To create opportunities for improvement of labor-management relations

3) Preparation of viewer-friendly illustrated manuals

Easy-to-understand and enjoyable teaching materials

4) Easy progress checking with the QC Flags

Going slowly and steadily while considering the local situation

In 2000, in order to check whether they were ready or not, I requested each department to organize a pilot QC circle and conduct trial QC circle activities. For that purpose, we provided 3-day education to all circle members and explained to all directors, general managers and section managers about the purpose of the pilot QC circle and the roles that should be played by them. Together with the administration office members and the supporters sent from the TQM Promotion Division, I visited the five pilot circles one by one to coach and give advice. And at last, the day came when they made a presentation at a company-wide presentation meeting. In front of a large audience, they made masterful presentations, generating tremendous excitement and getting an enthusiastic response.

Chart 15-16   Launch of pilot QC circle in 2000

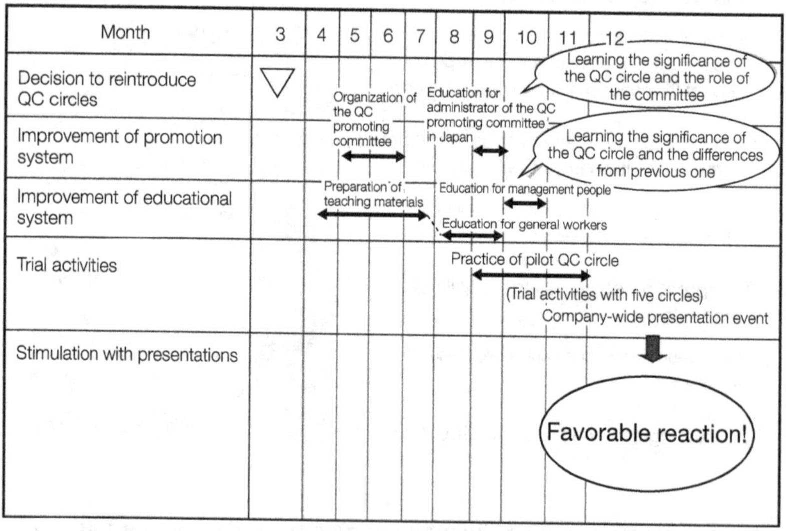

In 2001, the QC circle was officially positioned as the main event designed to inspire all employees of Toyota South Africa to feel a sense of unity, and thus, the company-wide full-scale QC circle activities began. A company-wide convention was held twice a year in June and December to choose the champion. Although I was initially worried about how many circle teams would enter when garnering the participation of QC circles, but I was really surprised to have as many as 39 circles' applications. A lot of employees seemed to have taken an interest in the activities after listening to the voices of pilot circle members saying, "It was enjoyable", "I was very happy", etc.

Chart 15-17　Opening of the first stage in 2001

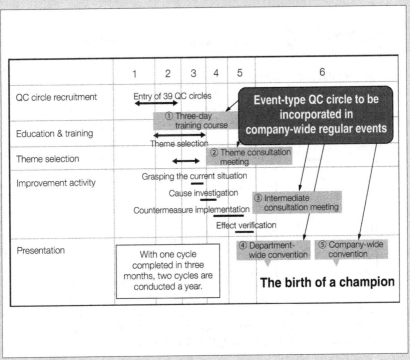

We divided the 39 circle teams who would participate in the next competition into smaller groups and provided a 3-day training course to each of them. For most of the members, it was their first time to leave the work site and receive such training. During the lessons, their enthusiastic attitudes with their eyes sparkling were impressive. They said that the curriculum, which included paper-craft airplane making and quizzes, were a lot of fun, and the text containing many pictures were very comprehensible. Also, a sense of fellowship among the trainees seemed to have been built up at a stroke. Apart from the training course for QC circle members, we requested all directors and general managers to take a half-day class for QC circle promoters for better understanding of the significance and procedures for QC activities, as well as the role of top management.

Chart 15-18

(1) Three-day training course - **Fun and Comprehensible Training** -

◼ Targeting all circle members

Day 1		Day 2		Day 3	
08:00	◎Opening ceremony Self-introduction	08:00	5. Problem solving procedure	08:00	8. Actual examples of activities
08:30	◎Paper-craft airplane making and flying distance competition				7. Role of leader
		10:05	6. QC method I		8. Role of members
08:45	1. Introduction				
	2. Definitions of terminologies	11:35	◎ Q & A ◎ Quiz	11:35	◎ Q & A ◎ Quiz
12:00	Lunch	12:00	Lunch	12:00	Lunch
12:30	3. Significance of QC circle activities	12:30	7. QC method II	12:30	◎ Case study
13:10	4. Concept of QC			13:25	◎Checking trainees' levels of understanding ◎Q & A ◎Comments on completion of training
13:55	◎Checking trainees' levels of understanding ◎ Q & A	13:55	◎Checking trainees' levels of understanding ◎ Q & A		
14:30	End	14:30	End	14:30	End

It was important to make everyone happy with their first training after entering the company.

The three-month activities started all at once, and each team began with the theme selection. It is said that the success or failure of the QC circle depends on the theme selection. So, the plant manager, the committee administrator, the TQM supporters and I visited all the circle teams to have a "theme consultation meeting", which also involved the respective section managers, supervisors and group leaders related to individual teams. The Japanese and white people carefully listened to the black people, visited each work site to see the actual items, and decided the theme through discussion. The communication between the white and black people, and between the company and union that had not been done properly before then, began to take place quite naturally through the QC circle activities.

Chart 15-19

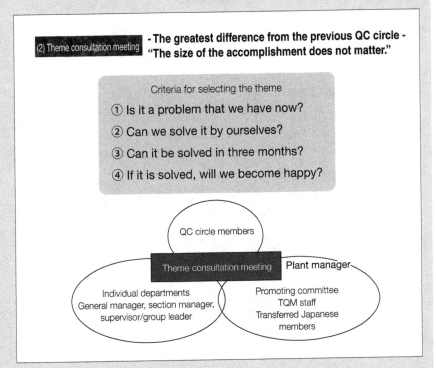

(2) Theme consultation meeting — **- The greatest difference from the previous QC circle -**
"The size of the accomplishment does not matter."

Criteria for selecting the theme
① Is it a problem that we have now?
② Can we solve it by ourselves?
③ Can it be solved in three months?
④ If it is solved, will we become happy?

QC circle members

Theme consultation meeting   Plant manager

Individual departments
General manager, section manager,
supervisor/group leader

Promoting committee
TQM staff
Transferred Japanese
members

At around the time when they started considering countermeasures after grasping the current situations and identifying factors through "why?" questions, we made a second-round visit as an "intermediate consultation meeting". The plant manager and I confirmed the progress through *GENCHI GENBUTSU*, while listening to the circle members, teaching necessary things and praising them for their good jobs. In that process, we began to open our hearts to each other and became able to have frank discussions. Also, it was another advantage that any superficial support by the managers and supervisors on the work site was clearly revealed through our visit to each circle team. The circle members' enthusiasm for improvement increased slowly and surely.

Chart 15-20

 **- All circles visited by plant manager, transferred members, committee staff, and TQM staff -**

1) Progress check through *GENCHI GENBUTSU* (on-site check of actual items)

If the progress is stagnating → Giving advice on recovery strategies
If they are worried about what to do → Teaching and encouraging them

2) Making opportunities for communication between top management and general workers

Exchange of mutual opinions while checking the process through *GENCHI GENBUTSU*

3) Putting spurs to the department and section managers who are getting lazy.

Visualization of those loafing around on the job

After three months, all the QC circle activities ended at the same time. Some circles which had stumbled in mid-course managed to recover somehow, and all of the circles made it to the finish line. First, a "department-wide QC circle convention" was held in each department, in which unique presentations were made in front of a large number of employees attended. Any fictional presentations were prevented by limiting them to the actual activities based on the "QC Flag". After the presentations, the improved status was checked through *GENCHI GENBUTSU*, so the effects were obvious at a glance. The department-wide convention reached its climax at the time of the ranking announcement. I was really touched by the scene in which black and white people hugged each other and shared the joy without any discrimination.

Chart 15-21

| (4) Department-wide convention | **- A big event for each department -** |

① "QC Flag" used as a presentation document

Time and effort for document preparation could be saved.

② *GENCHI GENBUTSU* check after presentations

The members were praised during the check of the actual status.

③ Award ceremony

This was a moment of excitement.

④ Building a feeling of unity with attraction!

The general manager warmed up the party.

Next, a company-wide convention gathering winners of individual departments' conventions was held as a major event of the company. All management and indirect department and section managers were also obliged to attend it, so that they got to know the difficulties and achievements in the manufacturing site for the previous three months. Presentations that demonstrated the results of improvement after strenuous efforts by using actual materials and data stuck in all audience member's minds and made a deep impression. Through the ranking announcement, award ceremony, commemorative photographs, and complimentary words, it became a friendly conference that greatly enhanced a sense of unity of the company. After the conference, a convivial gathering was held, and having a chat and snacks was also effective for deepening human relations.

Chart 15-22

(5) Company-wide convention **- Becoming the company's main event -**

① Attended by all management people

③ Award ceremony

② Unique presentation by each department's presenter

④ Commemorative photography

For this convivial gathering, I made some arrangements to make the QC circle activities become the subject of their conversations. I set up a "QC circle activity bulletin board" showing the pictures of the circle members together with their comments. It attracted attention, and many people looked at it amusingly. In a weekly message issued every Wednesday by the plant manager (also vice president), the objectives and fun of the QC circle were described in an easy-to-understand manner, and the group leader explained it to the group members in the Zulu language, resulting in the widespread penetration throughout the company. Also, a motivational speech from the Manufacturing Executive Vice President, who visited us semiannually from Toyota headquarters, was also great encouragement.

Chart 15-23   Other ideas to raise the interest of workers

① Related articles inserted in the internal newsletter

③ PR activities on the "QC circle activity bulletin board"

Installed in each department

② Issuance of vice president's weekly message

Explained by group leaders to members every Wednesday

④ Encouragement by an executive from Toyota's headquarters

Chart 15-24 shows four-year progress of the QC circles after the reintroduction. It expanded "slowly and steadily" as intended, with the number of circles increasing to as many as 130 in 2004. What is more important than anything is that about 2,000 people, about 30% of the total employees, took the 3-day training course and understood the importance of quality. The effect became clearly visible in the quality indicator and productivity index. As the awful state of "2S" was selected as a major target of QC circles, the plant landscape was greatly improved.

Chart 15-24   Rapidly increased activities after reintroduction of QC circle

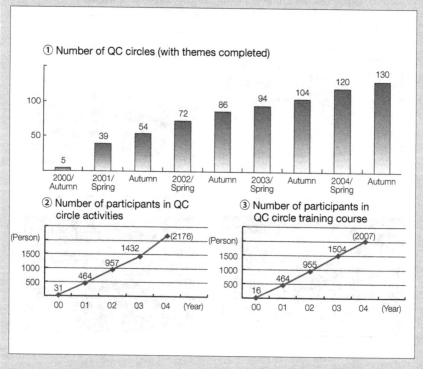

As a result of honestly, steadily and thoroughly making various kinds of improvement efforts through the reintroduction of the QC circle, we finally achieved the global quality goal in June 2002, and the export license was granted to us to export our South African-made cars. It took as many as five years. We shared the pleasure of achievement with all the persons in the company. Through the process of QC circle activities, the improved quality enabled smooth production, various bottlenecks hindering production were removed, and the enhanced cooperation between union and management reduced the number of strikes. As a result, productivity increased by 34%, and the company was reborn as a stably profitable company.

Chart 15-25   Results of improvement activities at Toyota South Africa

Results of steady improvement efforts including QC circle activities

1. Achievement of the world-class quality targets and start of exports in 2003

2. Improvement in labor-management relations, achieving no labor strikes in 2002 and 2003.

3. Growth of top management people who lead the next generation

Management personnel who experienced the effectiveness of the QC circle activities

4. Profit improvement through decreased number of employees and increased productivity

	Year 1996	Year 2003	Difference
Number of employees	9,151 persons	7,149 persons	-2,002 persons
Productivity	10.2 units/person/year	13.6 units/person/year	+34%

Chart 15-26 shows the results of "quality audits" conducted by the Quality Audit team of Toyota headquarters, which visited Toyota's vehicle assembly plants around the world. Previously, the quality indicator for vehicles made at Toyota South Africa was the worst among Toyota plants in the world, but with the reintroduction of the QC circle working as a trigger, the following improvements were made.

- Improvement in human relations between supervisors (white people) and general workers (black people)
- Improvement in the relationship between labor union and management
- Numerous improvements made by QC circle teams

Those improvements made it possible to dramatically improve the quality.

We achieved the target "quality equivalent to that of Japanese-made cars" in 2002.

Chart 15-26 ① **Achievement of the world-class quality targets and start of exports**

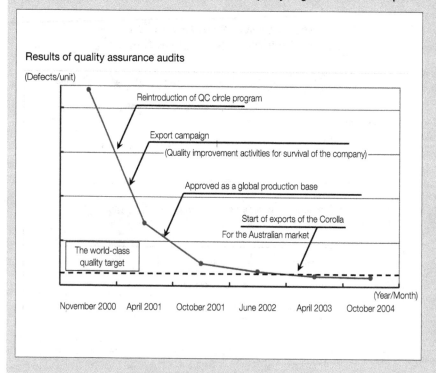

Results of quality assurance audits

(Defects/unit)

Reintroduction of QC circle program

Export campaign

(Quality improvement activities for survival of the company)

Approved as a global production base

Start of exports of the Corolla

For the Australian market

The world-class quality target

(Year/Month)

November 2000   April 2001   October 2001   June 2002   April 2003   October 2004

In addition, the working hours lost by labor strikes also drastically decreased. Previously, there were many cases where it was extremely difficult to accept the requests of the labor union, which was controlled by an external union headquarters, resulting in frequent labor strikes and production stops. To improve the situation, both the management and union sides agreed to solve the problems and matters inside the company only through internal discussion without outside interference and, as a result, staff restaurants, toilets and rest areas were greatly improved according to the union's request. Then, we requested the labor union people to directly participate in QC circle activities, and through continuous labor-and-management efforts for organizational improvement, a better relationship was established between both parties.

Chart 15-27 ② Improvement of labor-management relations

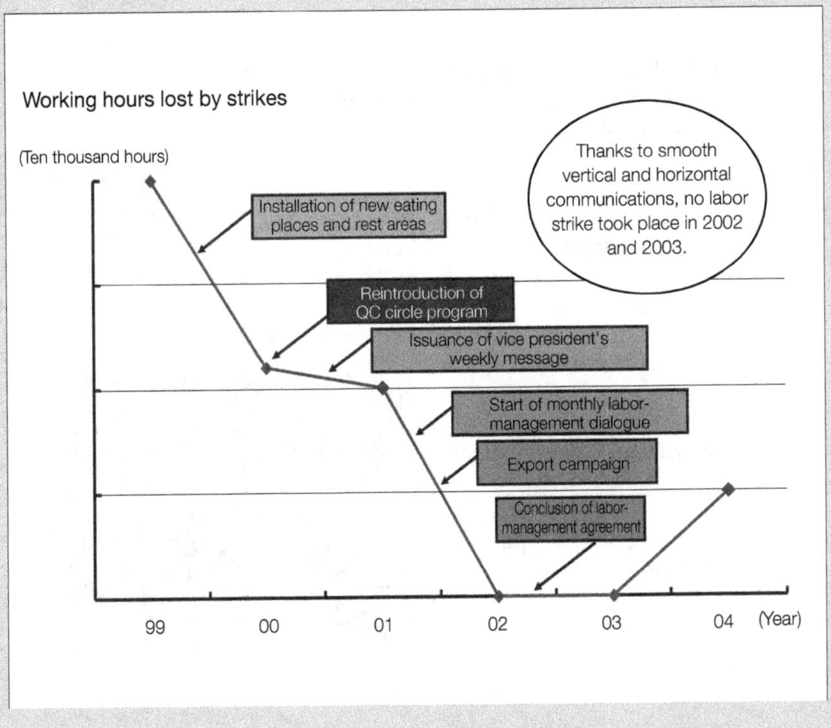

Working hours lost by strikes

(Ten thousand hours)

Thanks to smooth vertical and horizontal communications, no labor strike took place in 2002 and 2003.

Installation of new eating places and rest areas

Reintroduction of QC circle program

Issuance of vice president's weekly message

Start of monthly labor-management dialogue

Export campaign

Conclusion of labor-management agreement

99   00   01   02   03   04 (Year)

A major factor that made the QC circle activities successful in Toyota South Africa was the initiative and leadership of the local top management. After understanding the goodness of the QC circle, they played their important roles thoroughly and consistently. Under the strong leadership of Mr. Jansen (plant manager and vice president), superb teamwork was demonstrated by the supervisors (white people) and the workers (black people). The second factor was the support by experts sent from the TQM Promotion Division and the Tahara Plant of Toyota headquarters. The splendid teamwork between the Japanese and South African staff brought about big results.

Chart 15-28   Factors of successful QC circle program in Toyota South Africa

- Commitment and initiative by local top management
  They were more diligent and hardworking than
  the Japanese.

- Close support of TQM Promotion Division and
  various departments of Tahara Plant

Mr. Jansen,
vice president

- Steady efforts of the QC promoting committee and transferred
  Japanese members

- Enthusiasm of black members

- Adoption of event-type
  QC circle

TQM staff   Committee   Transferred
staff   member

In addition, the QC circle convention held as the main event to enhance a sense of unity of the company was very effective in promoting the activity throughout the company.

By deciding to hold the event in two seasons (spring and autumn) and incorporating it in the annual company schedule beforehand, it was possible to proceed with the plan without delay. The progress of each circle activity was visualized with the QC Flag installed at each resting place to check and prevent delays and omissions. Through the steps of "theme consultation meeting", "intermediate consultation meeting", "department-wide convention" and "company-wide convention", the employee motivation increased step by step.

Chart 15-29　Advantages of event-type QC circle

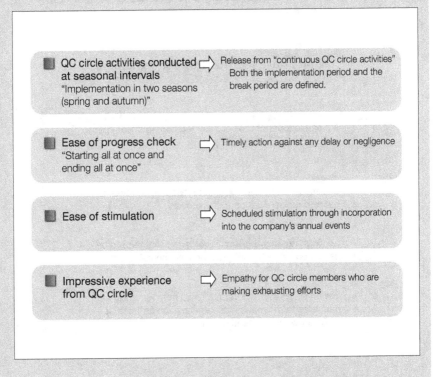

■ QC circle activities conducted at seasonal intervals "Implementation in two seasons (spring and autumn)"	⇨ Release from "continuous QC circle activities" Both the implementation period and the break period are defined.
■ Ease of progress check "Starting all at once and ending all at once"	⇨ Timely action against any delay or negligence
■ Ease of stimulation	⇨ Scheduled stimulation through incorporation into the company's annual events
■ Impressive experience from QC circle	⇨ Empathy for QC circle members who are making exhausting efforts

What I realized most when reintroducing the QC circle activities in cooperation with local top management was that the QC circle is a powerful management tool. The barrier between white and black people, which had been set up by the racial discrimination policy, was broken down by the QC circle activities. Also, the previous adversary relationship between the management and union turned into the mutually trustworthy one through the cooperative operation of the QC circle activities promoting committee. Even when every worker seems to be busy, a little arrangement for proper man-hour allocation made by the top management can bring about a big output.

Chart 15-30   Effectiveness of QC circle from the perspective of TQM

What I have learned through experience

1. A small amount of time of busy top management spent on it resulted in a large output.

2. It is effective not only for human resource development, but also for talented people discovery.

3. Solving "innumerable small problems" that tend to be neglected brings about great achievements!

4. It is an effective method for a small number of transferred members to move the local organization and people ... To show our existential value

If top and middle management people go to the work site, listen to workers while watching the actual things, discuss improvement measures with them, see results, and praise them, the following benefits are obtainable.

- Better human relations between the upper and lower position people
- Enhanced team spirit through the circle meetings and improvement activities
- Increased team motivation

As a result, both the quality and productivity are improved. The QC circle is a very effective tool to establish a bottom-up system. If it is used in combination with top-down management, major results will be obtainable.

Chart 15-31 [1] Small efforts bring about large output.

Top management's visit to QC circles for seeing, hearing and talking with the members brings about the following benefits:

Top-down

President

Bottom-up

Annual policy

General manager
Section manager

QC circle

Supervisor/group leader
Team leader   General workers

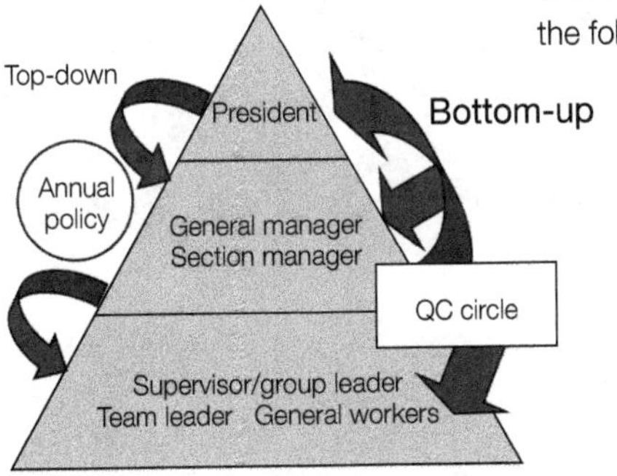

① Labor-management relations are improved.

② The workplace atmosphere becomes bright and cheerful.

③ It becomes the source of power of doing one thing in a group.

Very effective as a bottom-up approach tool

QC circle activities not only enable fostering of human resources, but also allow the finding of talented people.

• Evaluation of supervisors

The QC Flag indicates whether or not the relevant supervisors are properly and steadily teaching their subordinates. The flag can be used to check not only the progress of activities, but also the leadership capability of the supervisor.

• Evaluation of team members

The members who are actively leading the circle activities can easily be identified.

Chart 15-32 [2] Effective not only for human resource development, but also for talented people discovery

■ To managers and supervisors

① The top management people can easily find talented middle management personnel who are steadily making efforts.

② Also, they can easily find slipshod or superficial activities.

■ To team members

① The top management people can easily find high-potential employees by listening to their presentations and seeing the improved workplaces.

② Also, it is a great opportunity for them to directly convey their thoughts to general workers.

At the time of reintroducing the QC circle activities, the team members solved their own problems after choosing a theme that would make them happy. The innumerable "Y (difficult-to-do) work" and "K (tough, dirty, or dangerous) work", which had been neglected, were improved one after another through the efforts of all the circle members. The workplace atmosphere became bright and cheerful due to circle meetings, consultation meetings, and presentations, leading to great improvement of not only quality, but also productivity. I think the QC circle is a powerful management tool that can motivate workers.

Chart 15-33 ③ Solving a lot of small problems brings about great achievements!

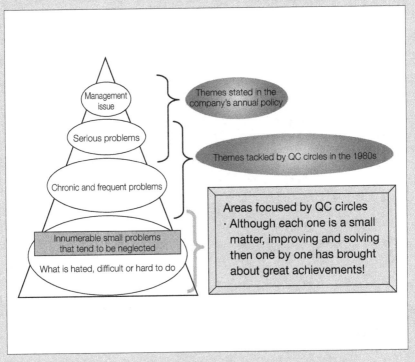

After a long interval, in September 2008, I was invited by Toyota South Africa as the "main guest for the Company-wide QC Circle Convention" and stepped on the soil of South Africa for the first time in six years. The convention was held early in the morning after the end of night shift operations so that both day workers and night workers could attend it. As the spring just began in September in the southern hemisphere, the temperature was low, and it rained unfortunately. Nevertheless, the convention place was filled with over 1,500 audiences. There was great excitement with passionate presentations by individual QC circles, cheering and clapping hands from the audiences, etc. I was really impressed by and felt proud of the fact that the seeds of the QC circle sown by the late Mr. Jansen (vice president) and me grew so much. During that journey, I re-realized the importance of the QC circle to improve teamwork, developing human resources and so on.

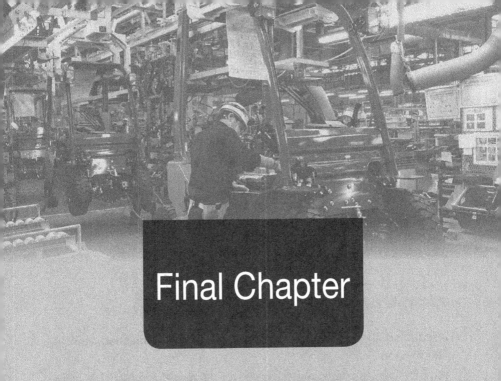

Final Chapter

Looking Back on Dantotsu Quality Activities

Under the belief that quality is the basic principle of Toyota, I worked on quality improvement for many years at the industrial vehicle division of Toyota Industries, and then, joined the group-wide "Dantotsu Quality Activities" in order to achieve quality that could overwhelm our competitors.

The results of our group-wide efforts accumulated for a total of nine years, through Dantotsu-I (2007-2009), Dantotsu-II (2010-2012), and Dantotsu-III (2013-2015), far surpassed the expectation of anyone who participated in them. Satisfied with such good results, overseas members acknowledged that the Dantotsu Quality Activity is a very effective quality improvement method, and kindly named it the "Nomura Method".

The results are described below.

1. Targets and results of Dantotsu Quality Activities

(1) Reducing the number of defects per vehicle in finished vehicle inspection

As a representative example, the results of the main line of the Takahama Plant in Japan are shown in Chart 16-1.

In the period of Dantotsu-I (2007-2009), there were major changes such as the start-up of a new model and the sharp decline in production volume due to the financial crisis of 2007-2008 (called "Lehman shock" in Japan), and at those change points, the product quality rapidly deteriorated. However, after 2010, when workers began to understand the basics of manufacturing, they became able to respond to changes, and finally achieved the target by reducing the number of defects in the finished vehicle inspection by 98% (Chart 16-2). Coupled with the decrease in defects, it became possible to deliver almost all of vehicles coming off the line without rework, eliminating the delivery delay problem. The waste of labor, materials, and space for reworking or repairing defective vehicles was drastically reduced, resulting in a great reduction in manufacturing costs.

One of the big achievements of Dantotsu Quality Activities was that six overseas plants also achieved a 91-to-98% defect reduction, allowing for stable production in the whole group around the world.

Chart 16-1 Number of defects per unit found in the finished vehicle inspection at the Takahama Plant

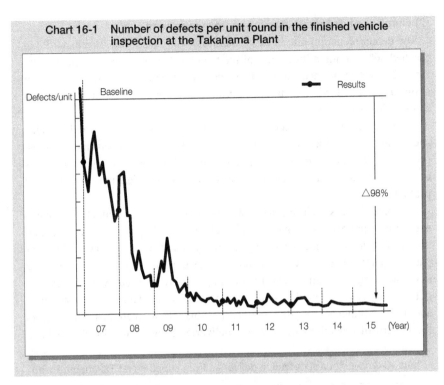

Chart 16-2 Targets for the both number of defects per unit found in the finished vehicle inspection and defective deliveries from suppliers

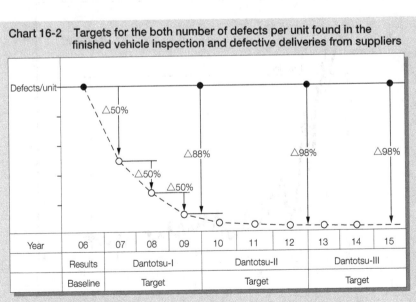

(2) Number of defective deliveries from suppliers

The defect reduction rate in deliveries from suppliers to the Takahama Plant reached 86%, falling a little short of the target 98% (Chart 16-3). Although the target has yet to be reached, the sharp decline in defective deliveries brought about a great reduction in trouble during assembly of the vehicle, enabling smooth line operation.

Meanwhile, on the supplier side, it became possible to significantly reduce such additional work as re-delivery, repair, screening of inventory items, preparing a countermeasures plan/report, etc. and the relevant additional costs of material, labor, and energy were greatly saved, leading to increased profitability.

In Japan, there is a close relationship between vehicle manufacturing plants and parts suppliers, like a parent-child relationship. Suppliers know well that they can steadily reduce defects by faithfully doing what was taught by their parent (plant). On the other hand, overseas parts suppliers and vehicle manufacturing companies have relationships based on equality, and there are not so many cases where the vehicle companies give guidance to parts suppliers about improvements in product quality. For this reason, there is a difference in the pattern of reductions of defective deliveries between the Takahama Plant

Chart 16-3   Number of defective deliveries from suppliers (at Takahama Plant)

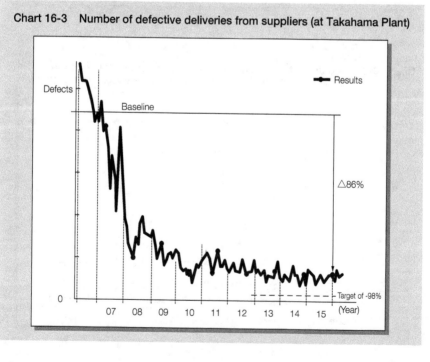

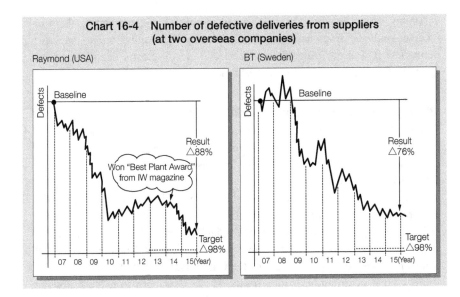

Chart 16-4   Number of defective deliveries from suppliers (at two overseas companies)

and overseas plants as shown in Chart 16-4.

In foreign countries, it is a common practice to purchase parts if their quality is good, and if the quality degrades, the contract is terminated and the parts are procured from another source. In such countries having a different culture from Japan, I visited some manufacturing companies supplying the worst quality parts, together with members of the "Supplier Quality Improvement Support Team" of our quality assurance department, and started giving guidance about "visualization", the "8-step procedure", etc.

Although the effects were hardly seen for the first two years, their interest in the activity increased gradually as they viewed the results (sharp decline in the number of defective cars) at the actual sites (in the vehicle manufacturing plant) through their own eyes (*GENCHI GENBUTSU*), leading to the increased number of companies starting to proactively conduct the Dantotsu Quality Activities. To further increase their motivation, we provided some excellent suppliers with an opportunity, at the annual supplier conferences, to make presentations about how to drastically reduce quality defects, in addition to other efforts, such as showing suppliers the actual quality improvement effects at our vehicle manufacturing plant and creating quality assurance texts based on my memo to teach them what to do. As a result of such continuous efforts made in the United States and Europe, the number of defective deliveries decreased similarly, as shown in both graphs. Raymond Corporation won the Best Plant Award from an American magazine, INDUSTRY WEEK, in 2014 and announced the details of "Dantotsu Quality Activities" at the award ceremony, attracting the interest of other companies and motivating them to receive guidance from us. That resulted in an 88% reduction in defective deliveries. It was the fruit of my honest and steady efforts dedicated to the Dantotsu Quality Activities for the past nine years.

(3) Target and achievement of market claim reduction

Using the data on the market claim cost and the total payment in 2006 as a benchmark (100%), we set a goal of halving it every three years, and encouraged each company to conduct Dantotsu-I to Dantotsu-III activities to achieve an 88% reduction.

As a result, as shown in Chart 16-5, the Company "F" cleared the target of a 93% reduction that had been considered to be unachievable. Next, Companies "D" and "E" approached the levels of 78% and 80% reductions, respectively.

For the entire group, we were able to reduce the total amount of market claims payments by 65%. Especially, the Claim *Asaichi,* which started in 2011, made a great contribution to this result. At the Claim *Asaichi,* the following activities were effectively conducted: Checking the claimed items returned from dealers every morning by all relevant persons, determining the person responsible for measures, and taking countermeasures promptly. In addition, new initiatives such as contamination reduction activities (involving suppliers) and weekly design related issue follow-up meetings, also brought about beneficial changes.

Activities described in Chapter 14 to prevent defect outflow to the market through the improvement in design quality and production preparation methods has just begun, but I believe the enthusiastic efforts at each company will bear fruit sooner or later. At each of those companies, individual section's SE Manuals are created; the quality check using the SE Checklist is performed at each step of design, prototyping, and production preparation; and various kinds of problems are solved at the "Best" (design stage) or "Better" (prototyping or production preparation stage) timing. If they become capable enough to solve the problems, a 90% reduction in claim cost will not be a dream any more.

The Dantotsu Quality Activities allowed for 65% savings in claim costs, which was a large amount of wasteful spending, making a big contribution to the improvement of profitability of the entire group. Moreover, decreased market defects have enhanced customer satisfaction levels, leading to expansion of our market share.

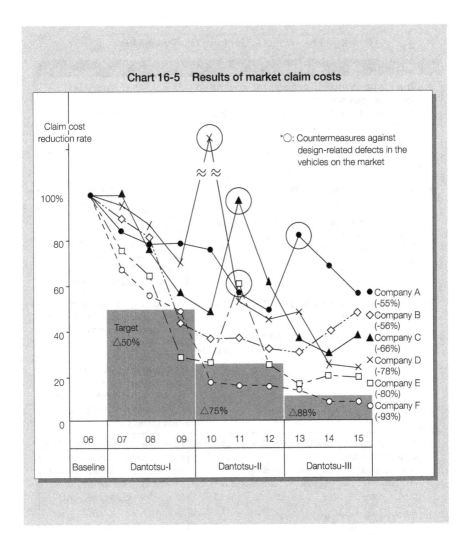

Chart 16-5 Results of market claim costs

2. Key words used in Dantotsu Quality Activities

The following are the key words for quality improvement that I repeatedly used at the time of guidance to each company through the Dantotsu Quality Activities. I strongly believe that these ideas and efforts were extremely important to globally apply the activities and obtain favorable results (Chart 16-6).

Chart 16-6 Key words in Dantotsu Quality Activities

No.	Keywords	Remarks
1	**There is no shortcut to or magic for *monozukuri* (conscientious manufacturing).** "Honestly, steadily and thoroughly improve" the problems indicated by quality defects. (*This is one of important concepts of TPS.) The word "honestly" indicates "Don't get by with slipshod work" or "Don't accept second best".	Quality cannot be improved overnight. You cannot reach the goal (zero defects) without accumulating countermeasures taken to solve the problems indicated by defects one by one honestly.
2	**Don't try to hide or smother any defect.** Reveal everything to take thorough measures! Even if you hide it, it will occur again as long as the root cause remains. Even if you smother it, it is only a matter of time before it is found out.	Even if you do not report it to supervisors, the same problem will recur soon because the root cause still exists. The first step of improvement is to report any defect without hiding it and take necessary countermeasures honestly.
3	**Take measures immediately and thoroughly.** "Speed" is the key! Nobody can tell when a defect will occur. If the root cause remains, a big accident may occur tomorrow!	A typical example is the JR Hokkaido derailment accident. A track defect (line width excessively enlarged by centrifugal forces), which had been neglected without repair, finally caused a derailment accident. That accident resulted in the resignation of the top management.
4	**Consider quality defects and trouble as a kind of financial resource.** A defect tells you a problem to be solved. Immediate countermeasures will reduce the negative cost to zero. Continue the efforts year by year!	If they are neglected, major claim and disposal costs will be incurred forever. Take measures against them one by one to reduce the waste costs zero.
5	**Defective items are like a mountain of treasure for finding hints for improvement** The occurrence of a defect tells us that there is some problem we should solve. Defects will surely come to zero if you investigate the causes through *GENCHI GENBUTSU* (on-site check of actual items) and take measures to prevent recurrence.	Before implementation of the Claim Asaichi, a huge amount of claimed items were stacked up in a warehouse. Whether or not finding hints from the "mountain of treasure" for improvement to save money is up to the leadership of the quality assurance department and the enthusiasm of the responsible departments.

No.	Keywords	Remarks
6	**Visualize and evaluate the quality activities in a long span of time.** **Five-year-term visualization of quality status** 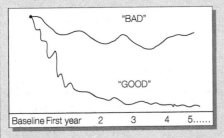 Visualize the activities over a time span of at least five years. If the defects are not reduced constantly, something may be missing or wrong. It's your job to find out the "something" and take some measures.	Generally, an annual target is determined based on the result of the previous year, but in many cases, the number of defects slightly goes up and down without approaching zero. Throughout the Dantotsu Quality Activities, when the stagnation continued for more than six months, we asked ourselves, "What is missing or wrong?", and changed something. That brought about good results.
7	**Think about whether you really did what you had to do as a manager or supervisor before blaming workers.** Quality will not be improved if supervisors make an excuse, such as "The workers' quality consciousness is so low that such a defect has occurred". In most cases, the real problems lie in the ways of standardization, education/training, and arrangement for processes, jigs and tools, which are attributable to the ability of managers and supervisors.	If managers and supervisors are very busy in full-time manufacturing together with all workers, the quality cannot be improved. Managers and supervisors should understand and implement their primary tasks, such as standardizing the procedures to ensure product quality, and teaching and training workers until they can do a good job.
8	**See the chart from the right side.** Right side = Clarify the goal or target, check the gap between the target and the current state, find out the real weakness (structural problem), and take proper measures. **Clarification of the current level of defect occurrence and real weakness** 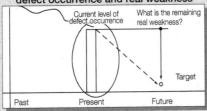 Just repeating the same countermeasure against a certain phenomenon will not lead to quality improvement, no matter how many years pass by.	Q: What does the word "countermeasure" mean? A: It means a measure to be taken for preventing recurrence of the same defect. Ten out of ten people can answer this question correctly, but in reality the same defects are repeatedly occurring. Paying attention to workers, and giving guidance about their work This is an insufficient measure, which will not make the quality get better even after ten years.

No.	Keywords	Remarks
9	**GENCHI GENBUTSU communication** Top management should visit the work site, and: • See the actual defects. • See the real work. • Listen to the workers and team leader. • Discuss with them and decide what to do after checking the actual defects. This is true communication required at the work site.	Listening to a plausible excuse in a conference room and giving instructions on it does not improve quality. This is because if the real problem leads to the disadvantage of the reporter, it is often hidden.
10	**"Try first before you say you can't do it."** **... Mr. Sakichi Toyoda** Trying and failing is far better than just saying theoretical reasons or excuses without doing anything. Exercise strong leadership in individual positions!	It is important to always think from the viewpoint of the company, not individual departments, and implement measures that lead to concrete results. Everyone must keep it in mind and work seriously.

3. Ideas and efforts leading to favorable results

Company-wide efforts must lead to satisfactory results. As a quality advisor, I describe some of the ideas that worked as driving forces of the Dantotsu Quality Activities and brought about such results.

(1) Motivation enhancement through global quality improvement competition

We standardized the quality targets and quality indicators for the six companies belonging to the Industrial Vehicle Division, for fair comparison, and made them compete with one another in global quality improvement (Chart 16-7). As a result, it became clear to all workers whether their company's quality was superior or inferior to others, so that every company became enthusiastic about its own quality improvement activities to aim at No. 1. Another change was the increased communication and closer relationships among plants. Previously, they seldom visited each other. After the start of the Dantotsu Quality Activities, however, upon hearing that a plant was doing good activities, others quickly visited the plant to learn something useful.

Initially, the Takahama Plant's Dantotsu Quality Activities were not very active. This was because they were too confident that they were far better than

Chart 16-7 Quality improvement competition through Dantotsu Quality Activities

	Until 2006	From 2007 (Dantotsu Quality Activities)
Scale of activity	In each plant	Global-scale quality improvement competition
Quality target	50% defect reduction from the previous year Poor results lead to the increase of the next target value.	A challenging goal common to six companies Based on the 2006 actual results To be reduced by 50% in each of three years (Goal change is not allowed.)
Quality indicator	Set by individual plant Comparison with other plants was not possible.	Common indicators to the six companies • Number of defects per vehicle in finished vehicle inspection • Number of defective deliveries from suppliers • Market claims cost Easy comparison is possible.

overseas plants in terms of quality. However, less than a year later, after the plant's director had visited some overseas plants, he said "We are losing to them." Then, they began to work hard on quality improvement. The best way to motivate a less enthusiastic plant is to let it know about other better plants.

(2) Setting of the order of steps in quality improvement and creation of texts

Based on the know-how accumulated through the quality improvement activities at the Toyota Motomachi Plant, Toyota Australia, and Toyota South Africa, I set an order of priority for the items of Dantotsu Quality Activities, and wrote each item on an A3-size sheet of text by hand. Whenever I visited overseas plants (once every four months), I explained each text and instructed the employees what to do based on them. The items of activities were conducted in the following order: "Visualization" (Chapter 2), "8-step procedure" (Chapter 3), "Standardization" (Chapters 4, 5, and 6), "Education and Training" (Chapter 7), and "Weak-Point Management" (Chapter 8). For the items that are difficult to teach only through paper explanation and on-site guidance, we showed actual things to trainees at the time of TPS training in Japan to deepen their understanding.

It is very important to steadily upgrade the training level step by step. For your reference, the memo Nos. 124 and 220 concerning the "8-step procedure" written in my notes are attached at the end of this chapter. These notes were written by hand. This is because I want you to feel my passion in the handwriting.

(3) Implementation of thorough follow-up activities

I visited each plant every four months and checked the progress of what I had taught them through *GENCHI GENBUTSU*. Staying a few days with eight hours a day in each plant, I checked the current state and pointed out what was missing or wrong on site. Then, I taught them the next step by using a text sheet. After returning to the hotel, I had to summarize the problems found on that day, think over the measures, and then, write down the next challenge to be addressed in English on a sheet of A3-size paper, which was given as an assignment to them. To create the A3-size text sheet, I was so busy in thinking about what to write and how to use pictures and tables to make it easy to understand, that I did not have enough time to sleep well. But that was my job. On the last day of my visit, I passed them a copy of my memo (text sheet), explained the details and confirmed what they would have to do. Then, I came back to Japan.

By visualizing what they should do with their promises written on the text sheet (homework memo), as well as by thoroughly implementing the follow-up activities, you can motivate even less enthusiastic plant workers to work on quality improvement.

Thank you for reading through this book while struggling through my poor explanation. I sincerely hope that you have found this book to be helpful to improve the quality in your company.

Last but not least, I deeply appreciate the top management of Toyota Industries, who not only authorized me to proceed with the Dantotsu Quality Activities for nine years long, but also fully supported me throughout all the activities. I would also like to express my sincere gratitude for all the people concerned in Japan and abroad with whom I really shared the joys of the amazing achievements made by us after a lot of hardship. The "Dantotsu Quality Activities" implemented in cooperation with them through many trials and errors are an "invaluable experience" to me.

品質不良再発防止 の 8つのステップ

NO.124
2009. 3. 5
藤村

不良再発防止の8つのステップを きちんと回せば、品質不良は確実に減少します。 しかし、
「再発防止の8つのステップとは何ですか？」
という質問に答えられない人が多々見られるため、再度、その詳細をご紹介します。
全社一丸となって この仕組みを回して、"不良をつくる"という大きなムダをゼロ化にチャレンジ
してみてはいかがでしょうか！ トップの強い旗振りで 不良をゼロにすることができます。

8つのステップ	誰が	いつ	やるべき事	キーポイント
① 不良状態の現認化	責任者 (チームリーダーズ)	即		※QAは、不良情報を受けたら直ちに現場へ（パトラ）で現認し責任工程へ報告する ※QAから各工程リーダー(TL)に連絡をとり、"品質不良の流出状況"を不良内容と 共に表示する。
② 在庫選別	責任者	即	他に同じ不良が無いか全工程を調査する。 左右を確実に押さえる 先頭を確実に押さえる	※目で見てわかる選別場所を会社として決める。 ※アレ以上に正しく数え絶対に正しい数が良いようにする ※QAは、ちゃんとやったか必ず確認する
③ 原因の追求	責任者	当日 (その日のうちにやる)	③ 現地現物で原因を追求する。 1) 初回不良の場合 (1)作業者に不良を流出したことを聞く 何が悪いめたことか悪いかを聞く (2) 標準作業手順書を確認する。 (3) 品質の関所の有無を確認する。 (4) 作業をもう一度、標準と比べてみる (5) 設備、治具、型を見て正常か見る (6) 材料を見る、もの置き方も見る (7) 変化点の有無を確認…人、材、設備 2) 再発不良、慢性不良の場合 過去の傾向履歴を確認する。 "履歴の見える化が重要" …テキストP.122 (1) なぜ再発したかをとことん考える (2) これまでの対策の履歴がどうなったのか (3) " がまちがっていたか (4) 決めたこと、やったことは正しいか？ 入り込むのをなぜ防げなかったのか？ 人の技能の不足か？ 等を現地現物で追求する。	※不良を流出させた工程の責任チームリーダーを中心に原因の追求を行う。(TLとラインキーを必ず) ※不良の発生情報を手際よくまとめることが非常に重要だ (不良履歴シートを見れば…) ※あわてることはない等々を洗い出し真因を1つずつつぶしていく ※単純な不良にしても…のムダ…
④ 対策の実施	責任者	当日	④ わかったこと を その日のうちに対策する。 1) 明日は、明日の問題が発生するので 決して問題をためないことが重要 "スピードがカギー！" 2) 対策に時間のかかる場合は、必ず暫定対策を決めて即実施して不良の再発を防止する。どうせ直さといけない不良なので 不良とみなされる損害が先行を行う。 ※対策は 発生源と流出源のそれぞれに対して確実に実行する。 3) 時間のかかるものは "問題と対策" 用紙に記入し、誰が いつまでに 何をするかを決めて、実施記録をフォローする。 4) 自動機のみで解決できない問題が多いので、技術部・設計部、仕入先の人間関係を良くするど 対策結果を早まるなどが必要	※要因がいくつかはカギツ不良は絶対発生させ流出はさせないようにつぶしこみ、徹底させていくが ※最後は人。人は 給料が高い利益で働いているから本気で動かない。テキストNO.106を参考に、人を大切にする良きロジを行う。
⑤ 朝市の実施	社長 工場長 係長 部長 (組織の大きさで判断)	翌日	⑤ 朝市の実施…毎日、時間を決めて実施 所要:20分生 朝市とは：前日発生した不良の原因と対策を責任TLが開き、再発防止対策として十分かどうかを判断。 不十分なら指示、指導 B的現地現物確認を行い再発防止対策のレベルアップを行うこと。 1) 前日の不良の原因と対策を 責任TLが前に立って説明 再発不良については、これまでの対策履歴と簡単に説明しこれ以上流出させないための対策をきちんと説明する 2) トップは説明を聞いて それで良いかどうかを判断すると共に、必要に応じて該当工程へ いっしょに行き、現物確認を行った上で…等がわかっていることを指示、指導する。 朝市の効果：きちんとやっている会社の不良は激減するが、やっていない会社ではいつまでたっても激減しない	※不良の話を聞くだけでなくそれで良いかどうかを判断することが重要。"信念"を持てなければ現地現物で確認をとり、たろうと判断する ※トップ、中間管理、現場がコミュニケーション行う絶好の交流の場。 この話しを通じてチームワーク、人材が育成される
⑥ 標準化と横展 (非常に重要)	責任者	当日 計画による	⑥ 標準化と類似の人工程への横展 ---発生工程だけでなく該当する全工程で不良再発をゼロ化 1) 作業 → 作業手順書の改訂やキーポイントの追加、重複防止や手順書の無いものは作成。(手順、ポイントと明記) 2) 作業の基本ルール →作業中のルール、異常発生時の処置ルール等 会社として決めるべきルールが守られてなく不良をつくり出しているものは、早期に図面やスペック追加 3) 設備、型、治具 → 対策の有る対策は、全設備、全型、全治具に横展する。 該当品のリストをつくり、計画的に対策を実施。	※標準の無いところに改善なし 現地現場で作った後、必ず標準化し、類似工程や設備、型、治具に横展して100%保証の作り方。※さらにつくり込む
⑦ 教育と訓練	責任者	当日 翌週	⑦ 標準化に応じて横展することを正しく教えるよう訓練する。 1) 標準化、基本ルール等、決めたことを関係者全員に正しく教えると共に実作業をやる者については、正しくやれるよう やれるまで訓練する。 2) 横展する設備を紙やすりなどでフォロー	※見た目でわかる標準書 読んで理解し入れなければ標準書は使われない、"誰でもわかるようにする"
⑧ 日常管理	責任者	毎日	⑧ 決めたことを 決めたとおりにやっているか日常管理する。 決めたことを守らせる。作業をしっかり見て、やっていない人へは厳しく指導 正常、異常を瞬時に見わける鋭敏のものさしを持つことが大事	※手を抜けば必ず現場が荒れる不良が出る前に手を打つブロク現場巡視をやろうぜ！

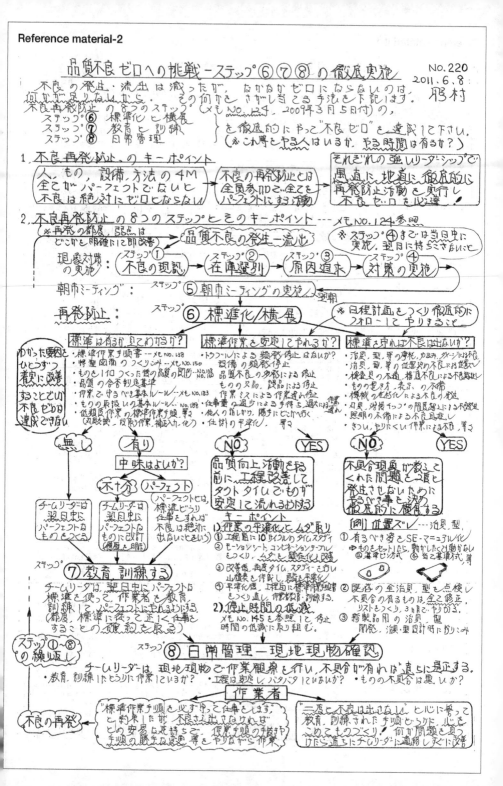

Index

[Author]

Sadao Nomura

Joined Toyota Motor Sales (now Toyota Motor Corporation) in 1965. Appointed as a section manager of Body Section No.2 of the Body Department of the Toyota Motomachi Plant in 1985, and promoted to general manager of the same department in 1993. Served as a quality improvement trainer for 13.5 years at Toyota Motor's manufacturing plants in Indonesia, Australia and South Africa while with Toyota.

After serving as a president of TECHNOL EIGHT Co., Ltd. from 2002 to 2006, led the "Dantotsu Quality Activities" as a senior advisor for the Industrial Vehicle Division of Toyota Industries from July 2006 to March 2014.

Now, he gives guidance to parts manufacturers as a quality improvement consultant.

[Edited by]

Toyota L&F Company of Toyota Industries Corporation

Toyota Industries Corporation (head office: Kariya city, Aichi prefecture) was founded in 1926 to manufacture and sell the Type G automatic loom invented by Mr. Sakichi Toyoda. Since then, it diversified its business by expanding into new business lines, such as textile machinery, automobiles (vehicles, engines, compressors for car air-conditioners, etc.), industrial vehicles and electronic products.

Toyota L&F Company is the Industrial Vehicle Division of Toyota Industries Corporation. It develops, produces, sells and services a wide variety of forklifts, ranging from 0.5-ton to 43-ton classes, and logistics equipment/systems. The company name "L" and "F" represent "logistics" and "forklift", respectively. Its forklifts, holding the largest market share in the world, are sold worldwide under the Toyota, BT, Raymond, and CESAB brands.